FOREIGN DEVILS
EXPATRIATES IN HONG KONG

Foreign Devils

Expatriates in Hong Kong

May Holdsworth

with additional text by Caroline Courtauld

OXFORD

UNIVERSITY PRESS

OXFORD
UNIVERSITY PRESS

Oxford University Press is a department of the University of Oxford.
It furthers the University's objective of excellence in research, scholarship,
and education by publishing worldwide in

Oxford New York

Athens Auckland Bangkok Bogotá Buenos Aires Cape Town
Chennai Dar es Salaam Delhi Florence Hong Kong Istanbul Karachi
Kolkata Kuala Lumpur Madrid Melbourne Mexico City Mumbai Nairobi
Paris São Paulo Shanghai Singapore Taipei Tokyo Toronto Warsaw

with associated companies in Berlin Ibadan

Oxford is a registered trade mark of Oxford University Press

Published in the United States
by Oxford University Press Inc., New York

British Library Cataloguing in Publication Data
available

Library of Congress Cataloging-in-Publication Data
available

ISBN 0-19-592437-1

Printed in Hong Kong
Published by Oxford University Press (China) Ltd
18th Floor, Warwick House East, Taikoo Place, 979 King's Road, Quarry Bay
Hong Kong

Dedication

Patrick Alexander

Anne Baker

Alistair Ballantine

Joan Barst

Ritchie Bent

Wendy Blackmur

Denis Bray

David Browning

Martin Browning

'Bruce'

Father Sean Burke

Nicci Button

Valerie Conibear

Liz Dewar

Anne Dickson-Leach

David Dodwell

Peter Edwards

Andrew Eldon

Michelle Garnaut

Dick Gazmararian

Deborah Glass

Chris Glover

Sister Mary Greaney

Anthony Hardy

James Hayes

Adrian Huggins

Janet Kaye

Sister Helen Kenny

John Lang

Margaret Leeds

Ian Lightbody

Noreen Lightbody

Piers Litherland

John Macdonald

Neil Macdonald

Peter Mann

Lindsey McAlister

Sisse McCall

Martha McGinnis

Mark Ford McNicol

Aman Mehta

Peter Moor

Alasdair Morrison

Stacy Mosher

Veronica Needa

Father Peter Newbery

Sister Gabriel
O'Mahony

Lavender Patten

Karen Penlington

Esben Poulssen

Ted Pulling

Jackie Pullinger

Gilbert Rodway

Andrew Russell

Reverend Carl Smith

Joyce Smith

Anne Sorby

Keith Statham

David Turner

Sami Wafa

Alexander Waller

Dan Waters

Carolyn Watts

Harry Wilken

Lord Wilson of
Tillyorn

Jason Wordie

Michael Wright

George Wright-Nooth

Miltinnie Yih

Pauline Young

Pat Youngberg

Allen Youngblood

Allan Zeman

This book is also for those who were generous and enthusiastic about the project but whose interviews we have not included. Simply, time and space ran out.

Contents

Introduction:
Who are They?

W hen we embarked on this book we had no doubt that an account of expatriates in Hong Kong should be told in the protagonists' own words. It was also clear that we must first grapple with the difficulties faced by all who attempt such a history—of definition, selection, and structure. The last problem turned out to be the easiest to resolve. Oral histories can be full transcripts or a patchwork of extracts, but as we were going to weave historical material and living recollections together, the latter approach seemed more suitable.

As to definition, a dictionary baldly states that the word 'expatriate' refers to a person who lives in a foreign country. By this description, all those in Hong Kong who are not Chinese nationals are expatriates.

They include the tens of thousands of people who carry American, British, Australian, or Canadian passports but are, if you meet them in the street, barely distinguishable by their appearance, language, and manners from the local Cantonese. Many of them emigrated in the years leading up to 1997, when Hong Kong ceased to be a British colony and was reintegrated into communist China. After securing their bolt-holes on Western shores, they returned to Hong Kong. Immigration figures put their number, as a proportion of those who emigrated in the decade before 1994, at 12 per cent; statistically, these returnees are expatriates.

And then there are the significant numbers of Indonesian, Vietnamese, and Malaysian nationals, who on closer inspection turn out to be overseas Chinese. They, too, fall into the foreign passport-holder category as far as immigration statistics are concerned.

The largest foreign group—in 2000 two-and-a-quarter times as many as the next category, Indonesians, and more than four times the size of the American community—is made up of Filipinos. Most of them are women, the 'indentured labourers', according to one author, and 'guest workers', according to another, whose contribution as housekeepers and baby-minders to local working families is incalculable and largely unsung. Others serve in restaurants and bars, and if it weren't for Filipino bands and singers, the nightlife in Hong Kong would certainly be less convivial.

Some residents of Hong Kong will also have come across Japanese and Korean businessmen and their wives, and not just on the golf course. These expatriates have their own associations, churches, and schools, but they also participate in the economic and social life of the territory.

A by-product of Hong Kong's colonial heritage is the presence of Indians and Nepalese. Many of the former, descendants of families who had followed the flag in the opium-trading days, were born and bred here and call Hong Kong 'home'. Some of the latter, from the brigade of Gurkhas which in the run-down of British forces before 1997 dispersed a number into civilian life, have taken up new careers as watchmen and security guards here.

So defining an expatriate by the book is easy but misleading. In Hong Kong, archetypal city of transients, it is especially problematical. Until the bamboo curtain sealed the border with China in 1950, even the Chinese population was a shifting one, moving back and forth between the colony and the Mainland as one crisis or another loomed and receded. The bulk of ethnically Chinese residents in Hong Kong saw themselves as emotionally detached from the territory, with no heartfelt allegiance to the place, the fulcrum of their patriotism still located in China though they lived under British rule. In that sense they too were 'foreign' to Hong Kong.

Who, then, are our expatriates in Hong Kong? It didn't take us long after starting our research to abandon the crude category of immigration officers. It would be far more interesting, we thought, to seek the kind of expatriate that resides in the eyes of the beholders. What emerged was a remarkable consensus. The expatriate as *perceived* is invariably an American, European, Australian, or New Zealander and, more often than not, white. In other words, he or she is instantly recognizable as foreign, in a way that someone of

Asian origin, being all but invisible against 95 per cent of the population, is not.

The stereotype is also quite often a blimpish senior civil servant or a well-heeled director of one of the British *hongs* (*hong* is a Cantonese term for a merchant company). This caricature is even cherished by some of the expatriates themselves, at least by those who disclaim affinity with the stereotype on the grounds that they're not as rich or, because most of their friends are Chinese, as exclusive.

It is inevitable that our dramatis personae is predominantly British. Survivors of Hong Kong's colonial phase, the civil servant and the *taipan* (the head of a large foreign company) are essential to this impressionist portrait. Selecting our other living witnesses was less straightforward. While trying to choose people who may be regarded as representative of their time and milieu, we nevertheless biased our account towards those who interviewed well.

Another problem of selection has to do with the fact that, with comings and goings and postings hither and thither, the expatriate population is in a perpetual state of change. For every interview we conducted face-to-face or by mail, there were several missed chances with people who had moved on to distant pastures before we could record their stories. The notable exception was Harry Wilken, caught on the wing between Bermuda and Italy one afternoon in the Royal Over-seas League in London, itself an entirely apposite venue for exchanging tales from the colonies over fish and chips and tea.

Sometimes, when Britons talk about themselves, their characterizations are laced with self-deprecation. This is of course an example of their famous sense of humour, which the possessors generally regard as a unique gift. When we started researching this book, a friend, Simon Heale, suggested that we called it *Gilded Mediocrity*. The image this conjures up of second-raters living in (undeserved) luxury recalls the traditional practice by British

families of shunting their black sheep or younger sons off to make their mischief and their fortunes in the colonies. Charles Boxer, a soldier and historian, remarked to the writer Emily Hahn in 1940: 'Hong Kong is the dumping ground for the duds, including me. Any old fool who can't be used anywhere else is dumped out here in Hong Kong. Look at them!'. His words embrace both the conventional view of colonies and the humorous self-disparagement we mentioned earlier. A more recent variation on Boxer's 'dud', with the same connotations as 'white trash', is FILTH (Failed In London, Try Hongkong), which cropped up in the local parlance in the 1980s. There was no escaping the suspicion that British mediocrity may have thrived in Hong Kong because citizens of the United Kingdom did not require permits to live and work in the colony before 1997, which gave them an unfair advantage over the nationals of other countries when it came to competing for jobs.

Not surprisingly, this image is occasionally held by the Chinese in Hong Kong—that is, if they think about expatriates at all, which many of them don't any more. But their mockery is part of the story. Over the short history of Hong Kong as a colony, local people have dreaded, misunderstood, detested, loved, and laughed at the foreigners in their midst. Today, expatriates have changed from being part of a dominant and privileged clique to a diffuse presence in a cosmopolitan city. And although some expatriates themselves are a little too quick to scent anti-foreign feelings when, say, an immigration officer is unco-operative or inefficient, they are more likely to encounter indifference than odium. They are still 'foreign devils' to the locals, but the term *fan gweilo* or simply *gweilo* is usually uttered in a neutral, ironic, or even an indulgent way, and hardly ever in tones of fear and loathing.

Starting with the two stereotypes, we went backwards and forwards in time to build up a picture of how a number of expatriates lived in Hong Kong, and what came out of their sojourn. In the foreground of this picture are the stories of some who passed through Hong Kong from the Second World War to the present. The background is filled in from the memoirs of those from an earlier time. Governors and merchant princes apart, most led ordinary lives, touched by the great events and dramas of the day but not obviously instrumental in instigating them. We made no attempt to pull them out of the shadows into the limelight. Each of the protagonists, though, found his or her own way of engaging with the place, the single mother of adopted Chinese babies no less than the Cantonese-speaking district officer. They are all participants in the story of modern Hong Kong, which developed out of the matchless synergy released when Western enterprise and Chinese ingenuity came together, and the whole historical panorama would have been very much less colourful without their commitment, talents, humour, and even, occasionally, their skulduggery.

They have been quoted at length. Some statements culled from old newspapers and memoirs read strangely today, but are more revealing of prevailing habits and opinions than any abstract comment of ours can be. In reproducing the words of those who were kind enough to write to us or let us interview them, we have deployed the lightest of editorial hands, confining ourselves to making only minor changes and conjunctions for the sake of clarity. Where a quotation is not attributed, it is either to respect a wish for anonymity or because what is expressed is a general view held by many. In one or two cases we were asked to use pseudonyms.

It has to be said that as research progressed, we ourselves were surprised by the sheer diversity of personalities and lifestyles revealed. At one point, realizing that we couldn't possibly capture them all, the book threatened to abort. We pressed on, if only because the tendency in these politically correct times is to deny that foreign men and women left their mark on Hong Kong. In a sense they were like the flowers of a plant whose roots extended deep into the subsoil of Hong Kong. That achievement is itself worth recording, even if the flowers eventually wither and die. Incidentally, Hong Kong left its mark on them. But that is another story.

Of course generalizations are always dangerous, and expatriates are not cast in a mould. Yet nearly all of them had something in common: they were in Hong Kong because they chose to be, and because they knew deep down that whatever their endeavour might be, the likelihood of their succeeding was greater here than anywhere else in the world.

1
'Braveheart' in China

The plaintive skirl of bagpipes wafts down a flower-bedecked staircase into the sumptuous lobby of Kowloon's luxurious Regent Hotel. There's no mistaking that this is the venue of the St Andrew's Ball. On the floor above, squeezed into the hall formed by the landing, burly men in kilts and sparkling women in silks and satin mill around each other. The sea of tartan, some of it stretched a little too tightly over expansive waistlines, reminds one of nothing so much as the Hollywood epic, *Braveheart*. We are not here, though, to celebrate a national hero or lament his lost cause (William Wallace succeeded in freeing Scotland from English rule but, branded a traitor by the English king, was hanged, beheaded, disembowelled, and quartered in 1305). The faces of the men are not daubed with war paint but will be, once the reeling starts, with the sheen of sweat. Yet the ball is a patriotic celebration of sorts, if only to laud the fact that 160 years after the first Scots came to Hong Kong, they are irrepressibly here still.

Beyond the double doors, in the ballroom itself, the walls are hung with the colourful regalia of the clans. The names emblazoned across the banners—'Armstrong', 'Haig', 'Strathearn', 'Bruce', 'Buchanan' and so on—are gaudily redolent of the romance of Scotland.

If the image of Scotland cherished by foreigners consists mostly of plaids, pipe bands, whisky, and haggis, generations of expatriate Scots must be held partly responsible. Emigration, to England and overseas, has been a theme of Scotland's history for over two centuries: 'In British settlements from Dunedin to Bombay, for every Englishman who has worked himself up to wealth from small beginnings, you find ten Scotchmen,' the statesman and Member of Parliament Sir Charles Dilke recorded in 1869. It comes as no surprise, therefore, to find a preponderance of Scots in Hong Kong, both in the established firms like Jardines and in the police force prior to the resumption of Chinese sovereignty in 1997. They themselves perpetuate the image when enacting such rituals as the St Andrew's Ball, Burns Night, and the Muckleshanter Ball—annual occasions at which Scottish expatriates revert to tribal form.

All the same, it is a form subtly transformed by distance from the homeland. On Burns Night, dressed in what Hong Kong barrister Adrian Huggins calls their 'Prada tartan', they gather in a room—according to Peter Edwards (another lawyer)—to eat haggis 'flown in by an English airline and washed down with French plonk . . . The whole followed by lamb cooked by a Swiss chef and finished off with American coffee'. As if that's not incongruous enough, the toast at the St Andrew's Ball is to the President of the People's Republic of China as well as Her Majesty the Queen. On top of the French plonk, a great deal of whisky is also invariably drunk. At one Burns Night dinner, an observer saw twelve bottles of whisky and one of Drambuie drained by a table of twelve before the speeches were over.

Adrian Huggins, himself the son of expatriates, knows that exile, even the voluntary sort, sometimes makes his fellow countrymen sentimental. They can also be defensively and assertively Scottish or English (or just British under different circumstances): 'When I was a boy at school in England, I used to be shipped off to my grandmother in Paisley for the holidays. Everybody could tell I was a Sassenach just by the way I spoke. Now I come to this sort of thing [the St Andrew's Ball], wearing tartan trews, something I'd never have done before. It's absurd but it has something to do with wanting to be part of the gang.' Indulging occasionally in exaggerated nationalism is very much in keeping with the expatriate experience.

Exaggerated nationalism is certainly in evidence on St Andrew's anniversary, which is more celebrated abroad than at home. The St Andrew's Society of Hong Kong was formed in 1881 in order, as its constitution affirms

> that there may be . . . a regularly constituted body of Scotsmen, under whose auspices and control the anniversary of St Andrew, the Birthday of Robert Burns and any other national celebration may be observed, and who may take cognizance of, discuss, and take steps in regard to any matters which possess a national and local interest by donations from the Society's funds, or otherwise. The Society shall also be a charitable association to relieve distressed and deserving countrymen, in so far as considered desirable and the funds will permit.

Beginning with the prominent merchant Phineas Ryrie in 1881, its list of 'chieftains' is a veritable roll-call of the great and the good in the territory.

Harry Wilken, a native of Elgin, joined the Society within two weeks of arriving to work for Jardines in 1972. One early autumn evening soon afterwards,

> the St Andrew's Society hosted a beating retreat of the Black Watch at the cricket ground in Central. It was attended by Sir Murray Maclehose, the Governor, and Lord Ballantrae, the honorary colonel of the regiment, who was in town and came as a guest. The Governor was a member of the Society anyway, being a Scot. By 6.30 there was no traffic and all had gone quiet. A screen had been put up in the middle. As dusk fell, spotlights were snapped on and the pipe band came out from behind the screen and they played the full beating of retreat. It was phenomenal—you suddenly realized this is something else!
>
> The St Andrew's balls were so well supported that I couldn't go in my first two years. A friend of my father's, deputy chairman of the Hongkong Bank at one time, used to go back and forth across the harbour on the Star Ferry, piping people to the ball

when it was held at the Peninsula Hotel. There were special
ferry sailings purely for people attending the ball, at two, three,
and four o'clock in the morning.

You get an inkling of how grand it all was. The very first St
Andrew's Ball in Hong Kong was held on 30 November 1877,
before the Society was formed. It took place at the City Hall, whose
embellishment for the occasion, far exceeding that of the Regent's,
was positively sumptuous. Six-foot high columns supported flower
stands in the entrance hall. Candles blazed and jewels flashed in
the light. You ascended the staircase through a mass of foliage, for
tendrils of lustrous evergreens were wound round its banisters, and
clusters of moss, ferns, and floral St Andrew's crosses adorned the
newels. These sylvan decorations were only the faintest adumbration
of greater splendours above. Three arches cunningly framed in
plantain leaves and draped with flags met you at the head of the
stairs. The middle one sported the Order of the Thistle in the shape
of an eight-pointed star picked out in ramrods and bayonets. It was
a prodigious design, measuring eighteen feet from end to end, and
surmounted by the Garter and motto *Nemo me impune lacessit*
('Nobody touches me with impunity'). Lieutenants Walker and
McCallum, who were credited with the decoration, clearly got

carried away. On the wall of the ballroom itself they had fixed 270 bayonets in a circle and festooned the device with flags. Today we would think it a parody of the officers' mess style, but for the large naval and military presence at the ball, it must have seemed positively inspired.

His Excellency Mr John Pope Hennessy (he had not then been knighted) and Mrs Hennessy arrived shortly before ten o'clock and opened the ball with Lady Smale, wife of the Chief Justice. Perhaps the repertoire of the Band of Her Majesty's 28th Regiment left something to be desired, for only one reel was played, although there were enough waltzes, lancers, and quadrilles to satisfy the most energetic of dancers. A letter-writer to the *China Mail* deemed the programme rather too select for the 'mixed population of a colonial settlement', and another complained about the scramble in the supper room, where the bill of fare was less than satisfactory, but on the whole the ball was thought to be quite one of the most successful assemblies ever given in the colony.

Waltzes are no longer included at the St Andrew's Ball, for the zealots of Scottish dancing would think them merely distracting. What's more, to ensure that all goes well on the night, practices are held three weeks before the event. A participant finds that they are taken very seriously:

> It is 6 p.m. and for some 150 dedicated expatriates the start to an evening of extremely sweaty activity. They are going to be put through their paces at the second practice of reels for the St Andrew's Ball.
>
> 'I have to say it's a very impressive turnout,' says a lady in a pink T-shirt over a droopy floral cotton skirt.
>
> Most men have come straight from the office, shedding their ties and their leather shoes as they enter the cavernous sports hall of the Hong Kong Football Club. In trainers and socks, they take their position for the Gay Gordons. The instructor, his own feet daintily shod in suede dancing shoes, speaks encouragingly into his microphone. The steps are simple enough, but it takes an inordinately long time for everyone to master them.

The Eightsome Reel absorbs another twenty minutes. By
then a rustling and murmuring is hinting at the spectators'
impatience. Not for them the Gay Gordons or the Eightsome
Reel, 'which the majority can do already', they claim. They are
anxious to move on to dances known as the Duke of Perth and
Machine Without Horses.

Sisse McCall, a Danishwoman married to a Scot, learnt to reel
at such practice sessions. 'It took ages really. Every year we'd be
sweating over these reels, getting frightfully worried and waking
up at four o'clock in the middle of the night wondering "how does
this go?" And then in the 1980s the Muckleshanter started, and
that really got us going. You then had two events a year. You get
into it better that way.'

A relative newcomer to the expatriate social scene, the
Muckleshanter Ball was launched in 1981 and has been held at
various venues ever since. In 1997 the officers' mess at HMS *Tamar*
was an evocative setting for Sisse McCall and others who

> came from near and far to be at this particular one—from Tokyo,
> Bermuda, France, and Britain. Yes, there would be another
> Muckleshanter but it would never ever be like that again. Here
> we were in the headquarters of the British Army in Hong Kong
> dancing under the portrait of the Queen. It had a very colonial
> flavour and was rather old-fashioned in that people had dinner
> parties around town or went to a restaurant beforehand. You

came only for the dancing and later ate an enormous army breakfast. It was in a way a sad occasion but also huge fun because so many old friends were getting together.

———◇◦◆◦◇———

Another powerful Scottish symbol is the national poet, Robert Burns. There is a long tradition of marking his birthday with a dinner followed by much drinking and several ribald speeches, the first, a toast to 'the Immortal Memory', being usually punctuated by snatches of verse.

What would a Chinese bystander have made of it all? To begin with, overlooked by a head-and-shoulders portrait of a fellow with a cravat, a man in a tweed skirt makes a baffling speech:

> Some hae meat, an' canna eat,
> An' some wad eat that want it;
> But we hae meat, and we can eat,
> An' sae the Lord be thankit.

Then an unappetizing-looking grey ball, reputedly containing the minced liver, heart, and lungs of a sheep mixed with oatmeal and onion, is carried in accompanied by a man puffing into a bag from which issues discordant sounds that pain the ear. Many of those grey balls, it is claimed, are sold abroad, and, although it seems hardly credible, an Edinburgh shopkeeper actually specializes in their export. A great poet even went so far as to immortalize them by writing an ode *To a Haggis*. What barbarous tastes foreign devils have, to be sure!

The ode intoned, the bearers and piper are thanked with a dram of whisky in a silver vessel, which they tip upside down over their heads once emptied. Later on, in a state of mild exhilaration after hot food and liberal quantities of drink, the diners settle back in their chairs for the speeches.

A veteran of many such dinners, Harry Wilken knows the form:

> Jardines had lots of Scots and the older ones would organize for the younger ones to attend the Burns dinner. If you were the

youngest recruit you had to give the 'toast to the lassies'. The
formula is that the Immortal Memory toast is the major one,
usually made by a senior figure, always a member of the St
Andrew's Society, then there's the toast to the lassies followed
by the reply. Traditionally Jardines would toast and the Bank
[the Hongkong and Shanghai Banking Corporation] replied.
The two hongs took it in turns.

Alasdair Morrison [who became head of Jardines in 1994]
gave the toast years before me, in 1972. It became legendary:
there he was, brand new, and he socked it to them. I remember
being taken round to meet the directors of Jardines and being
loftily asked 'Where're you from?', and my replying 'Scotland,
sir.' Of course that led the conversation round to the St
Andrew's Society, the ball, and the Burns supper. One of the
directors said, 'Alasdair Morrison did an excellent Burns speech.
He'll go far in the hong.' I hadn't a clue what they meant but
I certainly knew what they meant after I met Alasdair. Alasdair
had of course been to Eton and Cambridge; he came from
Dumfriesshire so he'd already got three out of the four things
right. He wasn't called Keswick but that didn't matter. If you
made a good Burns speech, you're remembered—your future
career depended on it.

Reciting Burns, wearing kilts, playing a pibroch—going
through these motions together for an hour or an evening
celebrates ancestral continuity and a shared consciousness. Yet
the appeal of Robbie Burns is not confined to Scots abroad, as was
resoundingly demonstrated to Patrick Alexander on a cold night
in Beijing in 1979:

I ran Jardines' China trade from 1978 to 1982. Jardines was the
agent for White Horse whisky throughout the Far East. One
January, I think it must have been in 1979, we arranged in
Peking a rather bizarre promotion in the form of a Burns Night
event. We held it in a hall which, like everywhere in China in
those days, was ill-lit and under-heated. Our people in Jardines'
office in Peking had found in one of the universities a professor
of English literature; in fact he turned out to be one of the world's
great Burns experts, who had translated the whole of Burns's

work from the Scots dialect into the Chinese of the early eighteenth century. Anyway, we arrived with cartons and cartons of miniature bottles of whisky and put one on each seat plus something printed—rather like the service sheet at a wedding— with the names of Jardines, 'Bai Ma Jiu' [White Horse Liquor], and the Chinese trading companies which bought this sort of thing. There must have been about a hundred people.

It seems the professor was a born showman. He went up on stage to make a speech and to toast the Immortal Memory. I shall never forget the sight of this man reaching into the pocket of his Mao jacket, fishing out a miniature bottle of whisky, and downing it at the end of his speech. Everybody stood up, not quite sure what to do or what to say, but many of us including myself took advantage of those bottles—to warm ourselves up as much as anything else! There was then an interval. In the second half the professor recited the poem *Tam o' Shanter* in Chinese. This is a long narrative poem about two drunken characters leading a horse home through a graveyard. Actors from a Peking opera troupe played the parts of Tam, his friend, and the horse while the professor recited the poem. It was a hoot! People who have seen Peking opera know what a highly stylized performance it is, and it was interesting to note how easily and skilfully they used mime, a traditional feature of Peking opera, to make the story of the poem intelligible and amusing for the Westerners present who didn't understand Chinese. It was a most extraordinary and hilarious evening.

2
Merchants

It is no wonder that events like the St Andrew's Ball are so well supported in Hong Kong. Like much of the British Empire, the creation of the colony was largely the handiwork of Scotsmen. Captain Charles Elliot, the man who started it all by taking Hong Kong on his own initiative in 1841, was a descendant of an Anglo-Scottish Border clan and cousin of the second Earl of Minto. He stood at the end of a line of British emissaries—from Lord Macartney to Lord Napier (a Scottish peer)—charged with the task of opening up China to foreign trade.

Diplomacy failed but force prevailed, and in the story of Hong Kong it was the flag that followed trade, not the other way round. Two Scots of a keenly commercial cast rendered the lion's share in this endeavour: William Jardine, born in Dumfriesshire in 1784, and James Matheson of Lairg, Sutherland, fifteen years younger and a graduate of Edinburgh University. To claim that the colony of Hong Kong owed its existence to them would be stretching a good story too far. All the same, if they had been able to sell opium in China unfettered by imperial edicts, and if Jardine's lobbying for gunboats had carried less conviction with the Foreign Secretary, Lord Palmerston, the first Anglo-Chinese war might never have been fought at all.

As it was, within days of Elliot's signing of the Chuanbi Convention on 20 January 1841, Matheson was able to attend the raising of the British flag over Hong Kong at Possession Point. He had little doubt of the island's potential, as he confided to his partner Jardine in London:

> I know not where else we could have got a harbour equally good, more especially for large vessels. Were we able to settle this in right earnest under the acknowledged and irrevocable protection of the British Government it could hardly fail to become a considerable Emporium. . . . Many prefer Cowloon Peninsula, but we ought to have both.

If he thought the scrub-covered peaks rising behind the harbour
reminiscent of the Highlands, he didn't say so, but other Scots have
undoubtedly felt some empathy with the rocky hills and beautiful bays.

He was to settle in Hong Kong for little more than a year. In
that time he arranged to build a Jardine Matheson & Co warehouse
in local stone, the first solid 'head office' of a foreign firm in Hong
Kong. He himself occupied, if not a grand mansion, at least a
bungalow, and on an unrivalled site nearby.

Other European settlers soon followed suit. One of them, a
Captain William Morgan, lived 'at the upper end of the anchorage
in a sort of palace he has there.' This was at East Point (roughly
today's Causeway Bay), acquired for Jardine Matheson & Co by
Morgan acting as their agent. Despite such creature comforts,
though, Matheson decided to return to Britain in 1842. He was
only forty-six years old, but he would not be the last Hong Kong
expatriate to leave because he had made enough money to retire to
a life of ease. Like Jardine, he felt all the classic urges of a *nouveau-
riche* nabob, for besides seeking political eminence (he was elected
to Parliament), he joined the ranks of the landed gentry by
purchasing the Hebridean island of Lewis for half a million pounds.

Matheson (and Jardine before him) would stand as a shining
example to the young merchants who still had their way to make
in Hong Kong. On the whole they fared pretty well, if Albert Smith
is any guide. Calling on the merchant J. D. Gibb one day in 1858,
Smith found 'four of his clerks at dinner, in good style, with a

punkah working over them, red pith wine coolers, claret, madeira, and an excellent dessert.' Their talk was likely to have been of tea, silk, and opium, but the one absorbing subject which united them all was money and the dazzling prospect of profit. Why else would they have exiled themselves from their own country? Not that the normal working day was anything like arduous. But for all that, and despite the fine dinners, life in the East was dull. Boredom could be a more pernicious affliction than tropical disease.

Albert Smith, an entertainer who brought his act to Hong Kong in 1858, was struck by their dreary routine: They 'have a sad mind-mouldering time of it. . . . They loaf about the balconies of their houses, or lie in long bamboo chairs, smoke a great deal, play billiards at the Club, where the click of the ball never ceased from the earliest morning, and glance over the local papers. These journals are mostly filled with the most uninteresting, incomprehensible and infinitesimally unimportant local squabbles.' On the other hand, if the 400-odd Europeans there became rich enough to buy estates in England or Scotland like Jardine and Matheson before them, the struggle would have been worth it. That parvenu ambitions were still being amply fulfilled as late as 1931 is plain to an editor on the *South China Morning Post*, who wrote:

> It used to be a Chinese saying, perhaps still is, that four long coats came out of Yaumati each year—i.e., that delightful suburb produces each year, from its opium and other doubtful activities, four millionaires. It might similarly be said that the foreign community produces each year a steady crop of taipans and near taipans, synthetic gentlemen and toadies, who acquire a position which must be kept up in the style to which they were never before accustomed.

As Jardine Matheson's founders both died childless, control of the company passed to collateral branches of their families and eventually to the Keswicks, descendants of William Jardine's sister Jean. At the time of writing, Henry Keswick is the chairman of Jardine Matheson Holdings. The story goes that he was once asked if it was true he owned a Moore. His reply was marvellously ostentatious, smacking of all the lordliness and condescension of a merchant prince: 'I have two Moores. My Henry Moore and my grouse moor. And my Henry Moore is on my grouse moor.'

Family connections matter to Jardines. Not only has the firm been controlled by the Jardines and Keswicks since its founding, but a high proportion of its senior managers have also been Scottish. According to Robert Blake in the authorized history of the hong, 'The Lowlands of Scotland do not have clans, but there is such a thing as "clanishness". In the Jardine homeland of Dumfriesshire everyone knew each other. Recruitment was by selective family and local patronage'. This patronage has spawned an insiders' lexicon: the area where the founders and their kin have settled in Scotland is Chinatown, and employees are gamekeepers, factors, or Johnnies (as in 'Jardine Johnnies').

Sentiment might have had something to do with this patronage, but underlying it was shrewd business sense. Jardines' success has depended crucially on its ability to hire and retain senior staff who would be hard-headed and loyal. Who better than Scottish Lowlanders, with their reputation for being mean, tough, and dour? It is said that they are as hard as the country they hail from, where the nights are long and where the denizens' capacity for survival is exceptionally keen. They are descended, after all, from men and women for whom poverty, hardship, and constant internecine warfare in centuries past made raiding, robbery, and murder a way of life. Recruiting from this area, firms like Jardines could more easily foster loyalty by building on existing feelings of allegiance and love for family and home.

John Lang (pictured), who hails from
Langholm in the Borders, classic Jardine
country, applied to the hong in 1973 after
his father sent him a clipping about
'Mandarins from Dumfriesshire' from the
Sunday Telegraph. It had a photograph of
Henry Keswick taken in the boardroom of
Jardine House on Pedder Street—the taipan
in the heart of his oriental business empire.

(There are several taipans, but only one is *the* taipan, a title arrogated
to the head of Jardines by the author James Clavell). John Lang was
then a graduate trainee with an engineering company in
Birmingham, acquiring a flavour of industry through a spell on the
shop floor. There he was on night shift, standing by a canal one
autumn evening 'in my overalls and hobnailed boots, sweeping the
aisles as a labourer', when the clipping fluttered out of the envelope.
Hong Kong must have seemed ineffably exotic in comparison.

Setting the scene for his own appointment to Jardines, Patrick
Alexander explains why he was headhunted:

> Around 1976 Jardines made the decision that they needed to
> recruit some people in addition to those they normally recruited,
> that is people who came straight from university. This was
> because Jardines had been rapidly expanding during the early
> 1970s and they probably thought they were short of middle
> management. So they deliberately went out to recruit people in
> their late twenties and early thirties rather than the usual new
> graduates. I was one of those contacted by a headhunter. His
> name was Dickie Dutton, I remember. Dickie rang me up one
> afternoon out of the blue and asked me if I would consider going
> to work in Hong Kong. Funnily enough, though he wasn't to
> know, because my father had been involved in things Far Eastern,
> this attracted me rather more than it might otherwise have done.
> Also life was pretty desperate in England at the time.
>
> One thing led to another and we—me and others no
> doubt—were put through an initial interview programme in
> London, and then we were asked to go out to Hong Kong,
> presumably for a final selection process. I remember landing on

one of Hong Kong's wonderful clear blue sunny days, and I was greeted at Kai Tak by Simon Murray [a Jardines executive who went on to become taipan of Hutchison] in a red sports car, and driven all round the island. And of course coming from what appeared to be the austerity of Britain, this was very seductive. I was asked to join and I said yes. I wasn't married, I was only thirty, and it seemed like an exciting opportunity which would never come again, so I took it.

Years later I asked Dickie Dutton how on earth he'd managed to find somebody like me; I was working for a molasses trading subsidiary of Tate and Lyle when he phoned me. He said, I assumed jokingly, that he'd looked through a directory of business school alumni in the UK—I think there was an Association of Business School Graduates or some such thing—and I fulfilled several criteria. My name began with 'A' so it was near the beginning of the book, Alexander is generally regarded as a name of Scottish origin, and I had graduated as a business student from Edinburgh University. All those factors made him call me before others! Jardines obviously had Scottish connotations. The fact that I had up till then spent only one year in Scotland, namely at Edinburgh University, and had no real connection with Scotland other than through my grandparents, proved to be irrelevant.

Harry Wilken confessed he hadn't a clue about Jardines when he applied as a chartered accountant in 1971; nobody, he said, warned him about 'the dynasty'. Arriving in Hong Kong, he was pleasantly surprised to be 'whisked away from the airport in a limo' and accommodated in a flat that came complete with resident staff. Invitations to an assortment of social events followed thick and fast. At work he found himself the only expatriate in the department, with a very competent Chinese as number two minding the office— 'like the Army, the sergeant major ran things'.

All the same, Hong Kong's noisy clamour, crowds, and climate are often a shock to a new arrival, while the emotional landscape can be equally alien and possibly lonely. Catapulted into this, the young expatriate initiated needs to have his social map defined for him. Long-lived hongs such as Jardines, John Swire & Sons, and the Hongkong and Shanghai Banking Corporation had known from the beginning how to hasten the process of adaptation. It was indoctrination of a kind, familiar to all those who had been to British public schools and the older universities. Bachelor recruits were accommodated in 'messes', a sort of extension of student halls or dormitories. An army of resident houseboys and amahs cleaned, washed, and cooked for them. Messes were fully furnished, and utilities were paid for by the firm. Graduate recruits stayed in them usually for no longer than six to nine months, after which they were posted to Japan, Thailand, the Philippines, Taiwan, and so forth. If they moved to a job within Hong Kong, they would vacate the mess after two years or so, making room for the next lot. Harry Wilken admitted that

> mess living spoilt you. You'd snap your fingers and say to your houseboy, 'Ah Ho, eight for dinner tonight. Can do?' And he'd answer, 'Can do', and in the afternoon a chilled leg of lamb was delivered which would be a roast joint on the table by the evening. If the price of lamb was, say, ten dollars, you'd be paying eleven for it including 'squeeze'. The houseboy or amah controlled the mess and they made money out of you, and you knew it. But they also knew a great deal about you, and they kept their mouths shut!

Young executives were quickly inducted into community life through boating on company junks, weekends at company bungalows on the outlying island of Lantau or in the Portuguese enclave of Macao, and sessions of inter-hong sports. 'Until the early eighties all those perks were for expatriates only,' Harry Wilken recalls, 'the logic was that being away from home they were the ones who needed the succour and relaxation.' Junk parties hosted by Hongkong Bank staff, who could lay on a chicken curry lunch for twenty just by ordering it from the office mess, were particularly jolly.

Team spirit was important too, and it was enough to believe that the Battle of Waterloo was won on the playing fields of Eton for the hongs to give the greatest encouragement to competitive games and athletics. Bestowing a sense of belonging to staff was vital, of course, but they needed to be physically fit as well—a

robust employee was patently more effective than one who was not. All this was simple logic, summed up by Harry Wilken as 'drink by all means, chase your bits of skirt, but keep your health above all.'

No doubt many did enjoy healthy diversions, though what often proved more appealing were the consolations of louche Wan Chai bars and a ready supply of female company, not to mention the multiple pleasures of Manila and Bangkok, only a short hop away by plane. Gone were the days when juniors were told to give a wide berth to local girls or to defer marriage until at least the end of their first 'tour'. Despite such inducements, however, some still succumbed to the nagging feeling that they were missing out on things at home, and others despaired of the vapidity of Hong Kong's cultural life. One Jardines executive distributed as Christmas presents a specially printed forty-eight-page pamphlet entitled *The Artistic and Cultural Life in Hong Kong*, of which forty-six pages were blank.

It is the fate of expatriates to feel constantly torn, to live with the culture of their homeland as their primary point of reference while surrounded by a culture that is entirely alien. Thus disorientated, many swore they would give Hong Kong only two to three years; just as many, though, found to their chagrin a decade on that the years had imperceptibly crept up on them, and it was too late, or they were too old, to join the job queue at home.

In retrospect it seems that the likes of Patrick Alexander and John Lang were very nearly the last of one breed and the first of another. By the time they arrived in Hong Kong, expatriate recruits to the hongs had run the gamut from Albert Smith's tea-tasters and opium merchants to privately educated graduates from Oxbridge or the Scottish universities. They were also some of the last to be taken under Jardines' pampering wing and housed in messes and company flats. On the other hand, with Hong Kong at the brink of a profound economic change, the reverberations of which coalesced for companies like Jardines into a wish to re-engage in commerce with the communist Mainland, they were about to become China traders again.

Jardines had signed away its China business to the People's Republic in 1951. Sir John Keswick, the last taipan to work in Shanghai, had this to say about the breach: 'After 120 years Jardines were out of China, but not without the hope of a new trading relationship in the future.'

The future did indeed bring a new trading relationship, heralded by Deng Xiaoping's launch of reforms in 1978. That very autumn,

Patrick Alexander accompanied Sir John and Lady Keswick and a party of their friends on a visit to the Yangtze valley, having stocked up on whisky, marmalade, Nescafé, and Coffeemate beforehand.

Middle China unfolded with novel landscapes and unfamiliar sights: rice paddies tended by hand, water buffaloes ploughing, loudspeakers bellowing homilies at passers-by, spittoons everywhere. In Wuxi Alexander breakfasted on warm rice gruel, pickles, eggy bread ('very good'), cold chicken, and 'a sort of *millefeuille* cake'; and at Jingdezhen, porcelain capital of China, the party visited three factories, as Alexander describes:

> At each factory we were greeted by a senior official, drank the usual tea and listened to how production was now improving after the ravages of the Gang of Four. It is quite obvious that the Party sends out through the length and breadth of China a standard line for use by all officials when dealing with foreigners. They even use the same jargon phrases all the time, which makes it difficult to know what is really going on.
>
> Two of the factories were actually making pots and figurines and the other was merely painting on blanks supplied by them. We saw two or three children whose ages were said to vary between nine and fourteen but they seemed to be there of their own accord and in all instances working with their fathers and learning the trade. One complete family was making a Goddess of Mercy Buddha figure which very closely resembled a rather Baroque Virgin and Child. Did they get the style from the missionaries or did it grow up independently? Nobody seemed to know the answer.

He also remembers sitting on the station at Shanghai 'surrounded by people all in Mao jackets. Sir John put his arm round my shoulder and said, "Patrick, I was once a director of this railway." I knew myself to be very lucky for having been to places in China which remained closed for many years afterwards.'

Patrick Alexander was to go on to run Jardines' China trade division and, among his manifold duties, to introduce White Horse Whisky to a country just emerging from a long period of communist temperance and discipline. Meanwhile, in London, two recent recruits to Jardines were told they would be sent to Cambridge for a language course. One of them, Piers Litherland, thought it was a real bonus to be sent back to university and, what's more, to be paid for it:

The great chance of China trade opening up had just been set in
train by Deng Xiaoping, and it was felt that Jardines should
show its commitment right from the start by training people to
speak Mandarin.

We went to Cambridge and started this Foreign Office
programme. The course was three terms and then a year living
in Singapore or Hong Kong or Peking. We only did the first
term which was all the basic grammar, but we were the only
people there whose promotion or livelihood didn't really depend
on how well we did. So we took it a great deal less seriously
than the people from the Foreign Office.

After Cambridge, work in Hong Kong proved a disappointment.
'You came with huge expectations of being given early responsibility
. . . and the biggest problem was just relentless boredom, because the
work was very routine. . . . It was a very odd existence; there was
nothing intellectually challenging about it.'

By the time Piers Litherland was sent to Beijing in 1984, the
China trade division that Patrick Alexander managed had become
a different set-up, but

despite six years of the Open Door policy, China was still
recognizably a communist country, still a command economy,
and trade was very much still conducted by huge ministries, great
monolithic organizations which foreigners had to go through.

We were doing two things really. One was representing
companies from the United States and Europe in their
negotiations, either for sales of equipment or projects. We had
twenty joint ventures of one sort or another ranging from aircraft
catering to printing books with the Cultural Relics Bureau. We
also took on a number of agencies.

He and his wife Jenny lived in an apartment vacated by his
predecessor John Hastings-Bass and rented from China's Railway
Ministry. They had no doubt of being under close scrutiny by public
security apparatchiks there:

Our things used to be gone through, I should think once a week.
You'd come back and find all the books in different places, all
the papers moved. . . .

We got used to it. When we had negotiations for companies like Westinghouse, whom we represented for nuclear power stations, we knew that all our negotiations were listened to and taped, so whenever you wanted to talk about prices, you went for a walk outside, or you turned the radio on and the taps in the bath and talked very quietly underneath all that. It was quite bizarre.

A lot of it was very unreal—all this sitting around drinking endless cups of tea, negotiating round and round in circles and all the games that used to be played; and the fact that it was never the person who conducted the meeting who really made the decisions, but someone else who was always the third person along in the group.

The trouble was, head office directors in Hong Kong were not always sympathetic to the oddities of the situation. One of them was particularly tiresome, although Litherland was not the first junior executive to come up against a familiar type of expatriate to be found in Hong Kong, the sort who fancied himself an old China hand just because he had spent a few years in the East. Litherland did, however, have a rather sportive way of puncturing such self-importance; he made this director the constant butt of his 'prep school' jokes:

It was very difficult in those days to ring into China though quite easy to ring out. One of the easiest things to do was to pretend that the telephone connection was not working. Whenever he raised the subject of revising the budgets or further economies to be made in the office, I'd crackle a piece of paper into the headset and pretend that we were about to be cut off, or that the line had gone dead.

On one particular occasion he came up to Peking and we had to scrabble around to get a high-ranking Chinese official or deputy mayor from somewhere to come along to a banquet. I don't think this director ever paid much attention to the reality of things in China, to the fact that any official who bothered to turn up to a dinner hosted by a foreign company couldn't— almost by definition—be worth talking to or meeting.

So we sat at the table, with me as interpreter between the Jardines director and the deputy mayor. Halfway through dinner my director said to me, 'Can you ask the mayor what he thinks China's Gross Domestic Product will be this year?'

Now that was a pretty stupid question: in the first place there were no proper statistics, and in the second I hadn't a clue how to translate 'GDP' into Chinese. So I improvised instead:

'My director says it's extremely hot for the time of year. Is it always this hot?'

To which the deputy mayor replied, 'You're right. It *is* very hot. It has also rained quite a lot this summer.'

Turning to my director, I said, 'The mayor hopes they're going to achieve six and a half per cent, but it will be touch and go.'

My director continued, 'Well, exports must be keeping up as a result of the Open Door policy. Does the mayor think the Special Economic Zones a great success?'

Again I turned to the mayor: 'My director says Hong Kong has had quite a lot of rain as well. It's unusual to see two places so far apart on the map with such similar weather, isn't it?'

And in this way the conversation went on completely at cross purposes for about fifteen minutes. It was a small, tiny, little bit of satisfaction that one got out of the whole thing!

―――――――◦◆◦―――――――

For Bruce (who wishes to remain anonymous), China trade has meant more than his fair share of adventure and stress, although he is as committed as ever. Now, nearly two decades after first putting his toe in the risky waters, he is actually living in Guangdong during the week.

Trained as an engineer, he arrived in Hong Kong in 1982 'essentially to work in a middle management position in one of the traditional trading companies which had maintained a presence not only in China but across all of Asia for sixty years. This particular company was not as grand as Jardines, but nevertheless shared the same culture.' For an expatriate even in the 1980s, such a hong was still the 'Promised Land':

Being a gweilo in Hong Kong then was like living in a gilded cage. You worked for a huge company and everything was done for you. We had a magic thing called the 'compradore account', and whenever you wanted some money you went down to the basement of the office, to a little cash counter, signed a chit, and somebody gave you the money. At the end of the month it was knocked off your salary.

Perhaps the mollycoddling palled. Certainly, within a couple of years, he was itching to do something more exciting. The Hong Kong and regional markets were all very well, he thought, but there must be opportunities in China for the sort of goods his firm was selling. These, 'let it be remembered, were fairly unromantic products like sewage treatment plants, oilfield equipment, and gas processing machinery. I was actually one of the mavericks who felt we should go to China and try and develop a model for determining what the Chinese would buy. So I volunteered for special duties!'

In the early 1980s China was still groping her way towards full-blown economic engagement with the rest of the world. Neither manufacturing in the Pearl River delta nor exports had taken off at that point. The country knew little about foreign trade or technology and had limited hard currency. Bruce suggested as much to his colleagues:

'Rather than apply a scatter-gun approach', I said, 'let's try and focus on what the Chinese will buy. It's clear they can only buy if they had the foreign currency, so they'd favour import substitution projects and anything that generated foreign currency. If you could identify products that would fit those conditions, you'd have a far better chance of selling them something.'

So, with the help of middlemen who had emerged to act as agents between us and the Chinese parties, we identified such key products as machine tools, onshore oilfield equipment, specialized manufacturing equipment, and started signing contracts.

When upgrading their devastated and backward industries, the Chinese concentrated on technology that wasn't too advanced. They wanted machines which would enable them to improve what they were making currently. In the Western world people were going into production processes that would reduce the reliance on labour. That wasn't necessary in China. They had plenty of labour with generally good skills.

Those were pioneering days for Western merchants, 'the romantic days', says Bruce, when there were no precedents or any recognizable way of conducting business. Even common sense or intuition was of no avail when it came to negotiating with Chinese representatives:

They were all dressed identically in faded blue jackets and you could never tell the pecking order or who the most important person was in a group. Frequently I made the mistake of being very respectful to the guy who somehow looked more distinguished than the others and he'd turn out to be the driver.

Understanding the Chinese way of business was difficult. At one point when the Chinese side was short of foreign currency, we were asked to enquire if the supplier, a small private company in Yorkshire, England, would accept any form of barter. We had to explain that barter no longer had a place in a Western economy, that 3,000 tons of rice in exchange for machine tools would not be a very liquid form of payment!

I have lovely memories particularly of places such as Wuhan where we would check into a hotel built in the 1930s, maybe in the Sino-Japanese era, and we'd talk through a haze of cigarette smoke and drink Chinese tea for hours and hours. You would wander through your vast hotel suite in search of your cherished little jar of coffee that you'd remembered to bring and sneakily make yourself a cup of coffee to masquerade as tea, and you'd find one of the Chinese party in your bathroom having a bath, and another using your toothbrush!

Then you'd go back to the smoke-filled room and continue discussions. That was the way contracts were negotiated. The Chinese had all the time in the world, their deadlines seemed to stretch infinitely, whereas yours were dictated by the fact that there was no computer flight reservation system and you had to go to the airline office to book your ticket on the day you wanted to go, so you were always worried that when you finished your meeting there would be no flight. We had people running backwards and forwards to the airline office all day long to try and get a flight confirmation so you could leave as soon as possible. Of course the Chinese knew perfectly well you were under pressure and that gave them an advantage.

Once, attempting to leave Shanghai, he found himself alone, without an interpreter, on a platform on Nanjing railway station:

That would have been in 1984. I couldn't get a direct flight back to Hong Kong; I could do it only through Canton, and the only way to get to Canton that day was through Nanjing. So I left the rest of my party and got on the train to Nanjing.

At the other end, I got out of the train and stood on a platform with my luggage surrounded by hundreds of Chinese who all stopped whatever they were doing to stare at me. I had very limited Chinese then, but somehow I had to get to the airline booking office or the airport itself.

Suddenly a man appeared out of the crowd, picked up my luggage, and gestured to me to follow him. He took me to a three-wheeled motor cycle with a wooden box of about one metre by one metre on its back. He put my luggage into that box and pointed for me to climb in as well. I concertinaed myself up and we set off down the road. I kept saying 'fei ji, fei ji' [aeroplane] and, unerringly, he took me to the CAAC booking office. Bicyclists who passed us on the road were practically crashing into each other as they caught sight of me crammed into this box, with my suitcase poking out on one side and my head on the other.

By the mid-1980s the Special Economic Zone established in Shenzhen was showing signs of becoming the leading manufacturing centre for southern China. Take-up for capacity there was breathtakingly fast; in fact the reforms were bringing such broad and profound changes that all those involved, says Bruce, 'could perceive a difference even at three-monthly intervals'.

When he returned to the China arena in the mid-1990s, having left the hong to pursue other business interests in the interim, he found the economic climate radically transformed. But although much had improved, no country proceeds that rapidly along the development path without touching off a host of contradictions, as Bruce discovered.

For a start, looks could be very deceiving. Assigned to restructure a Hong Kong–China joint-venture manufacturing company which had been 'haemorrhaging money' for many years, he realized that while 'the factory appeared well kept, there were great gaping holes in terms of ability in management.' He unearthed other grave problems: 'the machinery was breaking down, the designs were archaic; there was corruption as well as serious local competition through copying and plagiarism. Because the company was a foreign investment, it was seen by the local authorities as an easy touch for taxes, fines, ridiculous fees, and protection.'

He began by laying off much of the workforce, firing most of the Hong Kong-based managers who, it transpired, were just as corrupt as their mainland counterparts, and closing down all the branch offices in China. Pressure from the factory's creditors, some of whom had been waiting to be paid for over a year, was an equally urgent concern. To forestall any wayward tactics on their part Bruce decided to take the bull by the horns:

> I said to the managers I knew I could trust: 'Assemble a meeting of all the creditors and I'll talk to them.'
>
> They were aghast. 'You can't do that,' they said, 'the creditors are very angry. They'll lynch us or force us to shut the factory down.'
>
> But I insisted. When I walked into the meeting, I could see the mood was very ugly. One or two creditors were glowering at me and practically foaming at the mouth. I tried to stop the shouting and calm them down. To my interpretor, I said, 'Please translate everything I say exactly. If I say the 'f' word, use an

equivalent in Chinese. If I call myself an idiot, call me an idiot. I've got to get these people on my side.'

So I talked. I asked the creditors what they thought this stupid gweilo was trying to do. What was I up there for? I said I would answer the question myself. I was trying to save the company. If I saved the company, it was a win-win for all of us.

'But the moment I walk out of the door,' I continued, 'this company collapses and one of our major customers, whom I had brought in, will walk too. If I stay and keep things going, you've got a chance of being paid. Now what do we do? Will you take us to court and close us down next week, in which case I'll go back to Hong Kong and find another job, and nobody will get anything, or will you give us time to put things right?'

I made them laugh by speaking bad Chinese. Slowly the creditors calmed down. What I did would have seemed obvious in Europe or America, but in China frequently there's a reluctance to have an open dialogue. And maybe if you're Chinese it *is* difficult, but if you're a foreigner it can sometimes be easier. Still to this day, they'll show a certain respect for you, they won't perhaps be as blunt or rude as they would to one of their own. You can come out with a different approach, and that may help you to work out a plan that saves everyone's face and allows you to salvage the business.

Does that mean the expatriate still has a role in China, despite growing international exposure for Hong Kong Chinese and, to a lesser extent, mainland Chinese? 'Yes, we bring another perspective to the business and we bring in ideas. We know the international standards, the distribution channels, and the customers' viewpoint and their expectations. Somebody like me understands both sides. My contribution is to do with the fact that I've worked in Hong Kong for a long time, I've worked in China, but I also know what Western markets require, so I bring that mix. For all foreign managers working in China, be they Westerners, Japanese, or other Asians, the key is building on her strengths and complementing her weaknesses.'

———○-◇-○———

In July 1996 Chinadotcom was listed on the Nasdaq, the first Chinese portal to do so. Some would call this a defining moment, for though the old economy didn't exactly come to an abrupt halt then, that public debut did put the seal of approval on a new business that had seemingly appeared from nowhere before bursting spectacularly upon the investment scene. With apparently the same suddenness, terms like 'e-commerce' and 'e-merchants' began erupting in newsprint and conversations.

Chinadotcom was the brainchild of Hong Kong entrepreneur Peter Yip. Prior to its initial public offering, he bought a technology start-up named Web Connection with a view towards propelling the IPO. Web Connection, according to Neil Macdonald, is the jewel in Chinadotcom's crown.

Neil Macdonald should know, since it was he and two others who started it all. Son of an expatriate police officer, he spent his childhood in Hong Kong, went to boarding school in England, and returned to join the Hong Kong Police Force himself. Two years later he left, having decided that he really wanted to write screenplays and make films, and that was when he became involved in a company called Salon Films. As a production assistant to start with, he 'helped to run a film set which basically meant you made coffee for people.' But he did also work on location shooting for some glamorous projects such as the feature film *Noble House* and the television series *Round the World in Eighty Days*.

It was after he had left Salon Films and built up a business making corporate films that he met Ian Henry, another young expatriate. They got on very well, and the timing was perfect. The year was 1993, just as interest in the Internet was burgeoning and the market for corporate films went dead. Like other start-ups, theirs began with a good idea:

> We got talking about how the Internet was being used around the world and what it would mean to Hong Kong. We decided we'd be able to go to our corporate clients, people like Hongkong Bank, Mandarin Oriental Hotel Group, Singapore Airlines, Hongkong Telecom, for whom we'd made films, and tell them the Internet was the next big advertising medium. It was going to be the next big marketing tool.
>
> We were lucky in that we had very good contacts like the Mandarin Oriental who were prepared to listen. Our initial plan was to go to those clients and say, you need to go on the Internet, have some sort of Web presence. Pretty much to a man they hadn't got a clue what was going on in the United States and elsewhere, but they agreed it was something they needed to do.
>
> If we actually knew what was happening then you could say there was a design to what we did. There wasn't. We were complete novices, and we were making it up as we went along. There wasn't a pre-existing model to follow. The only thing we had was a good idea.

With modest profits from a marketing film they had made for the Mandarin Oriental Hotel Group, Neil Macdonald and Ian Henry set up Web Connection. It was to be an e-business solutions provider to traditional companies which were unable or unwilling to establish an online presence for themselves, and so 'we developed several dozen websites that we put into cyberspace.' But they also realized that

> nobody's going to visit a site that's simply listing companies; that would be very dry, very boring.
>
> Ian and I recognized very early on that the site should be content-driven. You had to have content that was specific to the location under which the sites were housed. We wanted people to understand that we'd created an environment to which they

could go to find out anything they wanted to know about Hong Kong.

So you need to provide all sorts of local information about the weather, places to eat, places to go, what's on at the cinema, all that kind of thing. You need to be able to offer horoscopes, financial updates, and people's opinions about Tung Chee-hwa. It's only by having interest in the site that you're going to be able to sell advertising. Companies are going to spend so many dollars a month having a banner on your home page only if they know you're getting hit several hundred thousand or even a million times a day. Without that nobody's going to advertise.

What content we had to start with we generated ourselves. It was the only way, because we didn't have the financial wherewithal to go to Reuters, say, for financial information, or to the *South China Morning Post* or the *Hong Kong Standard* for their leisure sections. With Web Connection still in its infancy, they might perhaps have let us have something, for example their restaurant listings, for a fee. But buying complete entertainment guides would have been too expensive.

So we were out there doing it ourselves, going to the restaurants to make sure they gave us their menus, and putting them on our site. We did this for free.

Cash flow was a perennial problem. Not being trained in graphics or programming, they had to hire staff, which added to costs. Macdonald makes no bones about what a harrowing time they had:

> It was very hard work. I know it's a Hong Kong story, but we did work every hour God gave. Eighteen- to nineteen-hour days were far from uncommon. During the day we'd approach the various groups which, for example, operated restaurants in Lan Kwai Fong. We'd have lunch at one of the restaurants, go back to our office in Wan Chai, get rid of the office stuff that needed to be done, and then in the evening we got on with writing up the reviews for the programmers to put on the site the next morning.
>
> I'd be lying if I suggested that all this didn't exact a personal toll. Ian and I were both in relatively young marriages at the

time. My son was barely six months old, and Ian and his wife were just about to have their first baby. Neither of us got to see our families.

At their lowest point, they went across to a bar, Carnegie's, to discuss whether to wind the company up:

> There was no money forthcoming. Neither Ian nor I as directors was taking a salary. We couldn't afford to, as every dollar we made went into buying new equipment or paying the staff, and even that was difficult.
>
> But I insisted we kept the company going. We also knew we had to find somebody who could help us out. Peter Hamilton, then a well-paid executive at Hongkong Telecom, was our first port of call. Way before the term was coined, he became our 'angel'. He provided us with sufficient money on a monthly basis to keep the company going, and eventually left Hongkong Telecom to come in with Web Connection.

Peter Hamilton, says Neil Macdonald, helped to take Web Connection in a direction that made it very attractive to Chinadotcom, which offered to buy the company. 'We did a straight share swap,' Macdonald explains, 'acquiring a percentage of shares in Chinadotcom that was to be listed in exchange for their total ownership of Web Connection.' By then he had decided that he wanted to return to film-making and the three founders agreed to 'an amicable separation'.

In the spring of 1999 he was given the option of selling a percentage of his shareholding. He did so at Chinadotcom's moment of glory, when the share price was near its height, and thus unlike some so-called Internet millionaires he escaped the bursting of the dotcom bubble and as a result is not merely paper-rich. He has gained the financial freedom to pursue whatever interest takes his fancy, and for that he is thankful: 'I don't know if "fortune favours the brave" is necessarily the right way of putting it, but we were lucky to do what we did before anybody else.'

3
Ministers and Mandarins

On 25 May 1999 the closure of Her Majesty's Overseas Civil Service (HMOCS) was commemorated at Westminster Abbey in the presence of Queen Elizabeth II. The Abbey was filled to the brim for this service, the Hong Kong contingent alone numbering 186. To say that there was not a dry eye in the house by the end would sound melodramatic, but there is no denying the emotive appeal of the last hymn, Kipling's *Recessional*:

> God of our fathers, known of old,
> Lord of our far-flung battle-line,
> Beneath whose awful Hand we hold
> Dominion over palm and pine.

The occasion undoubtedly had resonance, and Dan Waters (joined Colonial Service 1954, retired in Hong Kong in 1980) for one was moved. To a younger generation, though, 'Dominion over palm and pine' no doubt sounds obsolete and ridiculous: Pax Britannica was over decades ago, and Hong Kong, says Anthony Kirk-Greene in his book *On Crown Service*, is better viewed as the end of the end of Empire.

Yet it was not so long ago that the colonial administrator or District Officer remained at large. David Browning, one of those at the Westminster Abbey service, has the distinction of being the last British District Officer in the Empire. His penultimate posting before retirement—to Sha Tin in the New Territories (population in 1995: 570,000)—bore absolutely no resemblance to his first (Northern Rhodesia, to which he was appointed in 1960).

His own feeling about the Westminster Abbey service was that

> it wasn't a sentimental journey. There were no regrets; nobody was sad. I felt it was a nice culmination of a terrific effort by lots of people over the 150-odd years of the Service's history. But it's a period of history that's finished. The work's done. We think we've done a good job, and now it's up to the people in all these former

British territories to make the best of it themselves. I looked on the commemoration much more as a reunion of old chums.

I decided to join the Northern Rhodesia group, not the Hong Kong group, and I recognized so many people from thirty to forty years ago, and some of them remembered me though I was very much a lower form of pond life at that stage of my life. The main address, by Sir Richard Luce, Governor of Gibralter, put the emphasis on the value of District Officers in the days of Empire.

David Browning was one of an estimated 750 HMOCS members serving in Hong Kong in early 1997, and one of many who elected to stay on after the Handover. It was the third time he had seen the Union flag lowered on British withdrawal, having witnessed the independence of Northern Rhodesia and the New Hebrides, his second posting. Northern Rhodesia, which became Zambia in 1964, remains the scene of his most satisfying experiences:

> As an administrative officer it's always difficult to measure your achievement; you look back on life and wonder 'what on earth have I done?' Of course you can do things just by being there— keeping the peace—but it's not always possible to point to anything tangible.

By smoothing the country's difficult progress a little he made a difference in Zambia, 'and that felt good.'

Browning joined the Hong Kong Civil Service in 1981, two years after the New Hebrides became the Republic of Vanuatu. Hong Kong, Britain's last significant colony and journey's end for

a number of still-serving members of HMOCS, was a harsh contrast
to Africa and islands in the south Pacific. Ian Lightbody (Hong
Kong Civil Service, 1945–80) encountered some of the 'cadets who
transferred from the African territories as they "closed down" and
got independence. A lot of the administrative officers found it
difficult to adjust to Hong Kong because they were used to the
wide open spaces, going on safari tours and so on. Hong Kong was
very cramped, very metropolitan.' As Browning, speaking of his
penultimate posting, put it, 'The bush in Sha Tin was concrete,
concrete jungle, that is. There were no similarities between being a
bush DO [District Officer] and being a DO in an urban situation.
I didn't feel that the District Officer had an important enough
function, but the post was left in place to be a figurehead as the
main government representative in the district.'

Despite initial misgivings, Browning found as the years passed
that—almost to his own surprise—a sense of belonging had crept up
on him. Nevertheless, save for a handful who have chosen to retire in
Hong Kong, few expatriate civil servants felt called upon to decide
where their loyalty and future lay. They might serve beyond the
Handover, yes, but at the back of their minds they had no doubt they
would go in the end. 'I could have retired at fifty-five but I chose to
retire at sixty,' says Browning, 'because I wanted to go through the
Handover. I felt almost as if this was an obligation for me as I'd
experienced the transfer of power twice before. But once I got through
the Handover I felt there was a limited time that I should stay. This
was partly to do with localization and the increasing use of Chinese
language in government. Six months after the Handover I applied
for early retirement.' Exercising his prerogative to return home by
sea, he sailed off in the luxury liner *Arcadia*, a leisurely way to pass
from active life to retirement, from the East to the West. 'It seemed
a bit of an anachronism but was no less enjoyable for that. I got back
to exactly the same berth in Southampton that I sailed out from in
February 1960. . . . thirty-nine years and three months had elapsed
between the two voyages.'

⟼o◈o⟻

It was, of course, by sea that the first administrative recruits to the Hong Kong Civil Service came under a scheme instituted by Sir Hercules Robinson (Governor, 1859–65) in 1862.

Ian Lightbody explains: 'Back in the 1860s the Governor of the day felt the colonial authorities were badly handicapped because there was a complete lack of any reliable and authoritative translation and interpretation, which was not a good way of running a government in a Chinese colony.' Sir Hercules' scheme would redress this by recruiting graduates from Britain to be trained initially as government interpreters. As the author H. J. Lethbridge explained, these new recruits, or cadets as they were called, 'would have teachers provided for them; when competent, as they might be in three years . . . they should be considered preferable (after a further two years of experience in administration) to any office in the Civil Service that did not involve a professional training.'

In the event, the first cadets soon found their studies overtaken by the pressure of work so that they never became interpreters as such. The supply of cadets always lagged way behind the requirement, and as magistrate, superintendent of police, or registrar-general, they achieved rapid promotion. From the start they were expected to be what Ian Lightbody characterized as

> jacks of all trades, and they did pretty well everything at the senior level. The jobs were so varied and the posting range so wide that the Hong Kong government would have been caught out badly had it tried to specify qualifications and job descriptions. By and large you were expected to have a university degree, and candidates had to sit a written competitive examination, which was eventually replaced by an interview system. . . . the Colonial Office felt that exams weren't a very searching test of one's fitness for the job.

Selection by interview was introduced by Sir Ralph Furse, the Colonial Office's director of recruitment through the 1930s up to the immediate post-War period. An old Etonian, Furse had left Oxford with a third, and what he looked for in his recruits were perhaps attributes very like his own: the *esprit de corp* developed at public school, and common sense rather than academic excellence.

Interviews were more likely to tease out hints of such useful personal qualities as adaptability, doggedness, and practical reasoning.

The ruling establishment of colonial Hong Kong grew from these small beginnings. Sir Robert Hart, the famous inspector-general of the Chinese Maritime Customs, said in 1903 that foreigners in China could be divided into three classes—mercantile, missionary, and ministerial. In pre-1997 Hong Kong, the ministerial element was this administrative élite headed by the Governor. The way government was organized, the highest members of this élite (they were known as 'Secretaries') both proposed policies and implemented them, and so were ministers in all but name. Sir Ralph Furse was quite succinct on the subject: 'in most colonies the Civil Servant is the Government, and not the servant of the Government.'

Power wore a benevolent face on the whole, and those who exerted it 'definitely had a sense of mission,' according to Ian Lightbody. 'No-one instilled this. It seemed to be part of the ethos of the Colonial Service. The cadets felt responsible for their charges— that's how it was.' Austin Coates, the writer, speaks of the strange responsibilities of being 'the father and mother of the people'. In a similar vein, James Hayes, looking back on a thirty-year career in the civil service (1956–87) including several posting to the New Territories, notes that a District Officer

> was regarded as a 'Fu Mo Kwun', a 'Father and Mother Official', in the traditional mould by the New Territories' public, who saw us as officers with a clear responsibility to look after them and protect their interests.

Translated into everyday routines this meant government with a paternalistic, albeit light, hand. Provide the physical and cultural infrastructure of a civil society, and let people get on with their own lives—that was the principle. Sir James Stewart Lockhart (Hong Kong Civil Service, 1879–1901, Civil Commissioner of Weihaiwei, 1902–21) found this chimed rather well with the Chinese view of things:

> There is in China a saying that the art of government is to do nothing. While not attempting to follow such a short cut to successful government as that recommended in this saying, this

Government has taken as its maxim *Pas trop gouverner*—avoiding meddlesome interference with Chinese affairs, which invariably breeds trouble, creates friction, and ultimately leads to the creation of a large and expensive staff.

Sir James Stewart Lockhart had reason to be wary of meddlesome interference in Chinese affairs. Appointed special commissioner to inspect and report on the extension of the colony of Hong Kong in 1898, he was also charged with delimiting the boundaries of this extension, and it turned out to be no easy task to bring the New Territories and its resentful denizens into the fold of colonial administration. For centuries farmers in this area had looked not so much to the emperor, who was very far away, but to their village elders, and they baulked at suddenly becoming subjects of a foreign power. In fact they were all for taking up arms against their new masters until assured that their own laws and customs, not to mention their rights to land and other privileges, were not in danger of being overthrown. They got their way. Well into the 1980s, government policy conceded that the New Territories had to be treated as separate and different from urban Kowloon and Hong Kong. For the expatriate civil servant, this frontier area was the nearest thing to the 'bush' or 'out-station' that Hong Kong offered.

The leased hinterland was indeed a wild and unsavoury place in the early days. Here is a minute about his mat-shed office that Cecil Clementi, land officer and police magistrate in the New Territories, 1903–06, addressed to the Colonial Secretary; it was copied by a clerk, which explains the spelling mistakes and other errors:

> It is over-run by rats, cockroaches, white ants, etc. The stationery in the very drawers of my desk is urinated [on] by rats. I find today that one of the new rent rolls books, only completed last month and fresh from the goal [sic], has been gnawed all over by a rat. The other day I found a camphor wood box & its contents of paper partially destroyed by white ants. When it rains the rain comes through the roof and moistens everything. . . .

This was certainly an odd situation for a brilliant classicist and Chinese scholar to find himself in, but, nothing daunted, Clementi managed to acquire a detailed knowledge of local land law in the process. He proved highly adept as a linguist as well. Within a short time of arriving in Hong Kong, he was not only fluent in Cantonese but had also published a translation of Cantonese love songs.

Clementi had attended schools in Germany and England before going up to Oxford to study Latin and Greek. A grandson, David Clementi, has pieced together a picture of this clever, able, and charming man from the reminiscences of his father (Cresswell) and aunts (Dione and Cecily):

> My grandfather was strikingly tall, with a sturdy, athletic and dignified build, and can justly be described as an outstanding administrator, traveller, and scholar. What appealed to him in the Chinese was their capacity to work hard and to maintain a family life, both traits which were to be found in himself.
>
> Following university, in 1899 he joined the Colonial Service and his first posting was to Hong Kong. He always said that the happiest years of his life were spent in Hong Kong. . . .
>
> His main recreation was travel and he visited all of the eighteen provinces of China and mastered most of the languages. He was a keen geographer and details of some of his journeys, the longest being from the Indian border to Kowloon, have been published.
>
> In 1913 he married my grandmother at a service in Hong Kong Cathedral and shortly after left Hong Kong for duties in other parts of the world. Happily for him he returned to Hong Kong in 1925 as Governor and stayed for a further period of five years. His passion for walking and exploring continued and my aunt tells how, in the late 1920s, they would go for walks together, passing schools where the children were chanting their lessons, stopping to drink tea in a monastery courtyard and, when she got tired, being carried by my grandfather part of the way.

Everybody liked him. In 1910, as private secretary to Sir Francis Henry May, the acting Governor, he stayed with the May family at Mountain Lodge on the Peak. As far as Sir Henry's teenage daughters were concerned, he was 'our greatest friend'. One of them, Phoebe, left this portrait:

> He was a scholar and used to read poetry to us. He . . . was a most stimulating companion on any expedition. He spoke Chinese fluently and could tell us what the country people said as we passed through their villages. Once as we toiled up a steep hill the coolie who was carrying the luncheon baskets began talking to himself in mournful tones. Cecil translated his remarks, 'This work is bitter grief to me'. Ever afterwards that coolie was known as Bitter Grief.

He was a passionate man, too, judging from his poetry. It seems he fell in love with Penelope Eyres (pictured), whom he married in 1912, at first sight. She had accompanied her father, the commodore stationed in Hong Kong at the time, to dinner at Mountain Lodge. Cecil Clementi relived the moment of their first meeting in verse:

> The stars smiled welcome, the Peak loom'd dim,
> As up the path in your mountain-chair
> Four Cantonese men, lithe of limb,
> Carried you, swift thro' the night, to where
> Over the hill's black rim
>
> The lamp-lights gleam'd a-row in the hall:
> And there, in the porch of the hall, we met.
> Ah, fugitive moment! but, once for all
> Fix'd so fast, I can ne'er forget
> How Love then made me thrall.

Other academic high-fliers emerged from time to time; the field of oriental studies would have been poorer without them. Most of them had begun by acquainting themselves with local customs in the course of duty and, catching a glimpse of the richness of Chinese civilization, ended up by falling prey to the intellectual challenge of studying it. Sir Reginald Johnston, who served in Hong Kong (1898–1904), in Weihaiwei (1904–17 and 1927–30), and in Beijing as tutor to the deposed emperor Puyi (1919–25), was one such victim. He gave himself a literary name from the *Analects* of Confucius and chanted Tang poems 'just like a Chinese teacher,' according to Puyi, 'wagging his head' and with 'his voice rising, falling and pausing.' On leaving the East he became Professor of Chinese at the University of London. He had the requisite touch of eccentricity for a professor, too: eventually retiring to an island off Scotland, he punctiliously hoisted and lowered the flag of Manchukuo every day.

In Hong Kong, government service produced a crop of local historians who had all at one time or another enjoyed postings in the New Territories before development effaced the land's rural character. There they saw, as James Hayes did, 'the villages, the market towns and the resident boat people, all very much as they must have been at the end of the Ch'ing Dynasty, up to 1911. I am not exaggerating: that's what they seemed like at that time, owing to the lack of development.'

District Officer in the southern New Territories during the late 1950s, Hayes was put in charge of a large area which he visited regularly 'by car and by launch and on foot, meeting the various rural committees . . . and their members'. A typical meeting, as he tells his parents in one of his first letters home after his appointment and a year of language study, went like this:

> I arrive with Mr Lo, my right-hand man—a Chinese Special Grade Clerk but really much more, who has been twenty-eight years in the Southern District—together with a land bailiff and usually a demarcator. I am met, shake hands with people, walk round one half of the area, then go to the rural committee office, am formally welcomed, say a few words myself, and then we get down to brass tacks when they air their wants, views, and old moans! All the while, sipping Chinese green tea. Sometimes, a Chinese lunch follows (far too much for me, though I am getting used to Cantonese food now . . . it is very greasy), after which we go out to see the rest of the place.

Today, I met one committee for lunch, after two hours in the office and one and a half hours on a ferry; then went on to another island, watched the sports competition at a school and had to present the prizes and make a speech (in English and translated—I still felt unconvinced that I would be understood in country places, despite my year at language school!), after which I had a heart-to-heart talk with the committee of the island on a wide range of subjects.

One subject which greatly preoccupied him at the time was the government's plan to build a reservoir at Shek Pik on Lantau and the removal of two villages. Shek Pik village, he found, dated at least as far back as the fifteenth century, but when he wanted to know more about it, he faced a dearth of information. What *had* been written about the New Territories was either not in English or difficult to access in Hong Kong, which was why he started his own historical quest:

> I soon noticed that the temples and some other buildings contained inscribed tablets, sometimes about the repair of the building and sometimes about law cases in the long ago when the District Magistrate or the local people, after asking the Magistrate, had stone tablets put there commemorating legal decisions. I collected copies of these inscriptions and other documentary material, like land deeds, family papers, account books and genealogies. . . . I interviewed persons in their homes. . . . I persuaded other District Officers to get their staff to record these tablets, too, and built up a collection of inscriptions.

All this first-hand material was grist to the local historical mill, and that was how a group of expatriate civil servants, including also K. M. A. Barnett, David Akers-Jones, and Patrick Hase, opened up a new field of academic research and enriched our knowledge of the pre-colonial past. They might smile in self-deprecation if compared to the scholar-mandarins of imperial China, but one suspects that nothing would have pleased them more.

———⊃о⋄о⊂———

For all their varied skills, though, administrative officers remained generalists and could never support the whole apparatus of government alone. Their ranks were supplemented by professionals and technocrats. Michael Wright returned to Hong Kong as an architect and joined the Public Works Department (PWD) in 1939. His salary didn't improve dramatically: 'In England I was quite well paid. I was earning eight pounds a week which was something over £400 a year. In Hong Kong the starting pay was about £500 a year.' But living in Hong Kong was very cheap and he had a long family connection with the colony. He hoped to make his work as a government architect a lifetime career. Circumstances made for a gentle start:

> I hadn't really got a full day's work to do. The Japanese on the Chinese border and then the war in Europe inhibited the development of Hong Kong. Everything was very slow. The government was quite small, with PWD professional and technical officers numbering not more than forty or fifty compared to the several thousand when I left. Besides architects and engineers, there were subordinate officers like the inspectors or clerks of works who were on site full-time, and artisans like carpenters and joiners. They were all European. I am proud, incidentally, of appointing the first Chinese to one of those jobs. He was a Shanghainese who'd been to St John's University.
>
> It was the same in the commercial field. Seamail came once a week or even once a fortnight. You'd be very busy for a couple of days when the mail came in, and for the rest of the week you

wouldn't have enough to do. Most of the expatriates drank too much. I remember being taken to the Hong Kong Club where the men would be two deep around the main bar, knocking back their gin and tonics well into the afternoon.

Those thirsty businessmen were clearly suffering from the heat, air-conditioning being unavailable at the time. In the summer Michael Wright worked under fans with 'my sleeves rolled up, but my arms got so sweaty that they would smudge the drawings. And if you had the fan on too high it blew all the papers about. I remember the chief of the fire brigade coming to see me about a new fire station. We were both sweating profusely, only he'd been dyeing his hair and as we talked black streaks began running down his face!'

Behind the subtropical languor and calm routine lay an uneasiness, however. Europe was at war, although not everyone in Hong Kong believed that a Japanese invasion was inevitable. The attack when it came was swift and deadly and took most people by surprise. Fast on the heels of the bombing of Pearl Harbor, the Japanese launched air raids on Hong Kong. Wright and other members of the Volunteer Defence Corps were mobilized immediately:

> The press like to make out that we were swilling gin so hard we forgot all about the war. It wasn't like that. I was phoned up at about six o'clock on the Sunday morning that I was to be mobilized. Everybody turned up at Volunteer headquarters and all the volunteers and the regular troops were soon at their battle positions. I saw some planes coming over. It flashed through my mind that they might be Chinese planes but they were Japanese. Half an hour later we heard on the telephone that these planes had bombed Kai Tak airport. So that was how we knew the war had started.

At the outbreak of war in Europe Ian Lightbody was at Glasgow University. He joined up, went into the Indian Army, and was posted to south-west China: 'I had fifteen months in Chungking. They sent out forms and circulars to all units soliciting volunteers to man various military administrations. I volunteered and got a posting to join the military government in Burma, but having been

in China and speaking some Mandarin by then, I thought that would
be rather silly, so I arranged with my colonel in Delhi to be posted
to Hong Kong.'

Arriving in November 1945, Lightbody found Hong Kong
'absolutely ransacked by the Japanese. The population was only about
600,000. I remember the sound of wooden clogs—click, clack—as
people walked along the empty streets. Most of those who were
prisoners of war were in a very bad way when they were released from
camp. They were shipped back home to recuperate and we had to
take over their original jobs.' Michael Wright, who had been interned
in Sham Shui Po Prison Camp, nobly stayed on for three months to
help with the rehabilitation: 'One had to put windows back or in
some cases a new roof or a new floor. Floorboards had been ripped out
for use as firewood for cooking during the occupation.'

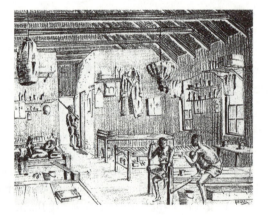

From south-west China came also a very young woman, Anne
Burrows (later Mrs Terence Sorby). Having been attached to the
cipher office of the Special Operations Executive station in
Kunming, she too was posted to the secretariat of the military
administration in Hong Kong. 'Everyone was in uniform in those
days,' she recalls. 'One reason why Hong Kong rose from the ashes
so rapidly was the fact that we had this wonderful naval Governor,
Admiral Harcourt, and some great administrators. There was a real
team spirit between the military, naval, and civil. Sir Mark Young,
when he returned as Governor, was another one who was able to
run a good team. It was all very inspiring. We were determined to

make it work, and work it did.' Ian Lightbody ascribes the impressive recovery to 'the Chinese people of Hong Kong, the merchants and traders who were so quick to cast around for supplies and to get normal trade moving again.'

Hong Kong people's quick-wittedness was sometimes manifested in unexpected ways. Shortly after the War Michael Wright went to live in Stanley, on the south side of Hong Kong island, with three other single men. Since having transport was essential to their jobs, two of them were proud possessors of a couple of 15-cwt ex-army trucks

> which we were able to hire for fifteen dollars a month. This enabled us to go to and from Stanley. There was no public transport at all out there.
>
> We let it be known through our servants that if anybody in the village wanted a lift into town, if they were outside the house by 8.15 in the morning they could get into the back of these trucks. We always had four or five villagers taking up this offer.
>
> Come Chinese New Year and the servants were off for a week's holiday. We were back at work sooner and the usual crowd of five or six were waiting for the lift into town. As I got into my vehicle each one came along with a dollar for me. It seems our servants had been collecting a dollar a time whereas we thought we were providing a free service!

Denis Bray joined the Hong Kong government as a cadet in 1950. Towards the end of his first tour, he was somewhat dismayed to be posted as District Officer to Tai Po in what was in those days a still rural, rice-growing New Territories where tradition pervaded living in ways that had long vanished from Kowloon and Hong Kong. His district was a large one, a curve of landmass defined on the west by spurs of hills facing an inlet called Tolo Harbour, and on the north and south by rocky peninsulas jutting out into an island-studded sea. It had few roads and most coastal villages did not even have piers.

As he looked at the map in his office, the huge extent of his jurisdiction dawned on him. There were villages scattered all over this terrain, some lying in their own folds in the hills, others looking seaward beside a sweeping bay, most out of easy reach by road. Intrigued and challenged, he decided to see village life for himself. He did this by long walks and rides on sampans, sleeping in village schools *en route*, finding out along the way how people contrived to exist despite the absence of modern amenities. If this 1950s version of the safari-under-canvas inspection tour into the 'bush' lacked romance, it nonetheless proved useful, for Bray soon realized what scope there was for improving the quality of life for those in his charge. Going from village to village, he asked about everything he could think of: crops expectations, housing, income, jobs people were doing. Everywhere he went, 'talk always reverted to the need for what we would nowadays call infrastructure, perhaps a rather grand name for a well, or a footbridge, or a pier, or an irrigation dam.'

On returning to base he checked the public works allowance for buying cement, knowing that the villagers could be relied upon to do the actual construction themselves. The kitty amounted to $13,333 a year. On this basis, what the villagers had asked for would require twenty years' supply of cement. 'Well, this was absurd,' he thought, 'even when I cut the list down to really essential works, the total came to two and a half years' supply—five thousand bags of cement, and the annual allocation was two thousand.'

Help came in the form of an agricultural officer, Norman Wright, who said to him at a party, 'Have you tried Horace Kadoorie?' It had never occurred to Bray that as a junior civil servant,

> I could approach this great man who was one of our prominent industrialists and doing so much to set up poor farmers all over the New Territories.
>
> Norman did raise it with Horace and the next thing I knew, the two of them descended on me in my office. In a very businesslike way Horace asked me exactly what I needed. Fortunately I was able to say 5,253 bags of cement—or some such figure. The Kadoories owned a cement factory. 'Done!' said Horace, 'You can have the cement if you collect it yourselves

from the factory.' Of course we hadn't a lorry but the Kowloon-Canton railway runs through the district, so with a little persuasion KCR kindly laid on a special cement train. They brought the cement down and put it in the sidings and the villagers came to collect it from there. I hadn't told the District Commissioner what I was up to and I was a bit worried about it. Fortunately he approved.

This turned out to be the beginning of a tremendous expansion in the local public works field, first by the Kadoorie Agricultural Aid Association. They did their own works, and to this day you can see the letters 'KAAA' in the cement of paths, bridges, wells, and piers throughout the old rural areas. Not to be outdone we put 'DOTP' [District Office Tai Po] on the works *we* carried out. Eventually, some years later, government money was boosted from $40,000 a year for the whole of the New Territories to over a million, just to show that we could match the charity of the Kadoorie family!

Those projects quietly transformed the villages. In certain respects, though, the tenor of life still followed ancient rhythms, with the calendar punctuated by gaudy celebrations of Chinese festivals. When the dragon boat festival approached Bray, having rowed at Cambridge University, began to wonder if he could 'beg a place on one of the fishermen's boats'. A colleague suggested that he raised a crew himself. As he recalls:

This proved so popular that we had to arrange a second crew, and we called ourselves by the irreverent names of 'fan gwei' for the mainly police and army crew and 'gweilo' for the civilian team—two common abbreviations for 'fan gweilo' or foreign devils. Tai Po didn't have proper dragon boats at the time: the races were rowed in Hoklo sampans. These were stripped of their fishing gear and accommodated a crew of fourteen: six oarsmen or paddlers on each side, a coxswain, and a gong banger. We did a good deal of practice and I began to get the hang of this novel style of paddling. The trick is to give the paddle a twist just before the end of the stroke.

Steering these craft with a long oar over the stern wasn't something that novices could do, so we engaged a fisherman for the job. When the great day arrived we were astonished to see massive crowds gathered to watch the foreign devils rowing dragon boats. Well, we were left at the start by the fishermen but we were gaining rapidly. It became clear that we weren't so much going to overhaul the fishermen as crash into them. So our coxswain boldly put his oar hard over to avoid this embarrassment and the effect was dramatic. The boat heeled over sharply, and all six men on the outside fell off. The sampan then filled with water and tipped the other way, so the other six fell off. And we sank. Our gong banger was a splendid Italian Catholic priest with a fine beard, and as he sank below the waves the beard floated up and he uttered not a word. The boat stabilized before he went under which was just as well. . . . We found out later that he couldn't swim.

⊃o⬦o⊂

If life in the New Territories appeared little different from pre-War days, the 1950s was nevertheless a time of tremendous change. For many a civil servant, resettlement, clearance, and housing were the most daunting concerns of the day. When China went communist, the first destination for most of the exodus of refugees was Hong Kong—but where were they to live? Ian Lightbody recalled:

For several years from 1949 onwards most of us had hoped that someday soon those refugees would do what Chinese had always done in the past, that is, filter gradually back to their villages

once things settled down. But this time it wasn't going to happen—there was no going back to communist China.

And then we all became aware that squatter huts were climbing up the foothills of Kowloon into every nook and cranny. There was a certain inevitability about it. We recognized that we had to find some means of coping. The fire at Shek Kip Mei squatter camp on Christmas night 1953 which left 50,000 homeless was the catalyst that settled the issue. That was when it all began, when the government took the very brave decision to rehouse the squatters and refugees, who thereby became Hong Kong citizens. When you were a government tenant, what more could you want in terms of being regularized?

Yet the resettlement scheme didn't amount to a housing programme for the poor. As Denis Bray was to explain in a report years later, it was 'a means to clear land for development.' A concrete box measuring twenty-four square feet per head in the newly built estate was available only in exchange for a squatter hut on the demolition list. Typically the flats were in a six- or seven-storey block with no lifts, no windows except wooden shutters, and only communal washing, toilet, and cooking facilities. But these resettlement estates, the first of which was built on the site of the Shep Kip Mei fire, provided weatherproof and fireproof premises, and rooms in them were much coveted.

But they were nothing if not basic, and were to become increasingly more overcrowded and squalid as time went on. Eventually they were declared unacceptable and Ian Lightbody (pictured right), appointed commissioner for resettlement in 1972,

was charged with setting up a greatly enlarged Housing Authority to initiate improvement to existing estates and to develop new ones. The human tide coming over from mainland China did not abate: 'Every Hour brings a New Refugee' ran a newspaper headline in 1972. Nearly all were permitted to stay, squashed into the estates or in the spaces between them. Lightbody remembers a startling sight when he visited an estate in 1971:

> There were resettlement blocks of solid concrete but between them, where there should have been open space, was a sea of squatter shacks.
>
> What had happened was that all sorts of commercial squatters had moved in, aided and abetted by Triad gangs, because a lot of intimidation went on in these areas. Resettlement staff had to recognize this. Many of the estates were like that so the poor residents lost all their open space. I realized there was quite a job to be done there. Eventually we cleared them all off, but it was a major operation, a military operation, getting them out. Our own staff did it. I depended heavily on a few junior administrative officers who were in charge of particular operations like squatter clearance. It took a lot of organization and leadership. We had one marvellous chap, an Irishman, who was absolutely the right man in the right place. He took to this job with a vengeance; he really had a missionary zeal about it. Gradually we worked through the estates and cleared them up; the end result was that the residents could look out over their open spaces and you could plant trees.

Hand in hand with the renewal of old estates was a new town development programme designed to disperse a sizeable chunk of the population to satellite communities conjured out of agricultural and reclaimed land in the New Territories. This was one of several forceful policies implemented by Sir (later Lord) Murray Maclehose (Governor, 1971–82). By 1979 the programme was well underway. Even so, Peter Mann found his first tasks as Assistant District Officer in Tuen Mun, western New Territories, quite testing:

> The most difficult part of new town development was the clearance of squatter areas, land resumption, and the fixing of

compensation. First there was the belief in *fung shui*. Indigenous village people were so smart. As soon as they knew which part was going to be cleared, they'd claim that our proposed change to the landscape would destroy the flow of beneficial influences they currently enjoyed. We'd have these meetings and you say you wanted to put a road through here or cut away a bit of the hill there; they'd suck in their breath and announce, '*Ayah*, very difficult, that's the dragon's head.' And if our road was going to cut the dragon's head off, we had to pay higher compensation.

As soon as word got out that an empty field was going to be compulsorily purchased by the government, miraculously it would spring plants and fruit trees overnight, because compensation was determined by how many fruit trees or squares of paddy you owned. It was an agricultural society, after all!

Nothing so clearly demonstrated the alarm and indignation of the villagers as the clearing of Mouse Island. Beside Castle Peak Road there was a big, strangely shaped stone. Chinese graffiti appeared on it just before the clearance operation began. It said, 'Man Pui Tak *dik fun mo*' (Man Pui Tak is Peter Mann's Chinese name); 'I had this translated by my liaison officer. It basically meant "It's your tomb, Mr Mann"! In those clearances you'd have the police tactical unit in front, and the hard-core people holding out for more compensation would be throwing pig shit and rocks at us.'

Like others who had worked in the New Territories, though, Mann can remember wonderful days out in the country. His district covered reservoir areas, hill ranges, and long stretches of the coast behind Castle Peak. Little villages sprinkled here and there were only accessible by footpaths:

You get to these villages and the people would treat you with such respect—huge 'face' that made one really feel like a 'Fu Mo Kwun'. One of our jobs was to organize the installation of generators for outlying settlements that had no electricity. I arranged for the auxiliary air force to fly a generator over to a village south of Lau Fau Shan, which was quite cut off and isolated. I remember the coastline with its pristine white sand beaches—beautiful. Landing by helicopter with the generator, I was greeted by the village chief as I clambered out. He said to me, '*Wah, Lei Mun Kwun* [Wow, District Officer]. You're very clever; you know how to fly a helicopter too!'

———————⊃0⬦0⊂———————

When Ian Lightbody moved to the resettlement department the *Government Gazette* would have listed few Chinese incumbents of posts at the director, deputy director, or even assistant director levels, not to mention more rarefied offices at the very top of the government hierarchy; they were invariably expatriates. Twenty years later, expatriates still accounted for about 36 per cent of the civil service's 1,300-plus directorate officers and just under half of the policy secretaries and department heads. In 1947 Paul Tsui Ka Cheung, a graduate of Hong Kong University, was the first Chinese to be appointed a cadet. According to Lightbody:

> There were a few more in the ensuing years but it wasn't really until 1958–60 that the numbers were enlarged and from then on there was a steady stream. In 1962 Anson Chan [Chief Secretary for Administration, 1993–2001] was one of our bright young local recruits. What we find so satisfying is that we see now people like Anson, whom we recruited way back in those far off years, running the place, and running it so well. We look back and we say, 'Well, we must have got something right!'
>
> We went to great lengths to promote localization: at one stage we set up a new law school at the University of Hong Kong and that was to maximize possible intake into the government legal department. But the private sector proved much more lucrative so many of those who qualified went to that, and time and again this was what happened. It was an uphill job and we just had to punch away at this bag and hope that someday we'd overcome it. My final appointment was as chairman of the Public Services Commission. Our standards were very demanding: with every recommendation for some promotion or job the Commission would probably have the head of the department up to explain why there wasn't a local candidate or replacement. This gave teeth to the localization policy, so the policy was very real but of course it takes time,

about ten to fifteen years, to produce someone who's sufficiently experienced to fill a senior post. One has to be patient but my feeling is that we did it in good time.

Critics would have argued the contrary, contending that localization of the top posts in government had long been perfunctory and slow, and that an accelerated pace was evident only after the signing of the Joint Declaration on the constitutional future of Hong Kong in 1984. If the top civil servants *were* the government, as Sir Ralph Furse claimed, it went without saying that come the transfer of sovereignty they should all be Chinese, not foreign.

But the Joint Declaration did not require those in the middle and lower ranks to be Chinese nationals too. As the countdown to 1997 began in earnest, expatriate civil servants started expressing their misgivings over job security. It was true that HMOCS members were guaranteed compensation payments for the loss of British protection in 1997, and indeed many took them and retired ahead of the resumption of Chinese rule. But it was equally true that others, finding themselves stranded in mid-career, wanted to be given the chance to work for the future Hong Kong Special Administrative Region (SAR) government rather than face the uncertainties of job-hunting at home. By most standards, they were well paid; with expatriate perks such as housing and other subsidies, they were *extremely* well paid. A survey in March 1993 by the Association of Expatriate Civil Servants found that two-thirds of their members working on contracts were willing to stay on past the change of sovereignty even if it meant forgoing expatriate benefits.

In fact the expatriates held a strong bargaining hand, for as morale dipped and the simultaneous and destabilizing retirement of senior officers from the civil service and the police force in 1997 became in prospect, alarm bells began to ring. Would their departure leave a dangerous vacuum? How could the depleted services cope? In the summer of 1993 Sir David Ford, the Chief Secretary, announced that long-serving civil servants from overseas who had acquired permanent residence in Hong Kong could have their contracts renewed if they transferred to local terms of employment.

Perhaps it was inevitable that the question of race should rear its ugly head. As local civil servants rushed to block this move, charges of racism flew about. Now the boot was on the other foot, and expatriates, having always taken preferential conditions of service for granted, suddenly found themselves subject to discrimination on purely ethnic grounds. It was a rude awakening, and some didn't hesitate to accuse the Chinese of racial prejudice. Matters were not helped when a number of well-meaning, liberal-minded expatriates joined the fray, hotly abusing the incompetence and unenlightened attitudes of their own compatriots, and weighing in on the side of the locals.

While all this was happening, a historic step in the localization process was taken in the appointment of Mrs Anson Chan Fang On-sang as the first Chinese chief of the civil service. But the controversy raged on all the same. There was a flurry in the press against the 'ridiculous colonial anachronism' of allowing retiring expatriate civil servants the expensive perk of going home by sea. But as one of those expatriates recalled, 'ironically it was the Chinese civil servants' association that backed the gweilos, because its members saw immediately in their very canny way that any erosion of gweilo perks would also mean erosion of *their* perks.' On an institutional level, there was pressure on 'gweilos to do the decent thing and retire', which was characterized by one officer as 'a Machiavellian piece of work'. Astutely, the government used an expatriate in the Civil Service Branch as its hatchet man; clearly acting on instructions from above, he interviewed expatriate administrative officers individually in his office. According to one of them, his message basically was: 'Hong Kong is going back to China, and you guys, your time's up: this is not your country, so why don't you accept the situation gracefully and leave?'

But one administrative officer chose to disregard this message:

A lot of people who were doing good jobs in the government were convinced by him, left, and some regretted their decision. Maybe it was inevitable. When I was interviewed, I said, no, I love Hong Kong, I want to carry on working here. Frankly, Hong Kong needs people like us. It was the dance of the dragon and the lion, the mixture of East and West, that made Hong Kong great.

So my line was that I wanted to stay. On the other hand, I hedged my bets by remaining on the old pension scheme, which meant I could go at fifty. Under the old pension scheme your retirement age is fifty-five but you had the option to go when you reached fifty. The new scheme brought in a few years before the Handover put your retirement age back to sixty; obviously you got more money, though if you left before retirement you got nothing.

Localization is likely to remain a fraught topic until white faces disappear totally from the corridors of bureaucratic power, as they must do one day. It continues to be a bone of contention in the meantime, as this officer maintains:

There's a difference in culture, education, training, whatever, between expatriates and locals in the civil service. Very few of us gweilos are left, but we are still more prepared to stick our necks out—you make a decision and you take responsibility for it. In the Chinese system you always avoid taking a decision because to have no mistakes is better than to have nine successes and one failure. And it's considered bad form to question one's boss, to debate, which I think is sad for Hong Kong. There's a huge mediocrity in government, particularly at the senior level, because what you have to do to succeed in this system is not to make mistakes, and the easiest way of achieving that is to do nothing; whereas Hong Kong never got to be the wonderful place it is through caution and fence-sitting. It's always thrived on taking a gamble.

4
Some of the Governors

When Edward the Prince of Wales visited Asia during his Empire tour in 1922, his easy manners charmed most of the people who met him. But on one occasion his informality went a little too far. To the consternation of the British Ambassador in Tokyo, he was heard to remark at a reception that the Governors of Hong Kong and Singapore were 'fossilized clerks who ought to be kept in a cupboard in Whitehall'.

No doubt he was being facetious. But like any job a Governor's daily lot must contain as much humdrum administration as excitement. 'Much of my day, every day,' writes Chris Patten (Governor, 1992–97), 'was spent being in effect the mayor of Hong Kong, running the civil service that managed the affairs of a rich and sophisticated city.' He echoes a comment made about Sir Frederick Lugard's administration by Margery Perham, Lugard's biographer:

'the greater part . . . was frankly and often sordidly municipal'. Lugard himself said, 'my role is to perpetually functionalize . . . to endure fools gladly, to sign my name perpetually and agree to the faultless suggestions of the Honourable the Colonial Secretary'.

Lord Wilson of Tillyorn (Governor, 1987–92) describes the Governor in his practical role of running a government, supported by the Executive Council and an enormous civil service, as 'the chief executive'. A chief executive makes decisions on policies and their implementation. But whether he is dealing with housing, schools, hospitals, industrial infrastructure, transport, reservoirs, or protection of the environment, the chief executive of Hong Kong must still try 'to make an assessment of public opinion, because when you're running what was then not—it's not now—a fully representative, democratic, elected system, then you've got to make sure you can be in line with what the public is looking for—hopes for—and if you are, then the territory will run smoothly. If you go badly out of line, as sometimes has happened in Hong Kong's history, then you have serious social disorder and riots.'

By any standard, being Governor is a colossal job, and a strange one: 'There's nothing like it in the world,' says Lord Wilson, 'On paper, if you read the Letters Patent and all that sort of thing, it carries a huge amount of power, and in reality the Governor does have a great deal of influence. But if you're sensible, you don't use all the power you've got. You govern by consent and through consultation.'

The power enshrined in the Letters Patent and the Royal Instructions, which together formed colonial Hong Kong's constitution, was sometimes hinted at, but then only symbolically, when a Governor assumed his ceremonial role. His gubernatorial 'uniform' and plumed helmet (which Chris Patten abjured, saying it made the wearer look like a recently deceased hen) were the last vestiges of imperial grandeur. In 1907 Sir Frederick Lugard arrived in Hong Kong by steamer to a salute of seventeen guns. His wife Flora had 'dressed herself happily in gold and white'; he, on the other hand, 'had struggled unhappily into the full levée dress uniform, which had cost him a hundred guineas'. Margery Perham tells us that this consisted of 'a heavily braided coat—Lugard called it his armour plate—the feathered hat and tight breeches in which Governors of British colonies grace the tropics'. Forty years on, Sir Alexander Grantham (Governor, 1947–57), who travelled by air, changed at the airport in order to alight at Queen's Pier to his reception by local dignitaries in a morning coat and top hat.

Plumed helmets are the sort of thing, Lord Wilson admits,

that everybody takes photographs of and laughs at and draws
cartoons of, but although it looks odd and you feel odd in that
sort of uniform, I don't think one should simply laugh at it.
What struck me was that when you were doing things with,
say, the disciplined services like the police, when you were going
to a passing-out parade, they had taken immense trouble to look
as smart as they possibly could be, and I felt that the least I
could do was to turn out looking smart too—maybe slightly
odd, but in uniform—and that was a courtesy to them.
Ceremonial matters.

Occasionally, the pomp and circumstance and being under the
constant eye of security guards can feel suffocating. One night during
his governorship Sir David Wilson succumbed to the temptation
to break out. He was in the garden of Government House with one
of his sons, 'and we thought, here we are in this goldfish bowl . . .
so we hopped over the wall, wandered around outside for about an
hour, and then walked back through the front gates. The expression
on the face of the policeman on duty at the guardhouse was
wonderful! The reason I never confessed this before is: what does
this say about the security of Government House?'

On the whole, though, having a member of Special Branch in tow was more convenient than not:

> Sometimes when you wandered around, as I did in the New Territories, somebody would come up with a petition, and either trying to understand properly what the person was saying—my Cantonese is serviceable but not as good as my Putonghua—or accepting bits of paper, it was much better to have somebody with you. . . .
>
> Never did I ever feel under personal threat in Hong Kong. The only time there was even the slightest problem was when legislation was going through about pig-farming and the pollution of rivers in the New Territories. Pig-farmers were brought in by bus to protest and they surrounded the Legislative Council building. When I was about to leave, the police advised me not to go. After a bit I said, 'Why can't I just walk out? I don't think it's right that I should be holed up here as though I couldn't move around Hong Kong.'
>
> I got into my car and we drove very slowly through this huge crowd of demonstrators. Some of them were so close they were touching the car as we passed. What worried me was that, however slowly the car was moving, somebody might slip and be injured.
>
> But what I found so charming was that the next morning I got a message of apology from the protestors, saying they were terribly sorry to have inconvenienced me!

Perhaps the most oppressive aspect of living in 'a goldfish bowl' was the endless social round, an essential part of the gubernatorial week. It certainly was for Lugard, who not only had to learn to dance the lancers but to attend more dinners, concerts, bazaars, sporting events, and so on, he complained, than could be dealt with in 365 days. He chafed at having 'to stand first on one leg then upon another with a glazed grin on my face, or bowing like the Chinese image on the mantelpiece whose head wags for an hour if you touch him under the chin.' To the more urbane Sir Alexander Grantham, if a social duty irked the answer was to change it. At one of the annual Queen's Birthday garden parties at Government House, he and his wife, Lady Maurine, found themselves shaking hands with guests without stopping for an hour and a half. 'I don't know how many people this was. I should think about 2,000,' he observed. This became intolerable, so they simply 'shook hands no more but mingled with the guests on the lawn'. He coped briskly at cocktail parties too, sticking to a set routine:

> We would arrive promptly at, say, 7 p.m.—and a Governor must always arrive on time, neither a minute late nor a minute early (to arrive early is the crime of crimes)—and at 7.15 p.m. the ADC would come up to me and say, 'Excuse me, Sir, but you have another engagement and it is time to leave'. This suited the host, for as long as the Governor was there, he could not feel free to attend to his other guests. The Governor had been invited to give prestige to the party. The same thing applied to charity balls which were an almost weekly feature of Hong Kong winter life. If the sponsors could say the Governor would be present, many more tickets would sell. Since the charities were one and all worthy of support, we did not mind being used as bait.

Apart from the ceremonial and municipal roles, there was a third aspect to governing, according to Lord Wilson,

> which was the sort of wider connection with ordinary people in Hong Kong. It's difficult, I suppose, for a Governor. You're up on a pedestal, you're in a goldfish bowl, but I found a tremendous thrill, a sort of rejuvenation, in being able to walk around in Hong Kong, and I don't mean formal or organized district visits when there were huge crowds of people and masses of cameras which made them so artificial. When I'd been working very long days in Government House and got a bit fed up with the paperwork, I would sometimes just go out at night and walk around the streets in Hong Kong or Kowloon, and because it was dark, until you were quite close to people, they didn't see that it was the Governor, and when you did come close, they always gave you a tremendous welcome. There would be people saying hello, and being prepared to chat, and you felt the bustle of Hong Kong—the people working late at night. You go past little alleyways, and there were printing presses clattering away, and little restaurants with people eating bowls of noodles out on the street. You could feel the liveliness of the city which frankly you

don't get from bits of paper. Every time I did it, I came back thinking, 'Gosh, it may be very tiring working away on papers, but here's what I've been working for: here's the living city; here are the real people.' What can be more worthwhile than trying to do whatever you can for a territory of five million people?

⸺⸺◦⸺◇⸺◦⸺⸺

One of the objects of Prince Edward's scorn was Sir Reginald Stubbs (Governor, 1919–25). With thirteen years' experience in the Colonial Office, Stubbs had indeed been a Whitehall clerk. But this Governor, son of the influential English historian and Bishop of Oxford, William Stubbs, and an Oxford double first himself, was no dried-up bureaucrat. By the time he assumed his post in Hong Kong, Stubbs had turned into a tough-minded proconsul whose recommendation for dealing with Chinese troublemakers was to give them a sound flogging.

And there were plenty of troublemakers during Stubbs's governorship, remembered today for a series of strikes which all but crippled Hong Kong. The first, by engineers, occurred within seven months of his arrival, but the action of the Chinese Seamen's Union in January 1922 was much more catastrophic.

At the beginning the seamen wanted nothing more than higher wages. When their European employers failed to respond, the disaffected seamen and dockers decamped to Canton, and in their wake other low-paid workers in foreign employ such as servants, coolies, tram drivers, and electricians—some 120,000 in all—struck in sympathy.

Shipowners and the government, convinced that the strike was backed by left-wing elements of the Kuomintang, decided to stand firm against the labour unions. By March, what had started as a disagreement between workers and employers was spiralling into 'a war directed exclusively against the non-Chinese section of the community', as one newspaper editorial put it. Plunging the colony into an 'atmosphere of despondency and gloom', the strike was seen to be deeply humiliating 'to British pride and prestige.'

Eventually, rather than let the strike drag on, the government and employers had to swallow their pride and offer terms. As things turned out, this was not the end of the story. An even more severe strike erupted in 1925, set off by a wave of anti-British feeling after some Chinese demonstrators were fired upon and killed in the Shanghai International Settlement by policemen under the command of a British officer. This incident reverberated throughout the Treaty Ports, and public indignation was further fuelled by another burst of protests which resulted in fatalities, this time in Shamian, Canton. The mood in Hong Kong was no less hostile, with workers again downing tools and marching off to the Mainland. On top of all this, a boycott of trade between Hong Kong and Guangdong province was organized, bringing the economic life of the colony almost to a standstill. There was again gloom and despondency, and nervous whispers of an impending takeover by Canton radicals and communists.

Lord Wilson describes the mid- to late 1920s as a period of 'huge tension. . . . There were three occasions when Britain almost went to war with the Kuomintang, and in a way only didn't because the Kuomintang split and Britain didn't know who to go to war with!' That period of history formed the subject of his Ph.D. thesis and was to provide useful insights later on:

> When you look into the papers on both sides—Foreign Office papers and as many as one could get of Kuomintang ones, and even the local newspapers in Canton at that time—you could see complete misunderstanding between the two sides. You could see how those conflicts were built up, and sometimes you could see how people of great skill could resolve the conflicts or deal with the problems. The British Consul-General in Canton, Sir John Brenan, was brilliant at doing that. All this made it an extremely interesting study and taught me something about that period of history and how differently facts can be interpreted on different sides of a conflict.

The strikes and boycott aptly illustrate a central fact about the governance of Hong Kong: the colony had always been only one motif in the pattern of Anglo-Chinese relations. Grantham felt that Hong Kong should have been 'placed under the Foreign Office instead of the Colonial Office, but with staff seconded from the Colonial Service which, unlike the Foreign Service staff, is trained in administration. . . . Practically every major issue that arose in Hong Kong, and on which London had to be consulted, was a matter of foreign policy.' These major issues usually ramified from political and economic disturbances in China, when Hong Kong would find itself used as a sanctuary for dissidents and refugees. It was at times like these that colonial administrators suddenly needed to become diplomats and politicians.

The Governors in office during three politically sensitive moments in the twentieth century were Lugard, Grantham, and Wilson. Lugard steered Hong Kong through the fallout from China's republican revolution of 1911; Grantham presided over the closing of the border in May 1950, soon after China went communist; and Wilson shared the horror of Hong Kong's citizens at the Tiananmen crackdown in 1989, a confrontation between government and people on a scale unprecedented in the history of communist China. Fortuitously for our purpose, Lugard's career is detailed in a magisterial biography by Margery Perham; Grantham wrote a memoir, *Via Ports*; and Lord Wilson was amenable to an interview.

As the last and most exhaustively documented Governor (1992–97), Chris Patten has gained his place in history. But although Hong Kong's return to Chinese sovereignty at the end of his governorship was undoubtedly a pivotal occasion in the territory's history, in a broader context it is more difficult to say whether it will be ranked by China as of equal or greater importance than a number of other events, past or future, not least the recovery of Taiwan.

———— ⋙◆⋘ ————

If administrative ability, sound judgement, and political skills are what's required of a Governor, how then is he best prepared for his task? According to Lord Wilson, there is no real training for the job. Some of the early Governors of Hong Kong had come via India and service with the East India Company. One or two had risen from the ranks of the cadet service: Sir Henry May, Sir Cecil Clementi, and Sir Alexander Grantham, for example, all began as administrative officers. From the late nineteenth century onwards we see the emergence of the career colonial Governor for whom Hong Kong was merely one posting in a series of increasingly exalted appointments. Those with gubernatorial experience in other possessions of the Crown included the likes of Sir Arthur Kennedy (Governor, 1872–77), who had been in Gambia; and Sir James Pope Hennessy, successively Governor of Labuan, Sierra Leone, the Bahamas, the Windward Islands, Hong Kong (1877–82), and Mauritius. Sir Frederick Lugard was different. Soldier, mercenary of Empire, and administrator from Africa, he had pursued a unique, adventurous, and occasionally dangerous career before his Far Eastern posting, and it was to Africa, his real love, that he subsequently returned. Sir Murray Maclehose was cast in yet another mould. He and the two Governors after him, all with experience of working in China, were appointed from the Foreign and Commonwealth Office (by 1971, of course, the Colonial Office had amalgamated with the Commonwealth Office which was in turn absorbed into a single Foreign and Commonwealth Office). Finally, and unlike all his predecessors, Chris Patten was a politician who by his own admission owed his job more to the loss of his Bath seat at the General Election of 1992 than 'to the experiences gained in the foothills and on the mountain slopes of a conventional diplomatic career'.

On the face of it, David Wilson's Foreign Office career was conventional enough. But in fact it didn't altogether proceed along beaten tracks, and his involvement in China 'like a lot of things in people's lives, was accidental'. His road to governorship had its share of twists and turns:

I joined the Foreign Office from university and was given a posting in London in what was called the South-East Asian Department. That was a bit unusual. Most people were sent to learn a difficult language but I was put into a job straight away. That was partly because I'd originally joined the Foreign Office without taking the exam. I'd been travelling while I was at university and met people from the Foreign Office and that led to the suggestion that I should join. The idea was that I could take the exam after I'd been there a year—if I passed I'd stay and if I failed I'd leave.

Doing his year in London, he longed to go abroad, and the easiest way to do so, he thought, was by volunteering to learn Arabic in the Middle East:

I drove to Beirut in an old American Army jeep I'd bought for £25, stopping to go climbing in Austria on the way. On arriving in Beirut, I was asked to go and see the director of the language school, and this very serious-looking man behind the desk said, 'Where have you been? The Foreign Office has been looking for you for the last three weeks!'

I said I'd been in the mountains in Austria.

'I've got very serious news for you,' he continued. I thought something awful had happened—perhaps my family had been wiped out or something! But his 'serious news' was that there had been a threatened North Vietnamese invasion of Laos and it was felt the British Embassy in Vientiane needed strengthening. They were going to strengthen it by sending an aeroplane for the military attaché and one junior officer—a third secretary— and I was to be that third secretary.

So I left for Vientiane in what I stood up in, which was my ordinary clothes, carrying an ice axe, and went to South-East Asia instead of the Middle East. Once I was there I said to the Foreign Office, 'Look, please don't send me back to learn Arabic. I find Asia far more interesting. Please send me to learn Chinese. Instead of London, will you send me to Hong Kong?'

David Wilson became the first Foreign Office language student to go straight to the University of Hong Kong for all his language training. Previously, the course of training had been split between two or three locations, usually London, Hong Kong, and Beijing:

I spent two years as a language student which I adored. I had classes all morning, and in the afternoon or evening I wandered across the hills trying to learn Chinese characters from little slips of paper with the character written on one side, the phonetics on another, and the translation on the next bit of paper. It was immense fun wandering over the hills learning these characters, or sitting on the beach writing characters in the sand, waiting for the waves to wash them out and then writing them again.

The problem was that in the early 1960s the number of native Mandarin speakers was limited. All my teachers were from northern China but around you people were speaking Cantonese. Eventually I found a family from Tianjin who were prepared to have a foreigner living with them, in a tiny flat in Wan Chai.

And so began a lifelong engagement with the affairs of China. From being a third secretary in the British Embassy in Beijing, he proceeded in the fullness of time to the post of second secretary. But he was always pressing back the boundaries of convention, even then:

> Foreigners, particularly diplomats, were very restricted. You could hardly go anywhere except the main cities. Otherwise you had to ask permission from the Foreign Ministry, and almost always the reply was *'Bu fangbian'*—not convenient.
>
> In my second week, I thought the weekend's coming round and what I'd really like to do is to go off to the Western Hills and look at some of the more distant, old temples which I'd read about in books. As they were outside the circle that foreigners were allowed to move in, I submitted an application to the Waijiaobu, the Foreign Ministry, and got no answer which was normal. Then I rang up and got hold of the duty officer in the protocol department who, predictably, said, *'Bu fangbian'*. But then he added helpfully, 'Have you climbed Meishan?'— he obviously thought that this little ornamental mound behind the Forbidden City was a good substitute for the Western Hills!
>
> In those days the old British Embassy in the diplomatic quarter had been taken over and the Embassy had been moved to a modern villa outside Jianguomen, and all the diplomats were living in a block of flats in a sort of foreign ghetto, which was miserable, frankly, and totally divorced from ordinary life in China.

When he announced that he would ask the Waijiaobu to let him live in a house in town, his colleagues at the Embassy 'laughed and said, don't be stupid, of course they won't let you.' But to everybody's astonishment, this time the Foreign Ministry was co-operative:

> And I was given the most beautiful two-courtyard house just off Wangfujing, right at the centre of the city, and there I lived as a bachelor for half a year until a new first secretary turned up.

Alan Donald, who was to be my predecessor as Political Adviser in Hong Kong, had four children. The Embassy said, 'He needs the house more than you do. You're rattling around in it. Very sorry, but you'll have to go back to the diplomatic compound.' So I went back to the Chinese Foreign Ministry and said, 'I'm terribly sorry. I had to give up my house. Could you please find me another which has only one bedroom?' And again, to everybody's surprise, they did, and I got a tiny little house in Ganyu Hutong, and there I lived for the rest of my time in Peking. That gave me the sense of being in China, however difficult contact was between foreigners and people in Peking or anywhere else. You felt you were part of the living city. You weren't totally isolated, and when you went home at night you could hear the city all around you, and that helped to give me a tremendous affection for China.

Posted back to London and working in the Far Eastern Department of the Foreign Office from 1965 to 1968, he was in charge of the China desk when the Cultural Revolution broke out.

During this 'very exciting, difficult, and dramatic time' he found that he was being treated as the resident expert on China in the Foreign Office and in Whitehall, a role which he felt he couldn't adequately fulfil because 'I didn't know nearly enough about China'. It came to him that he ought to learn some more, and he thought the way to do that was to study for a doctorate 'on the earlier period, before the War, before the communist victory, because that was a big gap in my own mind'. But when he approached the personnel people in the Foreign Office, he was told he could have only one year off. He responded to that by tendering his resignation, 'which was considered in those days a very bad thing to do—not that many people resigned from the Foreign Office'. All the same, he moved seamlessly to the editor's chair at the scholarly journal, *China Quarterly*, taking over from Roderick MacFarquhar (now a professor at Harvard). With his base at the School of Oriental and African Studies, London University, he was to edit the journal and work on his Ph.D. at the same time.

Much of the work for the Ph.D. was accomplished during a year as visiting scholar at Columbia University in New York. Academic life proved less than totally absorbing, however, and in 1974 Dr Wilson rejoined the diplomatic service as a full-time career member, thereby creating another precedent, because up to that point nobody had been taken back by that service except on contract. His first job on returning to the fold was in the Cabinet Office. When, three years later, the Foreign Office proposed a posting to Portugal, he demurred, 'and I thought I'd ruined my career yet again, and lo and behold, what happened? I was asked instead to go and be Political Adviser to Sir Murray Maclehose in Hong Kong. Obviously I jumped at that. There couldn't have been a job I wanted more to do.'

Hong Kong's first Political Adviser was appointed in 1947. Sir Alexander Grantham, would-be recipient of the advice, was dubious about the presence of a seconded member of the Foreign Service on his staff. He feared that the Political Adviser would be seen by his senior government officials as trespassing on their turf. In fact he needn't have worried, for the Political Adviser had no administrative or executive duties, and he was fortunate to be assigned 'a succession of first-rate Political Advisers who were careful not to tread on the toes' of their opposite number in the government secretariat.

David Wilson saw the Political Adviser role as providing 'a sort of semi-independent, mini Foreign Office for Hong Kong, dealing basically with China but also South-East Asia.' He loved the job: 'It was a very interesting, fun thing to do at a time when Hong Kong's direct connections with the Mainland were at long last unfreezing.' In 1979 he accompanied Sir Murray Maclehose on

a historic visit to Beijing, the first official visit to communist China by a Hong Kong Governor:

> That was when we first broached the question of how to handle the ending of the lease on the New Territories. We also came back on the first through train from Canton to Kowloon—that was the first time the through train had been re-established.
>
> As one looks back, it strikes me that people forget how totally cut off Hong Kong was from the Mainland until 1979. Not only was there no official contact—the Chinese government would never talk about 'the government of Hong Kong' but only 'the British authorities', avoiding the word 'government'— but there was no direct transport. You had to take the train to Lo Wu and walk across the bridge to get to the other side. Nor was there a boat service or an air service. I think the first air service was resumed in 1976 by chartered flights to fly Shanghai crabs to Hong Kong, and the first direct train service was that in which Murray Maclehose came back from Canton after his visit to Peking.
>
> I can remember, having done all the negotiations with Guangdong on the reopening of the train service, reporting back to the Foreign Office on the outcome. About a month later I got a letter back saying, thank you very much for your report, very interested to know the direct service has been reconnected, that sounds a very good thing, and so on. Then at the end, handwritten by the head of the Far Eastern Department, was

this postscript: 'I'm really rather sad that you no longer have to walk across the bridge carrying your own suitcase!'

After four years as Political Adviser, Dr Wilson returned to London and moved to a completely different desk as head of the Southern European Department. But soon he was back on his old beat, and as Assistant Under-Secretary of State dealing with Asia, he monitored that sweep of the world which in Foreign Office terms stretches 'from Afghanistan across to Mongolia and Korea, down to Australia and New Zealand, and including obviously Hong Kong and China'.

Meanwhile, negotiations over the future of Hong Kong had begun. And before long Dr Wilson became involved, initially at the London end, and then, for 'a couple of very, very hot months in Peking the summer of 1984', as head of the British team drafting the Sino-British Joint Declaration on the future of Hong Kong. It was logical—and was indeed part of his job—that he should in turn be the first chief of the Joint Liaison Group, the body of Chinese and British officials responsible for resolving all practical issues leading up to the transition and beyond. Then, unexpectedly, came the news that Sir Edward Youde (Governor, 1982–87) had died, and after a few weeks David Wilson was asked if he would take over as Governor.

This represented a great leap up the career ladder, for he was young and had not yet been an ambassador. So his first reaction was surprise: 'I had never imagined that I would finish my career being Governor of Hong Kong. And then, no hesitation whatsoever in saying yes, of course I'll do it. If you're asked to do a job like that, I don't think you would ever say no or let me think about it.'

Not that he had any illusions; after his initial surprise, he realized that the office was going to be 'a bed of nails':

The Joint Declaration had been concluded, political life in Hong Kong was changing, and there would be the shadow of the transfer of sovereignty in 1997. It would be a very different role—I knew that perfectly well—from the one that a Governor like Murray Maclehose had, before the whole question of the future had been discussed, let alone settled. . . .

But for somebody like me, with most of my adult life involved in Hong Kong and China, there can't be a better, more challenging, more thrilling job to be offered, so of course I accepted it.

───────◦◦◈◦◦───────

The resumption of the Kowloon–Canton railway service in 1979 had a resonance beyond its part in the transportation network. Indeed, it's not too fanciful to use the train as a prism through which to view how China's recent history bore upon Hong Kong.

In April 1910 Frederick Lugard drove the first engine from Kowloon to the border, and just over a year later the first through train trundled into Canton. That triumphant moment marked the end of a saga. The building of a railway from Kowloon to Canton which would, it was hoped, link Hong Kong to the heartland of China, had been a pet project of his predecessor, Sir Andrew Nathan (Governor, 1904–07), and Lugard proved no less enthusiastic when he took it over. But, fraught with problems, from its sheer expense to the engineering challenges posed by the New Territories' hilly terrain, not to mention the Chinese authorities' suspicions of foreign involvement, the line took the best part of two years to complete.

Over the border, meanwhile, the Manchu dynasty was losing its grip and the republicans were taking over the country. Well aware that the revolution might overflow into Hong Kong, British troops were on standby for an immediate move to Shanghai if necessary. On 6 November 1911, less than a month after the Wuchang uprising, the Viceroy of Canton asked Lugard to suspend the railway service from Kowloon. This was followed by the arrival of the Viceroy himself, fleeing the revolutionaries and putting himself under British protection.

Revolutions might rage in China, but Lugard's concern was Hong Kong, and his duty there was above all to keep order. He was watchful not only over the citizenry, who were generally supportive of the revolutionaries and eager to celebrate their victory, but also over hooligans and agitators coming from the Mainland under cover of the turmoil. By the end of the year he was able to write thus to his brother:

> The situation here demanded active measures. I introduced a special Ordinance—passed it in one sitting—did not consult the S[ecretary]. of S[tate]., but introduced 'the Cat' for all offences of violence and intimidation etc. . . . I had daily route marches of troops with fixed bayonets through all the crowded thoroughfares, and adopted a thousand minor performances. . . . The result is I believe the thing is fizzling out rapidly, and what might have been a serious crisis, will escape almost unnoticed. The Europeans got into a bit of a panic, and I hear many stayed away from the St. Andrew's Ball in the fear that the place would be blown up by dynamite! The Chinese have gone off their heads (the lower classes). Even the Prostitutes have announced in posters and in the press that they are paying half their earnings to 'the Cause' and inviting extra custom from patriotic motives! Where but in China would you find it an act of high patriotism to fornicate?

In fact the situation stabilized so quickly that the train service to Canton was soon reopened. Thirty-eight years later, the next Chinese revolution was to impinge on Hong Kong more critically. Southward advancing communist forces reached the border with

Hong Kong in October 1949. Shortly afterwards they suspended the through passenger service from Canton, as much as anything to prevent people from leaving China and escaping to Hong Kong.

Refugees, said Sir Alexander Grantham, Governor of the day, were nothing new in the history of Hong Kong. No barrier had existed at the border previously, and Chinese in Hong Kong as well as those in Guangdong travelled across it freely. Those who sought refuge in Hong Kong during times of trouble in China usually went back to their villages as soon as things had quietened down. But in 1949 there was no going back, and when this realization dawned in May 1950, the Hong Kong government closed the border against a further influx. By the time its hand was forced in this way, the numbers that had flooded in were already more than it could feed and house.

Fears that Hong Kong was under military threat were very real. Following a visit by the Minister of Defence from London, troop reinforcements were sent so that the garrison, boosted by Gurkha units and county regiments from England, was soon at full strength. Patrolling the border with the police, they were heckled by the communists through loudspeakers erected at the two crossings, Man Kam To and Lo Wu. One day a Hong Kong policeman who had inadvertently wandered over to the Chinese side of the border at Lo Wu was apprehended by People's Liberation Army soldiers. For a few days nobody knew what to do. Hong Kong couldn't make a formal approach to the Chinese authorities for the return of this hapless policeman since no official contact existed, while a rescue operation would clearly be unnecessarily provocative. In the end the tricky situation was resolved in a personal, face-saving, and quite 'Chinese' way. The Commissioner of Police, Duncan MacIntosh, had 'some contacts with, or to Canton', and he proposed to work through them. As Sir Alexander recalled: 'Within less than forty-eight hours he had fixed it, and the policeman was returned to us. One of the requests that the Chinese made was that the beam of one of our searchlights should not be directed into their barracks. It disturbed the sleep of the soldiers. We considered this a small concession to make.'

Cross-border tension was not the only problem. Mingling with the refugees were several thousand Kuomintang soldiers and agents who proceeded to do their best to bring about the discomfiture of the colonial authorities. So did pro-communist agitators, and no opportunity was lost in stirring up anti-British sentiments, the most fertile ground for political indoctrination being the trade unions and the schools. But with vigilance and discretion, Hong Kong managed to put out the smouldering flames of subversive activities.

At all times, and especially in cases such as 'the closure of a communist school, the deportation of an agitator or the prosecution of a communist newspaper for a seditious article,' observed Sir Alexander (pictured), 'we had to do a balancing act'. Faced with the fact that the new regime in China was 'violently anti-Western, anti-British, and anti-Hong Kong,' what should be, he asked, 'the guiding principles of our policy? On the one hand we did not want to be provocative; on the other we did not want to appease or appear to do so, to give way to unreasonable demands. The population of Hong Kong knew that the government across the border was unfriendly and strong. If we truckled to it we would lose the people's confidence and support; they might even turn against us.'

If there is one phrase to sum up the Hong Kong Governor's experience of dealing with China, it is surely 'balancing act'. Like Grantham had found in the incident of the trespassing policeman, Sir David Wilson also came to the conclusion that, where China was concerned, a non-confrontational way of doing things was often the best policy. This was a lesson from experience, and most instructive of all was his participation in the team that put flesh on the bones of the Joint Declaration. To get down on paper in as much detail and precision as possible how the agreement was to work in practice, the British and Hong Kong side

> started with a huge wodge of paper, something like the *Encyclopaedia Britannica*. The Chinese side started with— whatever it was—ten principles, saying that we didn't need anything else, just sign on the bottom line and we'd solve the problem. The drafting group had to bring these two positions together.

What he learnt very quickly was the importance of establishing a rapport with the Chinese negotiating team, headed by an ambassador-level official named Ke Zaishuo:

> We were meeting in the International Club in Peking in the summer of 1986. It was very, very hot, and there was no air-conditioning. The first thing I said to the Chinese team was, 'Do you mind if we take our jackets off?' And I did that partly because it was very hot, but also partly to try to establish an informal atmosphere.

Negotiating from very different positions and in two languages, the communication gap was sometimes apparently unbridgeable:

> We would present a section of, say, appendices dealing with the legal system, and it would be four pages long, and Ke Zaishuo would say, 'No, that's absolutely hopeless, just go away and do something else.'
>
> I'd ask, 'Where's the problem?' but he would simply repeat, 'It's hopeless, go away and try again.'
>
> We would then try and work out what the problem was. And then it very quickly became clear that part of the problem

was the draft's sheer length. Probably the Chinese may even have a limit on the number of characters to be used. So we became quite skilled at boiling things down to the minimum, to what really mattered to us, and writing it as briefly as possible.

But British prolixity was not always the only impediment: 'I found over time that if you could just establish what the problem was, you could very often—80, 90 per cent of the time—find a solution. The difficulty was establishing *what* the difficulty was.'

The objection could be to a word or an expression used in the text. And this fastidiousness on the part of the Chinese struck a chord with Dr Wilson, taking him right back to his research into the 1920s, when suspicion and misunderstanding had similarly arisen on both sides. He could see, sixty years on, the same mistrust. Chinese negotiators had looked at the British proposals for the Joint Declaration, he realized, and had thought to themselves, 'Gosh, these British are incredibly clever, they're terribly devious, they're very subtle', going on to put constructions on words which had never occurred to the British team, and were certainly never intended.

It was only when wariness over the choice of a word and its possible meanings was allayed could discussions continue. In Dr Wilson's experience negotiating in an atmosphere where trust prevailed also meant, more often than not,

> dealing with things privately and quietly and not shouting from the rooftops. Now there were times when in private you had to take a very strong line; sometimes you also had to take a tough line in public because people in Hong Kong needed to be reassured, but on the whole my own preference was always to try and do things privately even though the penalty—and I was well aware of the penalty—was getting criticized in the press.

Here was the rub. However effective this approach proves in negotiations, it can be seen by the public as flabby. David Wilson didn't emerge unscathed from a critical press, but he was prepared to take the flak,

> and all the sort of easy things that the press can say—'you're kowtowing, you're agreeing with China'— because they didn't

know (how could they know?) what was going on in private. I felt that was a price worth paying personally in order to achieve what seemed to me was best for Hong Kong and for the people of Hong Kong.

In the summer of 1989 all that slowly built-up confidence between Britain, Hong Kong, and China collapsed with the tragic consequences of the student and worker protests in Tiananmen Square. China believed that the demonstrators had been helped by the people of Hong Kong, 'and all the steeped underlying suspicions of the British which were always there but which gradually we were overcoming came to the surface again. It was a very difficult, very bad time.'

Despite Hong Kong's brisk recovery from the crisis, the remaining years of Sir David's term were difficult ones, darkened as they were by people's forebodings about their future under communist rule. Of all the Governors of Hong Kong, he had arguably the toughest time. Most challenging of all, perhaps, was the need constantly to test the limits of what his government could do and commit itself to for the future welfare of Hong Kong without calling down China's opposition and wrath:

> If Hong Kong was going to survive and prosper after British administration, major things had to be done, and if they weren't done, Hong Kong would sort of decay in a Macao-like way. Yet you had to take those decisions knowing that the benefit of them would only be reaped after 1997, after British administration had ended.
>
> The classic example is the airport. A decision had been taken earlier that Hong Kong was going to build a new airport. . . . then it was shelved. After I arrived we began to look at it seriously, and I laid down that we must make a decision by the end of 1989.
>
> By the time the decision was due to be taken in the autumn of 1989 we'd had Tiananmen. There was a huge crisis in confidence, and morale was very, very low. And the decision then for me and for the Executive Council to take was: faced with this crisis and the collapse of confidence, do we go ahead with this massive project or do we shelve it again?

We took the decision of course to go ahead, and I announced it in my Legislative Council speech in '89. There was great Chinese mistrust although they knew—we had told them what we were going to do.

China's reservations had much to do with the airport's financing, since repayments on loans and bonds were to be spread over a period well past 1997. Her agreement was eventually secured at a price, for the British Prime Minister John Major had to go to China, then a pariah among nations after the Tiananmen crackdown, to clinch it. Sir David took the view that 'we were right to do things for the future of Hong Kong, even though they were very difficult for the government at that time . . . In pragmatic, realistic terms, if things were going to bridge '97, whether it's political structure or a massive infrastructure project, you had to do them with Chinese agreement in some form, tacit or public.'

Although he would rather emphasize his contribution to the expansion of tertiary education and the amelioration of environmental pollution, the new airport—not least because of its size and expense—may well be remembered by future generations as the defining achievement of Sir David's governorship, just as Lugard is associated with the foundation of the territory's first university, and Grantham with refugee resettlement and the birth of industrialization in Hong Kong. The largest engineering project in the world at the time, Chek Lap Kok International Airport would have been a tremendous last fling of the British administration in Hong Kong had it been completed by the Handover. As it was, the controversial airport proved the finishing stroke for Sir David's governorship. He himself has denied the connection between the airport and, as some saw it, his premature retirement from office, and remains philosophical about the way his public service career had begun and ended:

At university . . . I'd wanted to join the Colonial Service. I had gone through the Colonial Service exams, and had been offered a post in Africa. When I went in front of the final selection board, I asked them what sort of career there would be for a young man like me. And these elderly and distinguished gentlemen all said, 'Oh, don't worry about it—no question that in your lifetime there will be plenty of colonies.'

In the previous year—1957—I'd spent my last long vacation on an Oxford University, two-man expedition to what was then British Somaliland and the UN Trust Territory of Somalia, travelling in the hills with camels. And I had seen for myself first of all that British Somaliland was totally unprepared for independence, that they had one university-trained Somali graduate in the whole country, and also that independence was nevertheless going to come pretty soon whether we British liked it or not. It was very obvious to me that the colonial empire in Africa was going to go or be changed very rapidly.

So when I got this comment from the selection board, and then was offered a job in central Africa, I said, 'No, thank you very much, but I don't think I will.'

It's ironic to me that having turned down the Colonial Service I should finish up as one of the last colonial Governors. Anyhow, there it was.

5

Money Makes the World Go Round

In the early days of the China trade, finance was handled by the banking departments of the merchant houses. Companies like Jardines, Dent & Company, and the American firm Russell & Company bought each other's bills for their remittances. This was a neat enough arrangement were it not for the fact that it left the smaller traders high and dry. To meet those traders' financial needs, it was felt that Hong Kong had to have its own bank.

This was easier said than done. A few joint stock banks originally established in India or England tried their luck in Hong Kong but scuttled out again. In 1864, a group of merchants in Bombay proposed launching a bank in Hong Kong and China. They called it the Royal Bank of China and appropriated to themselves the bulk of its share capital, leaving only one-fourth to one-third for subscription in Hong Kong and China.

'Well,' thought Thomas Sutherland to himself when he heard the news, 'if the people in China were so unpatriotic, were so lacking in public spirit that they would submit to a Bombay enterprise coming along in this fashion and putting them into this undignified position . . . they would deserve whatever fate might befall them.' (Of course by 'the people of China' he meant not the Chinese but other Europeans like himself clustered in the Treaty Ports.) It was galling all the same, and once he had calmed down he found himself wondering. Thomas Sutherland was Superintendent of the Peninsular & Oriental Company in Hong Kong. A few months earlier he had been on a small P & O steamer, the *Manila*, which plied between Hong Kong and Fuzhou, and had idled away the hours reading some copies of *Blackwood's Magazine* he had found on board,

> which contained articles on the subject of banking and I absorbed these articles; they fascinated me. I had never had a banking

account in my life. I had only an account with the Compradore which was generally overdrawn; but it appeared to me that, if a suitable opportunity occurred, one of the very simplest things in the world would be to start a bank in China more or less founded upon Scottish principles.

This idea lay dormant until the news of the Royal Bank of China— a 'communication of a most momentous character'—burst upon him. Almost at once, reflections on the unpatriotic attitude of the people in China gave way to a visionary plan. Perceiving the dazzling future of financial services in Hong Kong with a clarity that was truly inspired, he sat down and wrote out a prospectus for the Hongkong and Shanghai Banking Corporation that very night. Next day

I took the prospectus . . . to my friend Mr Pollard, who was at that time the most eminent counsel in Hong Kong, and I said to him, 'You may make a business of this.' He saw it in a glance, he saw a fee of 10,000 dollars immediately, and he took the prospectus round to all the leading firms in Hong Kong; and with the exception of Jardine, Matheson, every firm of repute and distinction at that time in China put their names down as members of the provisional committee of this Bank with its five million dollars of capital. . . . Within less than a week the whole of the capital that we could possibly allot to Hong Kong was taken up and stood at a considerable premium. The ambassador from the Royal Bank of China arrived a fortnight or three weeks afterwards. His name, I recollect, was Mr Noel Porter. He could not get anybody to take a single share in his

capital; he could not discover a possible director anywhere, and
... within an incredibly short space of time the Royal Bank of
China was wound up in Bombay with somewhat unfortunate if
not ignominious results.

The Hongkong and Shanghai Banking Corporation, on the other
hand, went from strength to strength, building on its unique status
as 'the most powerful banking organization of foreign interests in
China'. Just how international those interests were is amply illustrated
by the nationalities of the provisional committee members, including
as they did British, American, German, Danish, Jewish, and Indian.

————◦◦◦————

Thomas Sutherland's 'Scottish principles', if by that he meant
frugality, prudence, shrewdness, and diligence, have more or less
prevailed. To outsiders, the Bank has also displayed inordinate
caution and conservatism, an approach perpetuated by long-serving
staff. Many senior directors and chairmen in the past ten or twenty
years have worked there for decades, joining after the Second World
War and rising through the ranks.

Retired banker David Turner was born in Shanghai and spent
his childhood in India. His father was an official of the
predominantly foreign-administered Chinese Maritime Customs.
With that sort of background, it was not surprising that he chose
to work in Asia, and so, after school in England and a two-year
stint of National Service,

> I went along to the Officers Association which had a place in
> Victoria [London] where they helped ex-officers and ex-
> servicemen from the Army, Navy, and Air Force to find jobs.
> They asked me what I wanted to do, and I told them it would
> have to be a desk job as I had a bad leg and was still then receiving
> treatment—I got shot in both legs by Egyptian terrorists in
> Suez and was paralysed in one.
>
> Various possible jobs were mentioned—in Malaysia and
> Thailand, I remember—and they also mentioned the Hongkong
> and Shanghai Bank. I said I'd go home and think about it. When

I told my parents, their reaction was, 'Ah, the Hongkong and Shanghai Bank; well, that's really the best firm to work for in the Far East!'

A few days later the Officers Association arranged an interview with the two joint managers of the Bank's London office, at 9 Gracechurch Street in the City. I think I started very soon after they appointed me, so within a few weeks of leaving the Army I was in the Bank. After fourteen months in London as a trainee I went out by the P & O *Corfu* to Hong Kong, arriving in January 1954.

New recruits used to be sent out in pairs, and the sea voyage constituted a gradual and gentle introduction to Eastern climes and cultures. Mess accommodation at the other end eased things for the uprooted bachelor too, especially for someone from the Army who would have found close parallels between regimental life and communal living of this sort. David Turner remembers his luggage being taken up to the Bank mess on the Peak, where he was allotted a bedsitting-room, while he and his fellow recruit went to the office so that they could start work straight away. The mess as an institution has long vanished, however, for 'the number of young bachelors going out to the Bank in Hong Kong from the UK is substantially down from the level in my day, so the two or three of them that do go out probably share a flat now.'

All the executives of the Bank, he found, were British. 'Of course the Bank was much smaller than it is now; it had only four branches at the time—Central, North Point, Kowloon, and Mong Kok; now there are 250-odd. The clerks were Portuguese or Macanese, and the shroffs who dealt with the cash and accounting were Chinese.' A Chinese compradore guaranteed the probity of the shroffs. Then, as the Bank expanded,

> there was a mixing of the Portuguese and the Chinese staff, with the Chinese staff becoming clerks as well as shroffs. And of course the Portuguese and Chinese staff also became officers. They were called 'regional officers' [now 'resident managers'], meaning that they would only work in Hong Kong, whereas the international officers could be posted anywhere in the world

at twenty-four hours' notice. And you went! If you agree to be an International Officer you have to accept the bad posting as well as the good.

One example of this is particularly memorable. His chairman Michael Sandberg announced to him one Friday evening in June 1985 that he was to supervise the rescue of a local bank, the Overseas Trust Bank (OTB), starting at eight o'clock the next morning. The government, which had taken over the ailing company, felt that if a senior manager of the Hongkong and Shanghai Bank could be seconded to sort out the mess, the collapsing bank might have a chance of being restored to health. Over the weekend Turner rang colleagues as far afield as San Francisco, Toronto, Bahrain, and Britain, running one to earth in Scotland on holiday. His request was to the point: would they drop everything and join him at the OTB? They would—and 'were there ready for work on Monday morning'. By this time a subsidiary, the Hong Kong Industrial and Commercial Bank, had also failed, 'which meant I had two bankrupt banks to run, and this made life rather interesting! Not only was there bad debt but also corruption at the very top. Later on the former chairman, deputy chairman, and three senior managers went to gaol for fraud.'

During the first year or so at OTB Turner was ceaselessly at work—'I practically lived at the bank'—and at the end of 1986 he officially retired. But there was life after the hong. Offered a direct contract with OTB, he agreed to continue for two years and ended up staying for eight. The culmination of his tremendous efforts was the sale of OTB to Dao Heng Bank; and from this the government not only recouped its investment but also made a profit.

⸺⸺◇∘⸺⸺

One could be forgiven for speaking of Dick Gazmararian and Sir Paul Chater in the same breath—they share a common heritage as Armenians and one-time bullion traders, and both adopted British nationality. Dick Gazmararian's father, born in Jerusalem when Palestine still lay within the Ottoman Empire, became a naturalized subject of the Crown under the British Mandate. 'If he hadn't become naturalized,' Gazmararian says, 'I would be a Palestinian refugee, stateless.' Although Paul Catchick Chater's personal history before his arrival in Hong Kong in 1864 is shadowy, we do know that several generations of his family had been based in Calcutta, which also makes him a child of the British Empire.

But there the similarity ends. Chater diversified from his bullion business into other ventures, including property, docks, coal mines, and good works (which gained him a knighthood in 1902); for Gazmararian, however, the lustre of precious metals is far from dimmed as he continues to facilitate their movement across the world. He has worked in Hong Kong on and off since 1970: 'I first came to Hong Kong to set up Merrill Lynch's commodities department. My office was in St George's Building in Ice House Street and I used to drive up in my MGB, park right outside, and leave it there all day. Then I went to Beirut in 1974 and walked straight into a war!'

Back in London, he was asked if he wanted to run a gold company in Hong Kong. Precious metals, especially gold and silver, have been used as a medium of exchange since ancient times. Before there was paper currency there was gold and silver. In fact, Gazmararian asserts, 'modern-day bankers originated in the medieval goldsmiths'. Of course silver possesses an even greater historical significance for mercantile Hong Kong, for was it not because of silver, or rather the loss of it, that the Opium War was fought? And what a lot of silver! Chinese *sycee*, Maria Theresa thalers, Mexican pesos, US trade dollars, *piastres*—a cascade of coins, all 900 fine or 90 per cent pure—had set the wheels of China trade in rapid motion. And as for the ships plying restlessly to and fro, their

sails plump with monsoon winds and their holds heavy with treasure—they made fortunes for those who dealt in silver, and for Mocatta and Goldsmid above all.

This most venerable of bullion brokers sent Dick Gazmararian to Hong Kong in 1975. There had been no legal market in newly mined gold in Hong Kong until then. A member of the sterling area, Hong Kong imposed strict controls on the import and export of the metal but, as Gazmararian explains, these controls were frequently bypassed:

> In 1950 the government imposed a ban on gold imports. This was very peculiar considering that a gold and silver exchange had existed since 1908. Until the ban was lifted in 1974, the market was supplied by smuggling. What happened was this: gold ingots would arrive on a BOAC flight into Kai Tak Airport, go into a bonded warehouse, get transshipped to Macao, there broken up into smaller lots and then smuggled back into Hong Kong. The stupidity of the whole thing—or rather the law— was that once gold landed in Hong Kong and got made up into jewellery and so on, it became perfectly legal for ordinary residents to buy or sell it!
>
> Once gold imports became legal the international bullion houses moved into the market because now there was an opportunity to do all the various things you do with bullion like trading and arbitrage. Mocatta and Goldsmid was the first international bullion house to open in Hong Kong and that's why I came back in 1975.

Even when dealers talk prosaically of ingots, kilo bars, and taels, nothing tarnishes the emotional allure of gold. It is the stuff of bank reserves and a traditional hedge against unpredictable swings in the value of less solid currencies. There was a time in Hong Kong, with the collective memory still smarting from the rampant inflation, wars, and political instability of republican and revolutionary China, when it glittered more brightly than ever, possession of it being equated with the last airline ticket out in the minds of many. Dick Gazmararian tells the story of a woman who bought quite a lot of gold from him one day:

I asked her, 'What are you going to do with it?'

'I'm going to put it in the bank in case something goes wrong.'

When I said, 'You think China will invade during normal banking hours so that you can get your gold out from your safe deposit box?', she looked at me in absolute horror! It had never dawned on her to keep the gold at home.

There were those who, in the absence of safe deposit boxes, *buried* their treasure, which is what people did when the Chinese communists, taking power in 1949, called for the surrender of gold and silver in private hands. The communist government asked in vain. Out in the provinces, late at night when the fields and farms were wrapped in darkness, much of the silver that had been circulating as currency literally went to ground.

Three decades passed. And because an American named Bunker Hunt tried to corner the market, the world's appetite for silver was spectacularly revived, pushing the metal's price from a dollar and a half an ounce to $50. When the price reached $35 on the way up, somebody telephoned Gazmararian and said, 'By the way, have you been to Aberdeen lately?'

'No, why?' I asked.

'Well, all the fishing junks are coming in loaded with bags of silver.'

So I went down there, and sure enough men were moving sackloads of silver coins all covered in soil and mud. Barter was taking place right there on the high seas—electrical goods from Hong Kong for silver. The silver was 900 fine and worth a fortune. It was amazing. The coins had stayed underground all those years, from 1950 to 1980. When the price was $5 an ounce—nothing; $10—nothing. The moment it got over $35 an ounce people must have thought 'OK, I'm going to dig up my hoard and sell it.' Somehow or other the coins were mobilized from all over China and got to the coast, on to junks, the high seas, and through barter trade into Hong Kong! It's never ceased to amaze me how, with no Reuters machines giving quotations— in 1980 China was still pretty locked up—the prices filtered into the provinces to those farmers and ordinary citizens.

As soon as the price dropped back below \$35 it was like turning a tap off; the silver stopped coming out. Nobody knows how much silver is still buried in China.

The world is a safer place now, says Gazmararian, and inflation is low. But if investment demand for precious metals is negligible today, gold is no less desirable as jewellery. 'In the 1970s trading was a big part of the business but now that the price doesn't fluctuate much it's really become more of a banking business. Over the last fifteen years Hong Kong consumed, say, fifty to eighty tons a year to make jewellery.'

———◦◇◦———

It was no coincidence that Hong Kong people felt the world safer in 1978, for that was when China emerged from an isolation that had lasted for nearly thirty years. The effect of this opening-up on Hong Kong was more than psychological, however, for it gave the territory a new role to play—as China's agent to the capital markets of the world. And so while the colony remained an entrepôt, its trade became 'invisible', the more important commodity that now swirled in and out of the territory being money—not in bars of gold but as so many figures on pieces of paper.

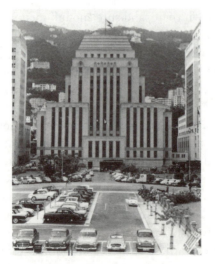

Hong Kong took to its new role like a duck to water, but though it drew to its shores a fair share of international wheeler dealers, not a few fortune hunters and very fishy corporate sharks came too.

In 1983 the territory reverberated with shock when a listed company, Carrian, folded with debts of more than US$1 billion. Carrian and the man behind it, George Tan Soon-gin, a Malaysian Chinese, had seemingly come from nowhere before their meteoric debut on the entrepreneurial stage. In fact George Tan had concocted an image of impressive assets and limitless funds for his company by one of the oldest tricks in the swindler's book. He had bought a number of small properties and offered them to banks as collateral to borrow money to buy bigger ones. These were then used as collateral to raise yet more money. Replaying this formula over and over again, George Tan was soon able to persuade gullible investors that his company possessed a real estate portfolio worth many times more than the value of the first small properties he bought.

Just as disturbing when Carrian's business was exposed as a fraudulent affair was the ensuing spate of scandals including a murder, a suicide, charges of bribery and corruption, extraditions, and legal wrangles, all of which were to keep officers of the police force and Independent Commission Against Corruption (ICAC) engaged more and more as the years passed, memories faded, and the prospect of bringing the guilty men to justice seemed increasingly elusive. Their investigations involved, among others, senior executives of George Tan's principal lenders, Bumiputra Malaysia Finance Limited and Wardley Limited, whose exposure to Carrian was estimated to add up to $7.25 billion. Not for a moment did the ICAC believe that all bankers were credulous, stupid, or negligent; for George Tan to obtain as much credit as he did with so few questions asked, some had undoubtedly been corrupt.

When Wardley, then the merchant-banking arm of the Hongkong and Shanghai Bank, was granting substantial loans to Carrian, its chief executive was a tall, spare, apparently respectable, and well-known figure in the financial community, Ewan Launder, who had been a stockbroker in Britain before moving to Hong Kong in 1973. In the circumstances, it didn't seem unreasonable to suppose that he 'had a lot of influence and control over the granting of loans'. This was the prosecution's allegation when the ICAC finally prevailed and brought him back to Hong Kong for trial in early 2000. The prosecutor further alleged that, to ensure Ewan Launder used his influence in favour of Carrian's applications, $4.5 million in bribes was given as 'a general sweetener'. These bribes landed him behind bars, to serve a jail term of five years, nearly two decades after the crime had been committed.

Scandals of this sort, as well as a highly volatile stock market that some likened to a casino, undermined Hong Kong's bid for international stature as a financial centre in the 1980s, for the shifts in its economy were accelerating, and by the second half of the decade the process of transition was about to succumb to overwhelming pressures from both within and without. Implosion duly followed when the stock market, set off by the Wall Street crash of October 1987, spectacularly crumbled. With the world of money in turmoil, Hong Kong's financial sector was starkly exposed as being totally out of its depth. And in the post-mortem which followed it became all too clear that credibility could only be restored if a framework were in place to supervise the financial industry of the territory. What came out of all this was the establishment of the Securities and Futures Commission (SFC), a body entrusted also with the power to investigate fraud and deal with corporate malfeasance. For staff with relevant experience the SFC cast its net far and wide, recruiting among others an Australian lawyer with a financial background then working in Switzerland, Deborah Glass.

She was in at the birth of the SFC in May 1989. As senior manager responsible for the section that vetted and authorized applications for unit trusts and mutual funds, she had her work cut out. The section's previous incarnation, a government department, had carried on in a mode that was nothing if not Byzantine. Case officers invariably sent long lists of inconsistent requisitions to each applicant, and when the answers came back, would pluck a few more dozen out of the air, apparently by individual whim. A backlog of other applications from perfectly respectable jurisdictions whose laws did not tally precisely with the wording of the Hong Kong code was given short shrift: as each application struggled to the top of the pile, the applicant was asked to make a detailed request for a waiver, even though the point had been considered countless times already. Out of this bureaucratic disarray, Deborah Glass and her assistants brought order. 'I came in fresh from the funds product department of an aggressive US investment bank,' she writes, 'and with a little application of teamwork and a lot of training and streamlining procedures, the backlog was cleared within months.'

In early 1993 what were known as 'B shares'—shares in mainland China registered companies tradeable by foreign investors—were listed to great fanfare. Less than a month later the SFC received an application for a B-share unit trust. The trouble was that only two stocks had been listed,

> and unit trusts must be diversified and may not put more than 10 per cent into any one stock. After some debate we authorized the fund, subject to full disclosure about the nature of the B-share market and the fact that investors would be paying a hefty management fee to keep their investments in cash until there were more shares around.
>
> A year or so later I was asked to put together guidelines for the registration of B-share rights issue prospectuses. The B-shares issuers had so successfully tapped overseas investor excitement that they could not resist coming back for more. Stories abounded of companies using their IPO proceeds to redecorate their offices. So in the registration guidelines we took the unusual step of requiring not only disclosure about the proceeds of the rights issue, but also what the company had said it was going to do with the proceeds of the original issue, as well as what it actually did.
>
> The pioneers of the SFC brought Hong Kong into the regulatory Premier League: we had our battles with vested interests, but we believed that right was on our side.

Despite periods of intense frustration and great stress, Glass found her job

> deeply satisfying for the nine years I ended up staying in Hong Kong. It carried a strong sense of achievement: a chance to make a difference. Idealism kept me going through the difficult

periods—that and, I suppose, a need to prove myself in the world of the expat British male.

I was terribly nervous when I first arrived and discovered that most of my new staff were male and older than me. But Hong Kong tradition stood me in good stead—I was the teacher as well as the boss, and neither age nor gender was any bar to loyalty. After those early days I wasn't particularly conscious of being a woman in a man's world. There were plenty of Chinese women in positions of power. As a foreign woman I was more unusual, but I rarely noticed it.

Occasionally the job intruded in embarrassing ways. She remembers one evening when a friend took her to dinner at the home of someone whom the SFC had been investigating. Only the week before 'I had been negotiating a tough disciplinary case' involving her host. 'Fortunately the discipline had been concluded and my unlucky host put on a display of perfect manners.'

Regulators such as Deborah Glass have made the industry more respected. Ted Pulling, a fund manager, observed, 'Anybody working here twenty years ago would have found Hong Kong a bit more of a frontier town, whereas now this is a world-class financial market; it's much more sophisticated. I suspect there was a more clubby atmosphere before. . . . Now it's much bigger, the volume's much larger, and you have international investment banks, bulge-bracket banks from the US, like Merrill Lynch, Morgan Stanley, and so on.'

———◦◦◦◦◦———

At the time of our interview, Ted Pulling was a fund manager covering the Indian and Korean stock markets for Jardine Fleming (which has since been sold to the American conglomerate, Chase). He will never forget the first break he was given in Hong Kong, a place which furnishes no less a welcome to youngsters who come without the backing of a job than to international officer recruits of the established hongs. Though armed with impeccable academic credentials—Groton and Princeton University—Pulling had majored in history, not economics or business:

My personal details aren't particularly exciting. Whoever would have thought that some stupid kid from the east coast of the United States would be working for a British company on an island in southern China investing billions of dollars in India and Korea? I guess Hong Kong is still very much a meritocracy, and if you're intelligent, and you're reasonably good at what you do, then nobody's going to say, 'You can't do this because you studied History at Princeton, you didn't study Hindi at Oxford'. If you're good, if you work hard, you can succeed here.

Up to the time he arrived in Hong Kong, the scope of his experience in Asia had been a summer internship at Shearson Lehman American Express after his freshman year, 'though to call the job an internship would be a generous way of describing it. My father helped me get the job . . . the extent of my duties was basically to read the newspapers, cut out articles and file them. And for this I was paid a minimal amount of money. I lived in the Luk Kwok Hotel in Wan Chai *before* it was refurbished, so it was classic Vietnam-War vintage with the same thirty-year old beds. It was the world of Suzie Wong without Suzie Wong.'

His return to Hong Kong could almost be said to be unpremeditated. To graduate from Princeton, he said, you needed to write a thesis. Since he completed this with about two months to spare, the end of his final semester was passed

> pretty much hanging out at my club, drinking beer, and playing cards all day. And what I noticed was that I would struggle up to the Ivy Club at around noon, at the same time that a lot of my friends would be coming in wearing suits, having spent the morning interviewing with Wall Street companies. I'd spent the morning less industriously in bed.
>
> Basically all my friends were out getting jobs and I wasn't. And lunchtime conversation would come around to what I was going to do, and somehow or other I'd concocted a story that I would go to Asia after I graduated.

His timing was disastrous. Typical of students on the eve of graduation, he had been partying most of the night, not sitting at home watching television. Which was why he was taken by surprise when, walking out 'to Nassau Hall in our robes,' he found a bunch of students there asking everybody to wear a black armband 'because the morning of our graduation was the morning after the tanks had rolled into Tiananmen Square and the students had been shot by the PLA'. In late June 1989, he recalled,

> Hong Kong was a pretty subdued place . . . I checked into the YMCA in Wan Chai. I had some five names that I'd gotten from the Princeton University Alumni records. I started calling them. Two of the people had already left, but a couple of dynamic Americans who didn't have a job for me gave me names of other people to contact and so the process started whereby you interview or meet somebody and you get a few names. Finally I met a woman who'd graduated from Princeton in 1985 and was working for Reuters at the time. She'd gone through the exact job search that I had, basically interviewing all the merchant banks. Mind you, I didn't even know what a merchant bank was. She gave me a comprehensive list and I started calling.
>
> One of the first companies I called was Jardine Fleming. I can remember getting through to someone with a very thick English accent. And I said, 'Hi, my name is Ted Pulling. I'm from Princeton University, and I'm out here looking for a job. I was wondering if I could come over and talk to you?' The response was, 'Do you really think you can simply telephone Jardine Fleming and obtain an interview?' I was very put off by that; my heart sank. At that point Hong Kong struck me as a very English enclave.

His reception at W.I. Carr, a brokerage firm, was positively warm by comparison. He had asked to speak to the head of research there and got put through to someone called Frank O'Reilly, who had a perceptible Irish accent, although at that time Ted Pulling could not distinguish an Irish accent from a Scottish or English one. Frank O'Reilly suggested an interview. It didn't start very well:

> When Frank O'Reilly asked me what I read at university, I interpreted that to mean, what was my major at Princeton. So I said, 'Oh, my major was military history, and I focused on English military history, but you must know a lot about that, Mr O'Reilly, being English.'

To which he replied, 'I'm not English, I'm Irish, and we've been on the receiving end of English military history for a hundred years!'—or something like that.

At that point I thought, OK, another job interview gone to hell. But instead he asked me to stay, and sent in somebody else to give me another interview. And in classic Hong Kong style, those interviews happened on a Thursday, I got a call on Friday afternoon from W.I. Carr asking me to come in on Saturday morning. I went in on Saturday morning for what I thought would be more interviews, but was in fact offered a job.

My starting salary was HK$10,000 a month, and I was pretty excited about that. The job was equity research. There I was, with absolutely nothing, living at the 'Y', and that company gave me a break. That was true Hong Kong style, I think. A lot of young Americans, a lot of young Brits, a lot of young everybody, have come here and used that same recipe to get an entry-level job. . . . The great thing about W.I. Carr was the people who worked there. They taught me about economics and how stock markets worked. They didn't begrudge the fact that you were young and inexperienced. If you were willing to work hard and you were intelligent, people would listen to what you had to say.

I spent two years doing equity research. I can remember writing a huge report on Hongkong Telecom, and my first one was on Dickson Concepts, which was a 'buy' report. I think Dickson Concepts underperformed for about two years after I put that report out!

On his starting salary, he could afford only a tiny room in a flat in Mid-levels. Even so, his living arrangement was the envy of his friends, for although he ostensibly shared with two others, he had the flat largely to himself. It turned out that one of the flatmates, his landlord, had been sailing very close to the wind,

and he exited Hong Kong rather suddenly one evening. I'd come home from work on a Thursday evening and he came in shortly after, grabbed some stuff, threw it into a bag and ran out to the airport to fly to the Philippines, saying he would call me at the weekend. Which he did, and he said, 'I'm not coming back to Hong Kong, so would you pack this and this and send them down to the Philippines?' Which I did. And he never came back. You could say I probably owe him about a year's worth of rent. But if he wasn't here, I wasn't paying!

Ted Pulling's landlord was employed by a English trading company which had provided him with capital to set up an office in Hong Kong. Instead he absconded with the money, and it was when the UK company's questions became rather too pressing that he bolted. The other flatmate, an English girl, was also somewhat unconventional:

> She had about five different boyfriends all of whom were either in the Army or the Police. The only time she ever spent two nights in the apartment was when the US Fleet was in town. Because then, rather than go home with one of her five squaddie or police boyfriends, she'd go out trawling for some American sailor and bring him back. I can remember a couple of occasions getting up in the morning and going to the kitchen to have my breakfast before work and meeting some pimply nineteen-year-old from Wisconsin or wherever, and the standard conversation would be, 'How do I get back to my ship?' And I'd say, 'Listen, just get this bus, or a taxi, down the hill . . .' and so on.

◦◦⟡◦◦

Time was when no Westerner would contemplate a job in Hong Kong without the full expatriate package. A housing allowance (or free accommodation), children's school fees, and travel subsidies were taken for granted. 'There's no doubt about it, the lifestyle here can be very good, with a lot of money and a huge housing allowance.' The likes of Ted Pulling spoilt the market by allowing themselves to be recruited on the spot and accepting the same remuneration as that paid to locals. But the market was changing anyway. Through the 1980s expatriate and local conditions of service gradually converged, a reflection partly of the increasing fitness of Chinese candidates to compete with expatriates for top management jobs. In the old hongs the distinction between international and local staff lingered on rather longer.

At the Hongkong and Shanghai Bank, for example, in return for cheerful acquiescence to constant moves, international staff are looked after exceptionally well, with the personnel department undertaking all their everyday chores from finding accommodation to paying income tax. This treatment did not elicit as much resentment from local staff as one might expect, certainly not since entry to the international cadre was opened to all. In the late 1970s, the Bank's 'Number One India', David Turner, came across

> five very bright young officers who were later sent to Hong Kong. Indian tax rates were very high in those days, salaries didn't go far, and I said to the Bank, 'Unless you promoted these officers you will lose them. Give them a chance and second them to Hong Kong.' Aman Mehta, now Chief Executive Officer in Hong Kong, was one of them. The current 'Number One India' is another, while two more hold senior positions in London and elsewhere. Four out of the five are still with the Bank twenty years later.

Aman Mehta explains how the division between resident and international staff has become less clear-cut over the years:

> There's a small cadre of international managers—they're now called managers, not officers—and there's a much larger cadre of resident managers. But mobility has increased in the sense that many more resident managers go on specific overseas assignments for maybe three or four years, and some actually convert to international managers.

I joined as a resident manager, and my first couple of postings out were as a resident manager. In 1987, at the end of a posting in Hong Kong, I moved straight from here to the Middle East. It was impractical for me to go back to India at that time, and I expressed a preference to join the international staff. And that was when I converted.

International managers at the middle levels tend to move more often than their seniors, but for those at the very top whose bailiwick is a continent or two, geography becomes almost irrelevant. 'I share my time between Hong Kong and the rest of the world,' says Aman Mehta,

I travel a lot, averaging a different country every ten days. I've done this in the last ten years. A job like mine doesn't give too much flexibility. It governs 90 per cent of waking hours in terms of what you do, whether it's at the office, or meetings, or other business-related activities. Even dinner parties, functions, or galas that I attend involve the Bank. I have lots of friends and acquaintances in Hong Kong, but they're mostly business associates. Obviously I've not been as engaged with Hong Kong as expatriates who have spent a lifetime here.

Unlike Aman Mehta and David Turner, few nowadays serve the same company for the whole of their career. Loyalty of that kind has been severely tested in the last quarter of a century as a result of the phenomenal growth of financial services in Hong Kong, providing opportunities, especially in newly opened branches of American banks, of earning dazzling salaries and even more breathtaking bonuses. Just before the so-called 'Roaring '80s' dawned, the Hongkong and Shanghai Bank had to compete for staff with those newcomers and began actively to recruit its international cadre direct from British universities. This is what a hapless employee, assigned to write copy for the Bank's first graduate recruitment brochure, encountered:

I thought it would be useful to ask one or two young international officers for their own experience of the 'milk round' at university, when companies make presentations to final-year students and solicit applications. The first department I visited was Current Accounts at the main branch, then run by a chinless wonder who promptly forestalled me by reading me a lecture on how irrelevant a university degree was to banking. Clearly he didn't have one. This stumped me, but I pressed on regardless. 'Could you tell me please if there are any graduates in this department?' I asked.

'There are none,' he replied. Then, after a pause, waving his arm in the direction of the back office, he said in a dismissive tone, 'Oh, I suppose there may be a few among the Chinese staff.'

Today fierce competition for plum expatriate jobs has roundly repudiated this officer's disdain of university degrees. Indeed a first or at least a good upper second is a prerequisite, and the few annual vacancies for the Bank's international manager programme are keenly sought by the most high-flying graduates. These vacancies appear all the more desirable after a rebranding exercise. Implying a sphere of operations confined to the East, the Hongkong and Shanghai Bank's name was seen as limiting, especially after its acquisition of countless European and American businesses, and so, breaking free from its parochial moorings, the Bank has emerged as 'HSBC', an acronym which sounds very much like the global group it is and might, in the minds of those with no historical curiosity, stand for anything.

To appreciate just how rigorous HSBC's selection process has become, we need only to turn to the story of Martin Browning, one of the international manager intake of 1999. Like David Turner, he comes from an expatriate family, a fact that set the seal on his own decision to work abroad: 'I was schooled in the UK and then attended university there, but really my home was overseas, be that Vanuatu, where I was born, Hong Kong, where my parents lived for eighteen years, or Colombia, my mother's homeland.' The prospect of commuting on the London Underground, day in day out, held no attraction at all. In his final year at the London School of Economics, while chilling statistics on the scarcity of jobs were bandied about by his fellow undergraduates, he cast his net among the hongs:

> As I had lived in Hong Kong, I of course knew of the famous trading houses, Jardines and Swires. These were known openly to graduates as having increasingly limited intakes for their international programme (the year I applied they were looking to recruit three people between them). Matters were not helped by the Asian economic crisis of 1997, which had severely dampened their enthusiasm for recruiting expensive expatriate staff. Anyway I applied, interviewed, and (in retrospect fortunately) failed to convince the recruitment officers that I was made of the right stuff for them.

Meanwhile he was looking into HSBC, a corporation with 5,000 offices in over eighty different countries, 'which had a cadre of some 400 generalist bankers and managers who were demanded to be fully internationally mobile. The first years were to be spent on a training programme, rotating every eighteen months or so between different functions and geographical locations.'

The arduous process of selection started with sweating over many drafts of the application form. In the next round, he had to submit himself to numerical and verbal tests at HSBC's headquarters in Lower Thames Street, London:

> A group of about twelve candidates entered the room for the tests, sat them, and were then told to wait in the reception area together until their names were called out. One by one the hopeful undergraduates were called in, and one by one they

would appear again, trying not to look upset . . . A few weeks
later came the dreaded 'in-tray exercise', an exercise that has
much to do with the pressures of day-to-day banking operations.
A short interview with the Human Resources department was
tackled, and again I crossed my fingers and played the waiting
game. The final round of the recruitment merry-go-round was
conducted at the Group's training centre in Brickett Wood, just
north of London. Six eager candidates arrived, and the fun
began—firstly with a couple of warm-up tests, both general
knowledge (of the Bank and the world outside it) and
psychometric tests. Following this, we commenced a series of
group exercises, whereby each candidate was expected to lead
the others in order to accomplish a set task, which was generally
impossible to accomplish in the given time.

In the evening we attended a formal dinner with extremely
senior members of the HSBC management. It was at this stage
that I became truly aware of the importance that the Group
placed on the recruitment. Around the table were men of
exceptional experience and seniority rising up to the Chairman
himself, Sir John Bond. Needless to say we were all on our best
behaviour! At the end of a long day we retreated into the bar to
see whether our social skills were as adept as perhaps our
numerical expertise.

The next day started bright and early, with a group
discussion around a table, problem solving. Following this were
the final formal interviews. We were left to sweat out the next
few weeks waiting to hear the outcome of the selection.

Offered one of the coveted vacancies, Martin Browning acquired
his first taste of retail banking in a local HSBC branch in the UK.
But his baptism of fire was to be at the training centre, where a
gruelling nine-week executive trainee development programme
awaited him and his twenty colleagues, whose provenance, he
remarked, reflected HSBC's global reach, for they came not only
from the UK and Hong Kong, but also Saudi Arabia, the Bahamas,
Argentina, Brazil, USA, France, and Japan. The course itself

covered personal banking, trade finance, accounting and finance,
lending and credit decisions, foreign exchange, as well as

managerial development. Towards the end of the nine weeks, it was time for us to find out where we would be spending the next twelve to eighteen months of our life. Having joined up to a prestigious cadre, and imagining exotic locations, the reality check hit us—for every Hong Kong and New York, there is a Baku and Tehran.

As a Spanish speaker, Browning had hoped for a job in South America, but to his own and his friends' amazement, the first posting was to Ras Al Khaimah:

> After I had successfully picked my chin off the table, and everyone had stopped laughing enough for me to gather my thoughts, I quietly gave my sister a ring. She had access to the Internet, a wonder of modern technology that assured us things were not as bad as initial damage reports had suggested. Ras Al Khaimah is one of the lesser Emirates. I had never been to the Middle East before, and had been given this golden opportunity.
>
> On 2 January 2000 I arrived in Dubai ready for a new career abroad. The first few weeks were among the most exhausting I have experienced—the stress of leaving friends and family behind and being on a continent where I didn't know a soul, let alone speak the language, was only part of it. I was here to run a department, manage people, and ensure increasing profitability. The challenge was only just beginning.

Some fifteen months later Martin Browning was told that he would be posted either to New York or to Hong Kong. If the choice falls upon the latter, he will become a second-generation expatriate in the territory, and the circle will have been traced.

6
Cops and Robbers

Colonial Cemetery grave inscription:
> Sacred to the memory of George McDonald, a native of Lewis,
> Stornaway, Ross-shire, Scotland, who was a member of the
> Hongkong Police Force and died at Hongkong on the 15th
> December 1886, aged 34 years

Hongkong Daily Press:
> George McDonald, died 15 December 1886
> Another useful member of the force, Police Sergeant George
> McDonald who had been in the force nearly 8 years, died on
> Tuesday. The deceased had long been suffering from chronic
> dysentery.

Colonial Cemetery grave inscription:
> Sacred to the memory of Harry Arthur Mills, acting Lance
> Sergeant of the Hongkong Police Force, a native of Battersea,
> London, England, who was shot while performing his duty at
> Yaumati on 24th February 1909, aged 30 years.

These and numerous other memorial inscriptions in the Colonial
Cemetery at Happy Valley are poignant reminders of the forgotten
lives of Britons who served in the Hong Kong Police Force after its
founding in 1844. It was a ragtag force in the early days, no more
than a band of officers, NCOs, and constables (some of them Indian)
drawn from the soldiery, navy, and merchant marine. In 1845 three
officers were recruited from the London Metropolitan Police to
organize a proper force, but only one of them proved to have staying
power. He, Charles May, became the first captain superintendent
and later police magistrate.

Charles May presided over a pretty disreputable constabulary.
Its members were a corrupt, drunken, and lazy lot, ready enough to
protect the European merchants and their houses but none too
concerned about the Chinese population. Anyone worth his salt

'had only accepted the position in the hope of something better turning up'. As for the rest, they were remarkable mainly for 'the readiness with which they yielded to the temptation offered by the many public houses about, and many of the deaths among the European constabulary were ascribed to their excessive indulgence in ardent spirits, a great portion of which, sold by the low tavern-keepers, was of the most abominable and deleterious description.'

It was a typically colonial force, comprising in addition to 'Caucasians of every stripe (although the majority remained British)' a good many Indians and Malays. Initially it had no Chinese constables, although by 1867 overall strength had reached some 590 men, including ninety Europeans, 370 Indians, and 130 Chinese.

That it wasn't the most exemplary law-enforcing bunch around may be readily gathered by the vituperations of Sir Richard MacDonnell (Governor, 1866–72). Not mincing his words, he said he could not remember seeing a body of men so ineffective in proportion to number, or so corrupt generally. His solution for rectifying matters was to recruit Scots instead of Englishmen, and to give preference to Punjabi Sikhs over Bombay Indians.

Inspector James Dodds was one of the Scotch contingent. We know that he was born on 19 October 1842, a native of Roxburghshire, that he joined the Colonial Police Force aged twenty-nine and arrived in Hong Kong on 11 February 1872. He advanced rapidly through the ranks, being promoted to inspector third class in May 1874 and inspector second class, at a salary of £200 per annum, in August 1875. But his luck ran out just as swiftly. Struck down by consumption, he died on 20 November 1876 and was buried in Grave no. 4268 at the Colonial Cemetery the very next day. And so, by removing himself from the scene, he at least remained blameless, for it transpired that the forty-five men from the Edinburgh City Police Force recruited with such high hopes by Sir Richard MacDonnell had feet of clay. In the frontier-town ambience, beguiled by the easy morals of the place, some of them had fallen upon seamen's drinking houses and Chinese gambling dens as places to run rackets and as sources of protection money with as much alacrity as the local toughs.

It took an Irishmen to sort things out. After Harrow and Trinity College Dublin, Francis Henry May had arrived as a cadet in 1881. Becoming captain superintendent of police (1893–1902) suited him perfectly. Efficient and authoritarian, he was to spend thirty-eight years in Hong Kong, his career spanning the whole spectrum from cadet to Governor. Sir Frederick Lugard, under whom May was Colonial Secretary, thought him a 'somewhat stolid, slow-thinking sort of fellow'. On the other hand Lugard thought him a man of sound character: 'quite good—devoid of vaseline—gives you rather the idea that you must play up to him than he to you. Plenty of sense.' May's abundance of sense (and deficiency in anything oleaginous) was much to the fore when he embarked on moulding a more disciplined and proficient force.

May undoubtedly worked hard, and there could have been little respite from policing for the captain superintendent in those days, even in off-duty hours, because his house was next to the gaol. One of his daughters recalled that apart from a spell on the Peak during the hot weather, the family lived most of the year at the Central Police Station, where 'we could see the Chinese prisoners exercising in the yard. At night we sometimes heard a woman prisoner wailing and were told that she was in a strait-jacket. Occasionally Daddy took us with him when he inspected the cells. I can remember how the prisoners stood with their hands up to show that they had nothing in them.'

As for Sir Richard MacDonnell's Sikhs, like others from the subcontinent they proved most effective in rural areas, and when the New Territories were leased in 1898, the Indian contingent was regularly stationed there. This worked well as long as Sikhs, Muslims, and Hindus were kept firmly apart.

Also boosting the ranks were Chinese infantrymen under British command from Weihaiwei, the British concession and naval base in Shandong province. Taller and more sturdily built than the average Cantonese, Shandong men continued to be recruited into the Hong Kong police right up to the fall of China to the communists in 1949.

Piracy along the coast and up the Canton delta was a particularly thorny problem in the 1920s and '30s. Highly adept and well informed on the movements of coastal shipping, marauding gangs plotted their raids with great precision, boarding vessels at the port of shipment, overcoming the crew, and finally escaping on the junks that met them with their plundered cargo or bullion. White Russians from Shanghai were deployed in a special unit to combat piracy and they, as well as Punjabis and Shandong men, regularly undertook guard duty on coastal vessels.

At the end of the Second World War, the force was so debilitated that it had to be virtually rebuilt. In time, with improved conditions of service, a new generation of officers were recruited into it. Better qualified than most who joined before the War, expatriate police officers no longer went into the subordinate ranks. Later, as Britain renounced its Mandate in Palestine, as one by one the African and Pacific colonies gained independence and the world for British and Commonwealth policemen shrivelled, it was inevitable that a number of them should drift *en masse* to Hong Kong, there to earn a little more towards their pensions—at least until 1997.

⤛>o❖o<⤜

When George Wright-Nooth (Colonial Police Service, later Royal Hong Kong Police Force or RHKPF, 1940–71) arrived in Hong Kong just before the outbreak of the Second World War, he had to make all the usual adjustments to life in an organization still entrenched in the traditions of an earlier age. One of the first things he learnt was the custom of leaving his calling card:

> I went along to see the Commissioner of Police, who had a white uniform in those days. . . . He asked me whether I liked to play cricket, which was his favourite game. As soon as I said 'No' I realized that I'd gone down in his esteem. I preferred to play rugger. It was the last time I really ever saw him.
>
> I was then sent next door to see his staff officer and all he was interested in was that I called on the right people. He gave me a list of all the important government officials and other people I had to call on and he explained to me that if there were two in the family I left two cards, if there was one I left one card, all of which I'd already known.
>
> I was given transport and told to go round calling straight away. The first place I must go round to was Government House, where I had to leave my card and sign the book. And that was really my first day.

His social obligations discharged, Wright-Nooth found he had no immediate police duties, for his first year was to be entirely devoted to the study of Chinese. But he was destined never to finish his two-year language course. Before it ended he was recalled to police duties, and instead of going on the beat he got embroiled in a war.

As he was sitting down to breakfast on the morning of 8 December 1941, his houseboy came rushing in from the verandah and announced in shrill tones, 'Master! Master! Japanese planes!' It was his first inkling of the Japanese invasion of Hong Kong. Afterwards, during the first chaotic days of the battle for Hong Kong, everybody's one fixation was, as he put it, 'securing the next meal'. On one occasion the shelling of a warehouse filled with rice set off a frenzy of looting. George Wright-Nooth found the only way he could stop it was to order his Indian police to plough into the crowd with fixed bayonets: 'We had to carry out our normal policing in order to stop looting. Looting was very, very heavy by the Chinese. They were ransacking empty houses. When a Chinese looted a house, not only did he take everything moveable out, but

he also took the window frames, every piece of woodwork, to burn
as fuel.'

He has a vivid recollection also of being ejected from police
headquarters, then temporarily located at the Gloucester Hotel, by
two Japanese officers:

> The Japanese officers' swords were dangling on the ground—
> they were tiny little fellows with great big swords, and they
> shouted 'Out! Out!'
>
> We all lined up in Des Voeux Road, carrying everything
> we could, and we were marched off down the road and locked
> up in a Chinese boarding-house. It was one of those flea-joints,
> a semi-brothel. We slept on the floors, six or seven to a room,
> and there were cockroaches dropping on us at night. After about
> two weeks we were told to form up and were then taken by ferry
> round to Stanley.

The beautiful Stanley peninsula had been one of the last lines
of defence. Now, all that could be seen behind the barbed wire and
sandbags was a scene of devastation, strewn with the ghastly scars
of recent fighting—dead bodies, blood, smashed windows, and
grenade marks. For the internees the first task was to clear up the
debris. What preoccupied them afterwards was food—or rather the
lack of it—as George Wright-Nooth records:

> Our basic ration was four ounces of rice for breakfast in the
> morning. The next meal was at about seven o'clock in the
> evening, and it was another four ounces of rice, with a teaspoonful
> of beans. . . . So a black market immediately started in the
> camp. You'd sell your watch for so many pounds of rice or bully
> beef. It even got to the stage where if you opened your mouth
> and one of the black market chaps saw you had a gold filling,
> they'd suggest you pulled your tooth out and sold the filling.

But he was not too hungry or enervated to involve himself in
some subversive activities with a former MI6 man called Alex
Summers and a colleague in the security service, George Merrimen.
Summers had a radio receiver which he kept hidden in the wall of
his room. Their three-man band was augmented by a Chinese

electrician who worked in the prison where internees arrested for
trying to escape were incarcerated. One of their schemes was to
disseminate news of the progress of the War to fellow Europeans in
the camp; the other was to smuggle extra rations to the prison
where the inmates would otherwise suffer severe malnutrition.
Wright-Nooth explains:

> Alex and George . . . listened to the overseas news at night. My
> job was to collect the radio reports and go and tell the European
> commandant of the camp what the news was so that he could
> pass it on to the other internees. I would also meet the Chinese
> electrician in strange places and hand parcels of food to him.
> He smuggled them into the prision. Through him I was able to
> feed the prisoners for the next three years.

Nobody had any illusions that this was dangerous, that they
were taking a risk by trusting the Chinese electrician, who might
have been for all they knew a collaborator or a Japanese plant.
Trustworthiness is a quality much discussed in police circles,
especially as different races and nationalities are a factor. In the
several periods of disorder that flared up in post-War Hong Kong,
feelings against foreigners sometimes ran very high. If any of the
Chinese members of the police force ever felt a conflict of interest,
though, he never allowed it to impinge on his performance. George
Wright-Nooth claims that during both the riots of 1956 and the
communist-inspired disturbances of 1967, local policemen's
allegiance to what was essentially a British-led force was unswerving.
'Throughout the time I served with the Hong Kong Police,' he
says, 'I got intense loyalty.'

—⟨⟩⟨⟩◆⟨⟩⟨⟩—

Like many expatriates who signed on with the Hong Kong Police
Force, John Macdonald came in 1959 intending to serve one contract
only, but he got married, had children, and ended up staying for
thirty years. As a uniformed branch officer, he was initially involved
in anti-narcotics work at the street and district level. A turn of

events then inducted him into the problem of illegal immigrants, for in 1962 he was posted to the Police Training Contingent (precursor of the Police Tactical Unit) at Fan Ling near the border with China. There was a rush of refugees to Hong Kong that year. Following the Great Leap Forward, a mass movement launched by Mao Zedong in 1958, China's grain output fell disastrously short of requirements and all over the countryside people began literally

to die of hunger. Fleeing famine, between 150,000 and 200,000 refugees attempted to cross into Hong Kong in 1962. John Macdonald was among the extremely stretched police force at the border when the influx was at its peak:

> My platoon was working with the Army on the frontier from Sha Tau Kok to Ta Kwu Ling. Volunteers Slope, an ex-army barracks and our camp at Fan Ling, was being used as a detention centre because all the border stations were overflowing with captured illegal immigrants. We ended one particular night with 5,000 camped out on the parade ground.
> Robins Nest is a mountain behind Sha Tau Kok. One day my orderly and I were driving to Sha Tau Kok, and as we went along the road we saw a huge mass of people on top of Robins Nest. Then all of a sudden they disappeared. I thought that was very strange and set off up the mountain to investigate.
> It was quite astonishing. Down a ravine cut into a side of the mountain by water flow from the top, we found various staging posts, in other words places for people to change into clean clothes brought by their relatives in Hong Kong, places

for them to sleep, places to eat. It was a natural amphitheatre of flattened brushwood, but hidden from any form of aerial reconnaissance. And the evidence was there that a massive movement of people had taken place down this ravine.

The government policy was to arrest illegal immigrants and send them back to China, which seemed to be a bit hardhearted. Those who evaded capture didn't surface until much later when there was more or less an amnesty and they were issued with identity cards.

Of course at that time the closed area of the frontier hadn't been extended, so the local population was able to drive up to the Sha Tau Kok Road, pick people up, and take them into town. It was understandable—lots of the refugees were their parents, brothers, wives, or children whom they hadn't seen for years. So it was a period of intense illegal immigration activity and also of astonishing compassion, because the chaps working with me realized the situation and were very sympathetic to the plight of the refugees.

Little, if anything, was done to stop the flow on the Chinese side of the border. The guards were even said to have encouraged it, looking the other way when people tried to leave and letting the repatriated ones make their own way back to their villages and communes, 'so it was far more attractive for them to try and get into Hong Kong again,' says Macdonald, 'In fact we did meet a considerable number of them repeatedly.'

But the crisis assumed such huge proportions that it finally compelled the Hong Kong and British authorities to act, first by officially soliciting the Chinese government's help in establishing tighter controls, and secondly by constructing a new border fence. Eventually the problem sorted itself out—rather drastically, as Macdonald recalls: 'On our last patrol from Sha Tau Kok to Ta Kwu Ling, we could hear shooting across the border. It wasn't directed at us; the Chinese authorities were clearly using firepower to deter people from crossing the fence. There was never again an exodus of that scale, although they kept coming throughout my service in Hong Kong, by land and by sea.'

⊰◆⊱

For the seventeen British recruits who landed in Hong Kong on 1 October 1966, the riots and random bombings which erupted in the spring and summer of 1967 were to be their baptism of fire. One of them, former Chief Superintendent Chris Glover (RHKPF, 1966–2000), remembers the edgy atmosphere then building up as the Cultural Revolution began convulsing China, and the spate of violence in Hong Kong:

> I'd passed out of PTS [Police Training School] in the middle of 1967 and was posted to Wong Tai Sin, which was where a lot of the disturbances were happening. I spent that time on the beat and also working with the military in the bomb squad.
>
> I think it was a Sunday afternoon when the first bomb went off. On the side of the road around the housing estates agitators had painted anti-foreign slogans like 'Fry the Yellow Running Dog' and 'Stew the White-skinned Pig'. We went up there with some labourers to paint out the slogans and found those agitators lobbing bombs off the old 'H' blocks [resettlement housing] at us. So we spent half an hour under our Landrover!

At such unruly times, it was the Police Tactical Unit (PTU) which bore the brunt. PTU men, normally distinguishable by their blue berets, are adept at riot and crowd control. Ritchie Bent (RHKP, 1977–88) has a clear memory not only of going into action in a stop-and-search swoop on a multi-storey building controlled by Triads, but also of the movements involved in dispersing a riot:

> A platoon of forty-one men would be formed in four lines. In the first line you had shields, batons, Mace (which is a chemical spray that causes people to cough and splutter). We called the second line 'smoke', and here you were equipped with pistols which would fire canisters of CS gas over a distance of a hundred, two hundred metres. The idea was to keep the crowd away from you in a riot situation. Those in the third line had baton shells. These were great wooden bullets; you fire them at the ground and they would bounce and spin and break the legs of the rioters. The fourth line of defence was Remington pump-action shotguns and AR15s.
>
> Depending on the situation you had to assess which level of force to use. It's always a warning first, and the minimum level of

force. If the crowds advanced you could scatter them with smoke. If they still kept coming and they were violent or had Molotov cocktails, you could use baton shells. And the last line of defence was the shotguns. Despite rumours that the Unit was vicious it was actually a very disciplined, carefully organized group.

The discipline and restraint the PTU exhibited at the height of the 1967 disturbances were afterwards much commended, for they had remained stoically composed throughout, though repeatedly taunted, assaulted, and spat on by rioters. Communist sympathizers found other ingenious ways to set upon policemen, as Chris Glover discovered when he went to Sai Kung, a sparsely populated but very left-wing area in the New Territories:

> I used to go once a week to relieve the one inspector in Sai Kung. He couldn't leave unless another officer went up and stayed there for twenty-four hours. We did a lot of raids there with Special Branch. There was a school where children were making bombs. When you went into the villages some of the old ladies would throw nightsoil over you. Yet in the houses you'd find commendations from King George VI for the assistance they gave to prisoners of war escaping to China during the Japanese occupation. There's a certain irony in that.

For some observers there was a certain irony, too, in the juxtaposition of events that followed in the next few years. In 1969 Queen Elizabeth II honoured the force for handling those riots so bravely and well by bestowing on it the title 'Royal'; in 1973 one of the heroes of the riots, Chief Superintendent Peter Fitzroy Godber, came under suspicion of corruption.

Power corrupts, and the power to turn a blind eye to illegal gambling, prostitution, and drug-peddling has often tempted policemen. There was a saying, according to Glover, which likened corruption to a bus: 'You could get on the bus, watch the bus go by, or jump in front of it. Most of us watched the bus go by, to be honest.' The existence of corruption in the Hong Kong police was more or less an open secret.

What did shock people rather was how rampant and organized it was. Sergeants and station sergeants, running what were virtually corruption syndicates, were thought to be the main culprits, but graft extended across ranks too, with subordinates paying senior officers for assignments to the 'richer' beats, the beats where opportunities for collecting bribes were plentiful. Equally shocking was the fact that Peter Godber was an expatriate, and in the popular mind of the time expatriates were assumed to be above such improbity.

When he served in the PTU in the early 1970s, Chris Glover coincided with Godber:

> Peter Godber was considered a good officer, but he was a bully as well. A typical question you'd get in an interview with him was: 'So you work in Wong Tai Sin. How many opium divans are there?'
>
> Well, you could answer this in two ways. You could say, 'I don't know', and he'd counter with, 'Why not? You should. It's your job.'
>
> Or you could say, 'There are six,' to which he'd retort, 'How come there are any? Why aren't you doing anything about them?' So whichever way you answered you were in trouble.
>
> In his office he always had a carpet on a slippery polished floor so that when you came to attention you might trip and fall over.

In early 1973 Godber was asked by anti-corruption officers how he had managed on his salary to acquire assets eventually valued at more than four million Hong Kong dollars. As Glover observed: 'Godber had lots of money, and he couldn't have got it all directly from drug dealers or gamblers or prostitutes. . . . He was the boss, the chief superintendent, and he was being paid by the Divisions. If they didn't pay, he could cause them a lot of trouble. So if you wanted a nice lucrative job you paid for it and you continued to pay.'

While his financial affairs were still being investigated, the suspect slipped out of the territory. His disappearance brought the issue of police corruption into sharp relief. Here was the glaring personification of venality and officiousness—for many members of the public it was the only face of the constabulary that they knew. If the police force were to redeem itself, people began saying, Peter Godber must be punished for his crime and divested of his ill-gotten gains.

But bringing Peter Godber to justice was easier said than done. He had escaped to England, and there it transpired he was inviolable. For though it was enough for the anti-corruption investigators in Hong Kong to show that he had been living beyond his means, no equivalent charge existed in English law to enable them to arrest and extradite him.

In the end, it was another corrupt police officer who provided evidence acceptable to an English court. Ernest 'Taffy' Hunt, then serving a sentence for corruption in Stanley Prison, was at one time divisional superintendent of Wan Chai, an area filled with bars, restaurants, and nightclubs and a favourite posting for policemen on the take. Hunt now came forward to swear that he witnessed Godber accepting a bribe. A sum of $25,000 was given, Hunt said, by a young Chinese officer to secure an appointment in Wan Chai. In exchange for his evidence Hunt and his wife were granted a total amnesty against any future prosecution.

Godber was duly extradited, convicted, and sentenced. (Released from jail in September 1977, he is currently believed to be living in Spain.) Meanwhile, the Independent Commission Against

Corruption (ICAC), set up by Sir Murray Maclehose at the height of the furore, continued to probe away at other cases of graft, going further and further back in time to encompass retired officers in their investigative net and making a great number of arrests. Peter Mann (RHKPF, 1976–79) remembers arriving at his station for an early shift one morning in 1977 and being met by an ashen-faced sergeant: 'He said to me, "Sir, we had big problem this morning." At dawn, my station sergeant, two other sergeants and something like sixteen constables had all been arrested by the ICAC. We just didn't know what to do.'

What the police as a body did was to stage a protest against the ICAC's continuing witch-hunt, tactics, and alleged harassment of suspects and their families. On the same day that Peter Mann found his unit decimated, thousands of policemen converged on police headquarters to present their grievances to the Commissioner. Some of the more aggressive members then peeled off to march on the ICAC's offices in Hutchison House and had what Mann describes as a 'punch-up' there: 'The beef among the police was that there was corruption in the rest of the government too, so how come the ICAC was just going for the police and not any other department?'

Senior Assistant Commissioner (retiring later as Deputy Commissioner) Peter Moor (RHKPF, 1949–84, pictured below) was in charge of Kowloon Command at the time and remembers meeting 300 inspectorate-grade officers with Roy Henry, the Deputy Commissioner:

He and I stood on the stage in front of these officers and took what was coming. It was a very emotional gathering. They were expressing how they felt, and they wanted people like us to listen. Their grievances were mainly against the anti-corruption branch. They felt they were getting a raw deal, and that the ICAC was concentrating on the police rather than other government departments. To them police headquarters was remote, and they wanted a greater rapport between senior and junior ranks.

It was potentially a very dangerous time, the tension defused only when the Governor declared an amnesty on offences committed before the beginning of that year. Looking back, Peter Moor believes that the whole exercise had been both a crisis and a turning point for the force: 'It was one of those things that had to be brought to a head, and we had to come out of it, pull ourselves together, and move forward. I think there was a much better atmosphere between the senior and junior ranks afterwards. . . . Part of our problem was that our recruitment and our pay left a lot to be desired.'

⎯⎯⎯⎯◦◦◈◦◦⎯⎯⎯⎯

A belief that the force needed to recruit a higher calibre of officers might have been behind the decision to seek out graduates. No doubt Peter Mann's degree helped his cause, although he only applied to the RHKPF as a compromise: 'When I came down from Oxford I didn't know what I wanted to do. I'd been to an interview for a short service commission in the Army, and I considered the Foreign Legion, so in the end the Hong Kong police seemed less extreme and more fun. I loved travelling and I wanted to get away from England.' He arrived in 1976 on one of those 'old-fashioned flights' that stopped in Rome, Bombay, Bangkok, and then Hong Kong:

We all got off the plane and were rounded up by a chief inspector for the Police Training School at Aberdeen. . . . The first thing I noticed as we drove in was a whole lot of men in shorts lying on their fronts, face down, on the concrete as though they were undergoing some punishment. We were shown our dormitories and left to unpack. While we were laughing and fooling around someone pulled out a *Penthouse* magazine that he'd bought at the airport.

Suddenly we heard footsteps up the stairs and the door burst open to reveal all these uniformed people (we thought they were our instructors) staring at us.

'What's going on in here? You think this is a bloody picnic?'

Of course they found the *Penthouse*. 'Whose is this? You're not on holiday! You guys have a bit of education to go through. Right, follow me!'

So straight after a twenty-eight hour flight we were marched out, lined up, and drilled for an hour. We were then put through an assault course—it was a full assault course where you had to wriggle through tyres and climb over barbed-wire fences. Then back for more drill. And all that time, we had a gweilo shouting at us like a sergeant major.

I remember him saying, 'See those blocks of flats up there? That's Wong Chuk Hang Estate. There are 30,000 Chinese living there, and they all hate your guts!'

This went on for about three or four hours till eight o'clock. And when you're jet-lagged you hadn't the faintest idea what was going on.

Eventually they marched us to the mess. At the order 'About turn!' all the lights in the mess came on and we saw everyone in there rolling about with laughter because the whole thing had been a set-up. Our drill masters weren't instructors, they were the senior squad of the PTS. The people lying at the gate were just to set the scene, to show us that we weren't coming to a holiday camp and life was going to be pretty tough. It was an elaborate hoax and we were entirely taken in—hook, line, and sinker. It was the best practical joke ever played on me.

Then they proceeded to pour five pints of beer down each of us, got us completely pissed, and took us down to Wan Chai.

A near contemporary, Ritchie Bent, had a similar initiation. He remembers the PTS senior squad dressed up as officers, the humiliating drills, a chaplain who asked embarrassing questions like 'Have you had any intimate contact with men?', and finally the mess scene where all was revealed to be a jape. From the PTS, the majority of new recruits 'get shipped out to the units, where you'd be looking after hawker control, drugs, traffic accidents, murders, suicides, and so on. Then you might spend a period in a vice squad, where you'd be working under cover.'

Working under cover poses something of a difficulty for expatriate policemen, but there are ways of 'compensating for being white and evident', says Ritchie Bent:

> We used to dress up as Mormons, in a white shirt with a badge on, and then we could walk around areas where expatriates aren't usually seen. There's always the risk that you might be recognized, but as we're normally in uniform and cap, we might have all looked the same to the man in the street anyway. The other thing we did was to patrol on private motorcycles. With a helmet on, you can move around without drawing attention to yourself.

While Hong Kong's citizens are generally law-abiding, there are some areas where they persist in breaking the rules. One of these is unlicensed hawking. Peter Mann had a memorable confrontation:

> The Jordan Road Ferry area was a particular problem. Hawkers used to sell seafood there. They would come up in boats and once a week we had to do an operation. But the hawkers had lookouts. As soon as you left the station everyone would know, and they'd quickly gather up all their goods, throw them into their boats, let the boats ten metres or so out into the harbour, and thumb their noses at you when you arrived!
>
> After this happened to me I thought, 'Aha! Marine Police!' And the next time they did this there was a marine police launch coming in so it was a good pincer operation.
>
> I remember struggling on the pier with this incredibly fat lady who was a hawker. For some reason a fish got dropped on my foot, and we found ourselves entangled with this fish, and in the struggle she slipped on it and fell into the harbour. The next day one newspaper reported the incident under the headline 'Inspector Pushes Hawker into Harbour'.

It turned out that not all these fisherfolk could swim, so it was 'shock, horror, panic' because this fat lady certainly couldn't and one of the constables had to dive in to save her. Meanwhile the crowd turned very ugly and started hurling insults like 'police brutality' and so on. I thought it was getting a bit out of control and started back for the station. There I went to my Sub-divisional Inspector and told him the whole story.

Meanwhile the mob had gathered torches and were marching on the police station, baying for my blood. Luckily my boss backed me, assured the mob that an investigation would be made, and eventually it dispersed.

Hawker control probably isn't the most thrilling job in the police force, but Peter Mann did see a seamier side of life, participating once or twice in exciting raids. On one occasion, while posted to a district vice squad, he chased a heroin dealer down ten flights of stairs in an estate in Kowloon and captured him. He also busted an illegal gambling den:

We were in plain clothes at that point, and I carried a .38 special in an ankle holster at all times. I never had to shoot anyone, but I did draw my gun once, on a raid of a gambling den.

Earlier, we had received information from Criminal Intelligence to target this particular flat. I had two men round the back, and two of us, me and my sergeant, were at the front. We kicked in the door. Inside were at least a hundred people including three or four big muscular, tattooed Triad bouncers. There we were, in plain clothes. And there were these guys. It was a double take—we looked at them and they looked at us. Two of the guys ran towards us and I had to point my gun and say, 'Mo yuk [Don't move]!'

They weren't really scared of the gun but for them it clearly wasn't worth the hassle to resist. Meanwhile our guys came from the back. We were hugely outnumbered so we had to call for backup.

We seized several hundred thousand dollars in cash that day. Back in the late 1970s that was quite a lot of money.

Ritchie Bent found plenty of excitement in his final stint in the police force, when he was part of the organized and serious crime group involved in criminal intelligence and surveillance, closely investigating the activities of gangsters from China as well as senior-level members of Triad societies. 'What happened was this: a gang in Hong Kong would pick a target, maybe a goldsmith shop or a bank, and then import guys from mainland China who would come in with their weapons, do the robbery, and slip back into China. That way the perpetrators of the crime would never be found. Our job was to ambush and neutralize those Chinese gun gangs.'

He and his team once stumbled upon a planned robbery in a most unexpected and gruesome way. It started with the discovery of a headless body of a man on a Fei Ngo Shan hillside. As the corpse had also lost its fingers, identification was difficult, but the police on the scene did pick up a key. And by the time detectives had done their work, the key was found to fit one of six Hiace vans in the territory. More surveillance and probing then narrowed the field to one—a van that did a suspicious run to the airport on a regular basis. It soon became obvious to the surveillance team that the van driver and his passengers were handling stolen goods.

To enter certain areas of the airport, the van driver and his mates were routinely asked to show their identity cards. Thus, by a series of measured steps, Bent and his colleagues succeeded in developing an exact portrait of a criminal gang:

We knew who they were from the identity cards, and we started watching them over three, four months—a very long time. We believed one of them was an organizer of crime, another had a record of handling stolen goods, the third had a record for stealing vehicles, and there were two more we couldn't identify, but from their complexion, haircut, and gait, they looked like Mainlanders.

One day we saw this group drive up, park in Observatory Road, and take a rather strange route through Tsim Sha Tsui. We also picked up bits of their conversation. They kept mentioning 'two together', which probably meant two goldsmith shops together. And in the circuit they'd done, there were only two places with two goldsmiths shops together.

All the pieces of the puzzle now resolved themselves into a date on which, the police knew, the robbery would happen. Very early that morning, teams of plain-clothes detectives drove to Tsim Sha Tsui and staked out the area. An inner and outer cordon of policemen, as well as a lookout, took up their positions and waited. Soon word came that the robbery gang had arrived at a teahouse in Tai Kok Tsui for breakfast. For Bent and his men, 'the decision had to be made whether we should take the gang out before, during, or after the robbery'. To minimize danger to the public, they felt that the only option was to do so before the robbery. They knew they already had enough evidence to convict the robbers, one of whom, after all, had been responsible for the body on Fei Ngo Shan. Although unconnected with the planned robbery, that discovery had been the beginning of the tortuous trail that led them to the gang.

The minutes ticked by, and before long a Mercedes Benz tailed from Tai Kok Tsui could be seen coming southwards down Carnarvon Road. At zero hour a white van driven by a plain-clothes detective swung out from Mody Road and 'accidentally' hit the Mercedes in passing. Traffic incidents might be an everyday occurrence in the crowded streets of Tsim Sha Tsui, but as the van driver jumped out uttering profuse apologies while the inner cordon closed in, the robbers were left in no doubt that they were caught in something more serious than a vehicle collision. As one of them reached for his weapon, he was shot through the window by a policeman: 'Bang—he's history. We arrested four of them that day, and got the fifth one later. So that was a good case.'

——◦◇◦——

Given Hong Kong's geography, it comes as no surprise to learn that its marine police is one of the largest waterborne law-enforcement agencies in the world. Pirates were the mariners' bane in the early days; later, waves of illegal immigrants from China and Vietnam kept them fully stretched. When John Macdonald moved to the marine police in the early 1980s, economic reform and the Open Door policy were just unleashing a surge of consumerism in China, and 'smuggling in Mirs Bay and around the Sai Kung peninsula became ridiculous.' Vessels with powerful outboards could 'do eighty knots while empty, but with a load of video cassette recorders and two or three Mercedes or BMWs, they still made sixty knots. That was a bit beyond the capability of our fleet.'

Since 'nothing goes to sea unless it has been loaded on land', John Macdonald once tried to intercept some stolen cars while they were being moved from shore to sea.

Information had come through the New Territories anti-crime people that three stolen cars were due to be sent into China from a pier just below Castle Peak Power Station. Macdonald was all too aware that with a stolen car, unless it could be proved that there was an intention of removing it permanently from the owner, the case would simply be classified as 'taking and driving away' and incur only a small fine. Loading it on a boat or ship, on the other hand, was unequivocal confirmation of theft.

When the anti-crime police asked him if he would provide a crane barge with a tame crew so that the stolen cars could be loaded, Macdonald agreed,

> and I got on to my harbour contacts and got a crane barge and a private crew willing to do the job. I put three of my men on board, armed, and they all duly went to the appointed place. Around the whole caboodle I placed a ring of launches as backup,

and the New Territories police were also in position on the land side.

Everything should have gone beautifully. We had the New Territories police on land, the marine police at sea, and we were ready to close in while the stolen cars were being loaded. We'd have the evidence—photographs and forensics and everything.

Sure enough the cars arrived and the loading began. The barge was in the middle of loading the second car when there was a noise of engine coming from the north. Then a boat heaves into sight and out of it and on to the barge clamber six chaps in olive green uniforms and caps with five-pointed stars on them, and all carrying a Chinese version of Kalashnikovs, Chinese A6 rifles. Oops!

Whether the smugglers were from the People's Liberation Army or People's Armed Police, they were personally making sure that what they'd ordered was safely delivered. They were also perfectly well aware, Macdonald thought, that they were in Hong Kong waters:

The barge meanwhile had cast off. I order Andy Birt, who's on the command launch, to close with the barge. Andy is an ex-Royal Marine lieutenant. He catches up with the barge, closes with it, and finds himself menaced by the guys with the A6 rifles.

He reports to me by radio, and I ask him, 'Well, what do you reckon? Any chance of boarding the barge and taking it over without undue harm?' But Andy tells me that if we tried to, those guys would shoot. I wasn't going to have anybody killed for three stolen cars. So I said, 'Just shadow the barge and see where it goes.'

Marine police launches shadowed the barge across the mouth of Deep Bay to Shekou, where it tied up. The next morning those on the watch could see the cars being unloaded and driven away. By then, Macdonald's three armed policemen had made themselves known to the smugglers and handed in their revolvers and warrant cards. They were taken away by the A6 rifle-carrying officers but returned through Lo Wu the following day. The whole episode was, Macdonald says ruefully, 'an attempted police sting that went wrong.'

By the time John Macdonald retired, the Joint Declaration had long been signed and the future for expatriate policemen was clear. Or was it? Until 1997 Hong Kong had always had a British military presence backing up the police on such responsibilities as security and peace-keeping. After 1997 the British garrison's replacement by People's Liberation Army troops must have caused a deal of heart-searching within the police force. Would the PLA soldiers be subject to civil law? How should political agitators be treated? With tanks and guns? Perhaps no expatriate officer would put it in so many words, but the question of loyalty must have lurked beneath the surface of his concerns. A conflict of interests had never arisen previously—most of the expatriate police officers were British or Commonwealth citizens, and Hong Kong was a British colony. But under the sovereignty of China, the thought of being at the sharp end of any potential confrontation caused distinctly more unease than before.

Few questioned the logic of localization as such, nor the reservation of the very top ranks of the force for ethnic Chinese officers. But the problems of allegiance and indeed the dimmer prospects of career advancement were disquieting nonetheless. The police force had been built up by the nationals of many countries, and disburdening the weight of that history was not something that could be accomplished overnight. The policy on localization in both the police and the government during the transitional period was, moreover, at best murky. After 1992 police recruitment of expatriates stopped and an early retirement scheme was proposed. Her Majesty's government agreed to pay compensation to her subjects serving overseas for the loss of British protection. These measures were swiftly followed by an official 'U-turn', as some would describe it, when the Hong Kong authorities began renewing expatriate contracts and granting local terms to anyone who would accept them. Prompted by fear that an exodus of expatriate civil servants and policemen would leave a ruinous void in the essential services that couldn't be filled by qualified locals for years to come, this change of policy provoked a rumpus, kicked up by local officers who wanted expatriates to vacate senior positions as speedily as possible. A spokesman for the Expatriate

Inspectors Association, voicing members' worries, tried to be conciliatory: 'Generally speaking, the membership is not too unhappy about Hong Kong being run by its indigenous population as long as they are not thrown out on to the scrap heap after twenty or twenty-five years of service.'

The other disciplinary body, the ICAC, had similarly embarked on localization. By the time Stacy Mosher, an American and former journalist, joined as an investigator in 1995, expatriates were becoming thin on the ground. Were it not for the fact that she spoke and read Chinese, she probably would not have been appointed. Ironically, her expatriate colleagues didn't feel entirely at ease with her either. For her part, she considered that it was

> probably the one job in which I allowed myself the illusion of contributing more than I might gain. But it was also the first time that I had forced a situation, and for once my timing was off. Or perhaps the possibility of good timing no longer existed for people such as myself. Ten years earlier things would no doubt have been different, but by 1995 the ICAC and other public bodies were moving towards localization, and if not for my knowledge of Cantonese and written Chinese, my application would not have been entertained at all. As it was, my Chinese was not adequate for me to function at the same level as a local person, but was good enough to place me under suspicion, and it became clear to me early on that some colleagues believed me to be some sort of spy.
>
> The great irony was that no-one of even the most vaguely spooky demeanour had ever approached me. A Malaysian friend once told me that in the eyes of Westerners I had 'gone native' and would never be considered completely trustworthy. It appeared that I had reached a peculiar middle ground where I was neither one thing nor the other.

Occupying the middle ground is not necessarily uncomfortable, but some expatriates still argued that the change of sovereignty robbed them of choice in the matter. Others accepted the situation, took their golden handshakes, and left in 1997, although a number of them, according to Chief Inspector Mark Ford McNicol, regretted it afterwards. Life in the constabulary back home after an active career in Hong Kong can be dull, and it is certainly not as well paid. McNicol is one expatriate officer who opted to change to pensionable terms and stay, but he knows he is in a shrinking minority. Currently chairman of the Overseas Inspectors Association (it changed its name from Expatriate Inspectors Association in 1996), he says, 'Totally in the force there are just under 500 expatriates, but when these officers retire they will be replaced by local candidates, so that number can only dwindle.'

7

Missionaries

'My God, it's an island!' exclaimed Sister Helen Kenny, standing with her two colleagues on the top deck of a Norwegian freighter as it chugged through Lei Yue Mun gap into Hong Kong harbour on a bright December day in 1958. It was little wonder she was surprised: the nuns had been told nothing about their posting before leaving the United States.

In their full-length white habits and veils billowing in the breeze like sails, they marvelled at the chaotic and noisy scene that opened before them. The harbour was teeming with boats, but unlike the port of New York, none of them seemed to be taking the slightest notice of traffic regulations, if there were any. It was an astonishing end to a journey that had begun not altogether auspiciously. At the start of it, they were told that no ship's captain liked conveying nuns, horses, and corpses, all of which were believed to bring bad luck. Fortunately the voyage was completed without untoward incidents, although there was one nerve-wracking moment before it was finally over:

> Once in the harbour the ship stopped mid-stream. In the choppy water below bobbed a collection of *walla-wallas* [water-taxis]. We'd brought with us a huge brass tabernacle which was to find a home in the yet to be built Maryknoll hospital. With great trouble and much shouting it was lowered overboard on

ropes. Then we followed down the rope ladder ourselves. We were incensed that everyone seemed more worried about getting the tabernacle down safely rather than us!

They crossed the harbour in the walla-walla and were driven to the Maryknoll Convent in Kowloon, joining a line of nuns who had first arrived in 1921. One of the pioneers, Sister Mary Paul, admitted that in those early days they felt like strangers, neither welcomed by the other orders who thought them unfit for missionary life, nor noticed by the colonialists who considered them socially beyond the pale. The nuns lived in a small cottage overlooking the railway tracks, and some remembered waking on their first morning to the 'click-clock' of pedestrians' wooden clogs tapping on the streets outside.

People in Hong Kong also found the nuns intriguing. A sister who had acquired a smattering of Cantonese once heard some bystanders whispering as she and a colleague passed in their long white garb:

'Are they men or women?' said one.
    'The big one is the husband and the shorter one the wife,' replied a second.
    'No,' said a third, 'they are Buddhists. Look at their prayer beads!'

As the nuns settled into mission life, Sister Mary Paul realized that to be self-sufficient and do something useful for the local community they needed to earn an income. Happily, Chinese entrepreneurship soon rubbed off on them, and with the help of a local seamstress—who later became the first Chinese to join their order—they turned their small dining-room into a workshop. There they made priests' vestments for sale in the United States. This mail-order business not only gave work and training to unskilled girls, but generated funds for their first kindergarten—in the garage. Eventually the kindergarten would grow into a distinguished school.

Evangelism apart, education, social welfare, and medicine have traditionally been fields of missionary endeavour. In Hong Kong it is no different; good works have always gone hand in hand with spreading the Christian gospel ever since the first missionaries arrived in 1842. Many of them positively welcomed work spurned by others—the more intractable the task, the more their faith was tested and strengthened. Valerie Conibear, a committed Christian, had no doubt after hearing an inspiring talk in London in the early 1960s that she had to go to Hong Kong 'to serve the Lord even though I knew there would be difficulties'. At the Sha Tin Home for Babies she came across another woman who had similarly experienced a 'direct calling' to work in Hong Kong, Wendy Blackmur. Together they set up the Home of Loving Faithfulness for severely handicapped children.

For the past thirty years the Home has been in a house near Sheung Shui at the northern limit of the New Territories. It is not a perfect site but 'the Lord doesn't always give beautifully wrapped parcels'. Wendy and Valerie have made the most of it all the same: there is a sense of hope and joy in the bright paint, pretty curtains, and walls adorned with photographs of the children at family outings. Visiting one of the day-care rooms, where members of staff talk and play with desperately handicapped children, is a moving experience.

In 1981 a charities funding body, the Keswick Foundation, donated a lift to the Home. When its founder Maggie Keswick asked about the Home's plans for the future, she was led to a chapel. There Wendy had lifted up the carpet and pulled out a stack of architectural blueprints. 'These are our plans for five extensions,' she explained. As for funding, she believed 'The Lord will provide.' Sure enough, He did. Two decades later, all the new buildings were there to be seen.

But the expansion programme had not proceeded without many a false start. Despite the Lord's largesse, the Home needed to take out a mortgage which it had difficulty paying a few years later. Faced with foreclosure, the two women plumbed the power of prayer. The sum they lacked was $200,000, and as the deadline for payment drew near, the bank manager

> wrote that we should consider selling the house. Prices having
> risen considerably, he said we should make a large profit which

would enable us to buy a piece of land and build anew. We prayed about this, and God very clearly said, 'My name is over this door and it is not to be removed'. So the suggestion to sell was rejected.

The day before the deadline, one of the few people who knew about their predicament rang to enquire. 'Don't worry,' replied Wendy, her faith unshakeable, 'today's post hasn't arrived yet!' On the day itself, the bank manager duly appeared to discuss the matter, but over a cup of tea disclosed that a few weeks previously he had received an anonymous donation for the amount owed. 'I dashed all over the house,' recalled Wendy, 'shouting "It's paid, it's paid!", leaving Valerie to be polite to the bank manager.' There were no recriminations for him, however; his failure to inform them promptly about the donation was simply 'a test of faith'.

Faith is what animates the Home. To this day it relies on individual donations, for no government funding is received. There is no fundraising, no appeals, just faith in God through prayer. Valerie points out that 'when people say we must have great faith I tell them that this faith itself is not ours but a gift from God. Not everyone is called this way. God uses those who earn salaries to support our work and other Christian ministries.'

Another committed Christian who refuses to raise money is Jackie Pullinger, well known as the Englishwoman who took the word of God to the criminals, drug addicts, peddlars, and prostitutes in the Walled City of Kowloon. As she herself described it, 'My mission was to help the Walled City people to understand who Christ was.'

Discovering what her mission was had been a long and confusing struggle. While still living in England, she was

told by God to go and for what reason, but not where. One night I had this strange dream of finding Hong Kong in the middle of a map of Africa and seeing very thin silhouettes of people who obviously needed help.

In desperation I went to see my local priest Richard Thompson. 'I think God is telling me to go somewhere but He's being very unhelpful about where,' I said. 'We've got to a stalemate, God and me.'

Richard just said, 'If God gave you your plane fare, a job, and an old age pension you wouldn't need to trust Him. Go and buy a ticket for a boat going on the longest journey you can find and pray to know where to get off.'

I thought I would love to do that but it would be cheating to do something so terrific.

She could not rid herself of the idea that it was necessary to suffer to do God's work until her priest reminded her that 'Abraham had left his country and followed God to a promised land without knowing where he was going.'

In 1966 the boat going on the longest journey she could find made landfall in Hong Kong. Her first sight of the harbour and its dramatic backdrop took her breath away: 'All the places we had passed by earlier on the voyage seemed so flat by comparison. Here was perspective. Here were mountains shimmering and fading into the mist in an Oriental painting. I found myself filled with peace and as I recognized that this was the place God had chosen, I said thank you.'

High mountains also rear behind the rehabilitation centre where drug addicts are treated through prayer. Overlooking the glistening waters of Tolo Harbour, the men's hostel is a collection of huts previously used as a police holiday camp. Over a lunch of steamed rice, baked beans, a little chicken, and fermented bean paste shared with twenty former addicts and some visitors, Jackie Pullinger observes that the tranquillity of their surroundings is frequently broken by disturbances: 'In fact if we didn't have a crisis that we have to pray for, or problems to talk through, then our addicts wouldn't learn anything. Once out in the world again they are going to have to face crises, difficult bosses and people, so really this is a new growing-up time for them.'

A young man, very pale, clean-shaven and in pyjamas, joins the group with a 'brother' (former addict). He had arrived the day before and this is his first full day of detoxification. Jackie refers to him as 'a new man in Christ' and looks at him approvingly as he manages a little steamed rice. 'If you looked at his calves you would see that his whole leg is covered with injection marks,' she says.

The marks showed that he had been 'mainlining'. Another way of taking heroin, known by the Chinese euphemism 'chasing the dragon', is to burn grains of the drug on a sheet of tinfoil and inhale the fumes as they melt. To rehabilitate drug addicts, Jackie puts her trust in what she calls 'praying in the Spirit'. When an addict arrives at one of the homes he goes through 'cold turkey' as he withdraws without medication to allay the torture. 'We don't even allow an aspirin and certainly not methadone which is much more difficult to kick than heroin.' The first few days of 'detox' are indisputably agonizing, filled with pain, sweating, maybe hallucinations. But always a 'brother' is there to help with prayers and guidance. A long-time addict recounted his own experience:

> Jackie told me there was no medication to come off drugs, only prayer. By the second day of withdrawal I was very uncomfortable, even when the others prayed for me. I was too shy to pray in front of them, but it seemed I had no choice— prayer is the treatment. So I prayed. When I said 'amen', all the pain stopped. I felt very comfortable and peaceful. It was as if I was on a quiet beach, alone and asleep in the sand.

A former Triad member who had spent his teenage years 'chasing the dragon' and going in and out of prison has no doubt that Jackie saved his life: 'I thank God that He brought her here. If He hadn't many would be dead who are alive today—I for one.'

⟶◦✦◦⟵

Angels of mercy come in many guises. To the tuberculosis patient on his bed of pain in the Ruttonjee Sanatorium they might well have appeared as nuns belonging to the Irish order of Columban Sisters.

A worldwide scourge, tuberculosis was responsible for over a thousand million deaths in the nineteenth and twentieth centuries. Death rates are particularly high in densely populated areas with low sanitary standards and exacerbated by wars or other sweeping catastrophes. In post-War Hong Kong the disease was the most serious threat to general health. Things were not helped by the humid climate, widespread poverty, and overcrowding, and rendered even more acute

when waves of refugees started coming from the Chinese mainland.
For years available facilities barely met the vastness of the problems.
But in trying to solve them, the Hong Kong government always
worked closely with religious and welfare agencies.

In early 1949 the Governor, Sir Alexander Grantham, officially
opened the Ruttonjee Sanatorium (pictured above). Its eponymous
Parsee benefactor, J. H. Ruttonjee, having seen a daughter die of
the disease, had established the Anti-Tuberculosis Association.
Ruttonjee and his fellow founders felt that continuous and dedicated
care would be ensured if a religious order were to run the hospital.
Just at that time, with China in the throes of civil war, many
missionary orders had been expelled from the Mainland and were
in Hong Kong either serving in the colony or awaiting new postings.
Mother M. Vianney, the Superior General of the Columban Sisters,
happened to be *en route* from China. She was immediately asked if
she would take on the administration of the Sanatorium.

By the time Sister Gabriel O'Mahony, a doctor specializing in
respiratory disease, joined the staff in 1950, the Sanatorium already
had 400 patients. She remembered her arrival in Hong Kong most
vividly: 'It was a glorious morning, one of those days that make
you want to shout the praises of God.'

The Sanatorium, however, seemed unbearably bleak compared
to the teaching hospital of University College Dublin, where she
had completed her medical training, and the institution in Boston
where she had done postgraduate work. 'It was spotlessly clean but

stark in its emptiness—just beds from the Army with white sheets and grey army blankets,' she recalled. The mattresses, also left by the army, were stuffed with straw. There were no bed tables either, so at meal times the orderlies would 'spread a sheet of newspaper on the patients' laps and place a tin tray on that with chopsticks and a bowl of rice and vegetables'.

But she didn't mind the austerity and wanted to work there. Until the advent of effective anti-tuberculotic drugs, rest under hygienic conditions, together with improved nutrition, was considered the best and only treatment, so patients lay flat on their beds. They coughed day and night. Then in 1952 the wonder drug isoniazid (INH) arrived on the market and the sisters one and all claimed it was the first time the wards became silent at night.

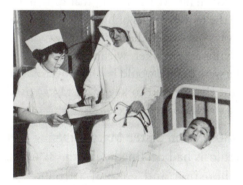

Few newcomers failed to be disconcerted by either the difficulty of communication or the strange mores of Hong Kong people. Sister Gabriel's introduction to these were typical of the experience of many expatriates.

As she remembered it, she had been but two days in the hospital when asked to take her first out-patients clinic. Crossing the compound, she met Sister Aquinas (then the Medical Officer) from whom she asked for a quick lesson in Cantonese. The two words Sister Aquinas taught her there and then were 'Jo san' for 'Good morning'. They would be easy to remember, Sister Aquinas assured her—'Jo as in Joseph and san as in sanatorium'. As it happened, her interpreter was nowhere to be seen when the first patient, a boy of six, appeared in the office, so she thought she would put her newly acquired Cantonese words to use at once:

> I cheerfully greeted him with '*Jo san*'.
>> 'Good morning, Sister,' came the equally cheerful reply.
>> Startled and somewhat disappointed that my phrase had proved unnecessary I fell back on my native tongue. But so did my little patient on his. Stalemate was averted only by the arrival of the interpreter!

One of her other patients that day was a young man of twenty-one, come for a checkup following his discharge from the hospital a month earlier. Sister Gabriel asked if he had been taking the prescribed rest since his discharge:

> With a twinkle in his eye he said no, that he found it impossible to reconcile the requirements of his health with the necessity of keeping always one street ahead of the police. It seems that he made his living as a hawker, without a hawker's licence. The penalty if he were caught would be the confiscation of his goods, which meant that he had to keep constantly on the move in Hong Kong's well-policed streets.

By the 1980s, when Sister Mary Greaney was the hospital's Matron, tuberculosis had declined with the availability of effective drugs, better housing, and general affluence, and its highest incidence was occurring among illegal immigrants from China. Up till 1982, if an illegal immigrant managed to reach the urban centre of Hong Kong undetected, he or she was then allowed to apply for legal papers and stay. Sister Mary treated many who risked their lives several times to get to Hong Kong: 'I remember one male patient who tried to swim from China three times so as to get treatment for his TB. Twice the police caught him and sent him back. The third time he was lucky: he made it and finished up in Ruttonjee for six months and made a good recovery.' Other refugees already infected with the disease by the time they reached Hong Kong were people who had fled Vietnam. Those patients, according to Sister Mary, 'were great—very accepting of their illness and very appreciative of the care.'

Like others of her order, Sister Mary was anxious to learn Cantonese so that she could communicate properly with her patients, especially the children, who 'couldn't understand why I did not speak or chat to them'. To begin with she went around with a little notebook jotting down Cantonese words. Then she took a full-time course at the Government Language Centre:

> My classmates were four English police inspectors, a South African, and a New Zealand physiotherapist. We were all very eager to learn the language. The course was geared towards the police. Consequently I learned some local terminology used on their beat! I made many good friends among my early patients, and am still in touch with some of them.

If TB is no longer a menace in Hong Kong, the influence of those clinical pioneers—the Columban Sisters—remains relevant, reaching out today 'to drug addicts, AIDS sufferers, prostitutes, and the dying'. In doing so they stand firmly in the old missionary tradition, the tradition of identifying needs, starting remedial projects, raising public consciousness, involving secular and government bodies in their efforts, and finally effacing themselves.

Not all missionaries shy away from fundraising. Salesian Father Peter Newbery has been brilliant at soliciting support and heightening awareness for his latest project, Youth Outreach, a service which 'helps runaway kids who are not making it. We try to show them life from faith. That doesn't mean prayers—don't talk to kids about spirituality! But I am presently looking at the possibility of engaging a pastoral counsellor who will be responsible for facilitating the kids' participation in programmes organized by churches of all kinds around Hong Kong.'

A jack of all trades, bilingual Father Newbery speaks north-country English peppered with Cantonese and a lot of laughs. He arrived in Hong Kong in 1967. Originally a teacher, he earnt qualifications in social work, counselling, and criminology and has

pursued a varied career including a stint as prison chaplain and chaplain to the Vietnamese refugee camp at Hei Ling Chau. In the 1970s Vietnamese boat people who were given temporary asylum in Hong Kong pending resettlement in the West were housed in closed camps which, though humanely run, provided only basic facilities designed to discourage them from overstaying their welcome. Many of them were still waiting a decade later when Father Newbery became involved.

'God works in the oddest ways, I'm convinced of it,' he said. God's odd ways pulled him into the Vietnamese community. At one time he was working with a Good Shepherd sister, and from her he learnt enough Vietnamese to manage a basic conversation. Soon he was hearing confession and saying mass at the camp—which was how he found himself in the middle of a riot in 1984:

> That was the most violent fifteen minutes I have ever experienced! Hei Ling Chau was originally a single men's camp with the northern and southern Vietnamese all herded together. The authorities were working on the principle that if the refugees were resettled they'd have to learn to live together.
>
> While the refugee authorities were humming and hawing about what to do, the Canadians came along and said, 'OK, we'll take 500. Anyone speak English?' That way, they picked out all the doctors and lawyers—the professionals.
>
> So the southerners were being resettled but nobody wanted the northerners. Then the northerners figured that if the

southerners got a criminal record no-one would take them either. Being used to resorting to violence as a means towards an end they decided to organize a riot on Chinese New Year's day. . . . They had been preparing for months before, sharpening up sheets of metal and taking iron bars from nearby building sites.

By that time a second camp for families had been opened at Hei Ling Chau. Since Father Newbery couldn't take two masses at the same time, he gained permission for the women and children to attend chapel in the men's camp. Unbeknown to all, the northerners had targeted a number of places for their rampage and the chapel was one of them:

> It was full of women and children. Just as the service finished, the northerners started the riot. One of them slipped behind the leader of the southerners and slit his head open like a watermelon. Luckily he didn't die. I was outside shouting in my best Vietnamese for the women and children to evacuate the chapel. There was a great deal of screaming and sobbing. It was terrible.
>
> Fifteen minutes later men from the Correctional Services Department [CSD] arrived on the scene, some in their pyjamas, others clutching helmets and shields. Eventually they transported the whole men's camp to prison where all the inmates were screened and then sent either to the camp at Chi Ma Wan or the larger camp for families at Hei Ling Chau, with the northern and southern guys split up.

Called to give evidence at the official enquiry into the riot, Father Newbery (pictured) was surprised when he was asked if he would like to be attached as prison chaplain to the CSD full-time. He was to perform that assignment for ten years.

His successor as prison chaplain was an American Maryknoll Father, Sean Burke. Father Burke had always had a clear idea of where his vocation lay: 'I didn't have a feeling for Latin America or Africa but I did for Asia. I don't know why—there was just something about China.' He first came to Hong Kong as a language student in 1974. Whenever his studies allowed him some free time, he would spend it helping Elsie Elliott, then an Urban Councillor. Previously associated with the Christian community known as Plymouth Brethren, Elsie Elliott (now Mrs Elsie Tu) has been an unwavering champion of the poor and dispossessed in Hong Kong since her arrival in 1951. Working in her ward office gave Father Burke a true insight into the real problems of Hong Kong, the severest of which was lack of or poor housing. The problem was particularly acute for the elderly, he discovered: 'When I came back in 1978 as an ordained priest, I was approached by Diane Coke of the Housing Department. She said there was a group of gweilo women who wanted to start a charity to rehouse old people. This was Helping Hand and I ended up becoming administrator of it.'

Father Burke's home and the Helping Hand office was a corrugated iron hut in the Lai King temporary shelter for the homeless. The shelter provided a roof over the heads, not only of old people who had no accommodation, but also families evicted from squatter areas waiting to be rehoused. It turned out not to be particularly temporary, however, for Father Burke was to stay there for the next ten years. At first it felt rather like camping out, he says,

> and after a bit you got used to the physical hardships. There was no running water in the hut. Outside there was a sink and if you wanted to shower you filled a bucket and used one of the doors as a partial screen. But it was still quite public. We used to collect a monthly five-dollar fee from each resident to pay for a caretaker. One day when I was showering the door was pulled aside and in came this woman. She didn't blink an eye when handing me her five dollars!
>
> We had to wash our clothes by hand squatting down over a bucket. The walls were paper-thin so you could hear every word your neighbours said. For cooking I had a little toaster oven and

a rice cooker—that part I didn't mind. What I minded most
was the heat in the summer. You could not have air-conditioning
as the electrical supply to that area was not powerful enough, so
I just had a fan. It was awfully hot and in the winter it was
terribly cold. Then of course there were the inevitable rats and
cockroaches that went with those sorts of areas. Otherwise it
was quite pleasant. I miss that place, the simplicity of it. It was
a great experience for me to live with elderly people.

He summed up missionaries' contribution to Hong Kong by
quoting one of Maryknoll's pioneering priests, Bishop James E.
Walsh: 'We go where we are needed but not wanted, and stay until
we are wanted but not needed'. He continued: 'We answered a need,
especially in the fields of education, medical and health care, and
moral formation.'

Answering spiritual needs are, of course, as important as material
ones, for is it not the missionaries' object to heal the soul as well as
the body? But many in the China field had strived to relieve the
suffering and misery of their converts only to see them walk out
without a backward glance—once the soup kitchen, school, clinic,
or orphanage had served its purpose. As far back as 1842, when the
Baptist minister J. Lewis Shuck and his wife Henrietta had set up
their 'native schools' in Hong Kong, the hope was that once young
heathen minds were opened to learning they would also imbibe
Christianity. But more often than not, as Mrs Shuck lamented to a
relative in Virginia, those 'perishing creatures . . . toil on, regardless
of eternity, and careful about those minor things which concern
the world.'

The worldliness of the Chinese and the constant need to separate
true converts from 'rice Christians' made proselytization somewhat
dispiriting at times. A deep gulf lay between the temporal morality
of Confucianism and the Christian concepts of sin and repentance,
and it was always a struggle to spread the idea, as Father Peter
Newbery put it, 'that concern for your fellow men is more important
than personal gain'. In Father Sean Burke's experience, however,
those helped materially often looked to the Church for spiritual
support as well. To decry missionaries' work as 'buying converts',

he said, is to fail to understand their real motive, which is to engage with the whole person—body, soul, and spirit. It is a simple equation as far as he is concerned:

> To help a person in need is to help Christ, as the Gospel so simply has it: 'Whatsoever you do for the least of My brethren, you do unto Me'.
>
> In return, we gain a sense of fulfilment of having served the Lord. In the early 1950s and '60s there was a great outreach to the poor, the sick, the orphans, the needy. Until 1962 there was no government social welfare department. Missionaries were able to share their faith with others. Growing numbers were received into the Church. That was certainly a cause for rejoicing. It was an exciting time for building and expanding, a time of great optimism. Of course, life was in many respects much simpler then. The 1970s and '80s brought more questions and religious doubt as the world and the Church changed drastically.
>
> Then the missionaries began to turn over much of their work to the local clergy. Chinese became bishops and staffed diocesan offices. There was even talk of missionaries being no longer needed here. Maybe it was time to move on. But a lack of vocation locally makes foreign priests still necessary and important. We bring an international dimension to the Church here and a reminder of its universality. And then there is always the reality of China to consider—can we ever return?

In the nineteenth century, the thought of the unredeemed Chinese dying without God at the rate of a million a month had drawn many ardent missionaries to China. Those early preachers had their vicissitudes, but perhaps none was more disheartening than being totally shut out by the communists after 1949. With the opening of China, however, the foreign mission presence in Hong Kong is, according to Father Burke, 'larger now than it was twenty years ago, mainly because of the dream and hope of working there once again'. In the meantime, missions in Hong Kong can 'serve as a bridge to China, financially supporting some church projects, visiting conferences there, offering short courses to church personnel, and helping to train future church leaders. It may be a long time before we're allowed to do direct church work . . . but there is such a spiritual

hunger in China and it is in danger of being smothered by materialism, as has happened in Hong Kong.'

An assignment to train future church leaders was precisely what brought the Reverend Carl Smith to Hong Kong. He was a pastor of the Reformed Church in Philadelphia when he applied to go into the mission field in 1960. His timing turned out to be impeccable, for it happened that the United Board for World Ministries of the United Church of Christ had just received a request from the Church of Christ in China for a teacher of theology in Hong Kong.

Carl Smith had scant preparation for this posting, for while 'every missionary was supposed to have two or more years of separate language instruction before going into the field, I did three months at Yale University of intensive Cantonese in which I was a very poor student.' He did, however, have another qualification up his sleeve—a background in genealogical and local history research— although it would not come into play until much later.

Greeted by the Chinese head of the church on arrival in Hong Kong, he was thrown in at the deep end immediately, his language difficulty airily brushed aside:

'You can teach through an interpreter and you'll pick up
Cantonese soon enough,' I was told. Well, I was an obedient
missionary, so I said I'd do it.

I was at the Ho Fuk Tong Theological Institute, at the first
theological training class that the Church of Christ in China
had held since the Pacific War, for only a year. I was the only
full-time missionary teacher, with a group of about a dozen
students who wanted to be trained for the ministry. It was
something of a two-bit outfit, although we did produce some
students who became church leaders in Hong Kong. Their
abilities were quite different. One or two had good English,
others had no English at all. Some were Mandarin-speakers trying
to speak Cantonese. My downfall in terms of language was that
when as a group we were sitting round a table, I would struggle
with Cantonese, and out of the kindness of their heart some of
the students would switch over to English, and in the weakness
of my heart I accepted that.

In 1962 the institute closed and its students moved to Chung
Chi College, forerunner of the Chinese University of Hong Kong,
where they became the first intake of Chung Chi Seminary. There
Reverend Smith was asked to teach the Old Testament and—'what
became significant in my future development in Hong Kong'—a
course on the history of the Protestant Church in China, of which
by his own admission he knew nothing:

> So I went to libraries to get books on the subject, and what I
> found was that most of the literature dealt with what the
> missionaries did and not who the Chinese converts were. . . .
> But I was not content to teach it just from the missionary
> standpoint. I thought to myself—the students are young Chinese
> who would be working with Chinese people, and they ought to
> know more about the origins of the Church as it affected Chinese
> lives.
>
> I thought I would try and get as much material as I could
> about early Chinese converts in the missions, particularly in this
> area of China, using the same methodology that I had employed
> for my genealogical research in the USA and looking at all the
> archives I could find.

During his first home leave and sabbatical in 1965, he spent happy if dusty days burrowing in missionary archives in London, Boston, Philadelphia, and Richmond, Virginia. Back in Hong Kong, his first project was 'to read the English-language newspapers published in Canton beginning in 1822, followed by those issued in Hong Kong when the British settled the colony and the press moved there. A second project was to go to old Chinese newspapers to look at the death notices in them'. From all these he collected much valuable data not only on local people connected with the Church, but also citizens prominent or wealthy enough to merit obituaries when they died. Similarly, he looked at land registry records, rate books, and government gazettes, and copied down gravestone inscriptions in colonial and Christian cemeteries in both Hong Kong and Macao:

> In compiling my records, I did everything by hand. For example, I was about a year and a half in the land registry, going there in the morning, staying until the afternoon, reading every land document seriatum. Each document was in a plastic folder and bound up in packets of fifty. It's easy to abstract such documents: you get the date, you get the property, you get the value, you get who bought it, who sold it, and who witnessed the transaction.
>
> Every day something leapt out at you—a name, for instance—and I'd start making connections with other material I'd seen, say in a newspaper or the tax lists. I did the same thing from rates and valuation records, copying out everything by hand. The period I covered was from 1844 to about 1885. I could have gone on.

It was around this time of intensive research that someone took a photograph of him at home surrounded by boxes of cards. Since then the boxes have multiplied to 140 containing a couple of hundred thousand cards. In addition, there are many file drawers filled with material on what Reverend Smith terms 'a sort of grassroots history' of Hong Kong. A duplicate set of his card file, gathered together as the Carl Smith Collection, is now stored in the Hong Kong Public Records Office and retrievable by electronic media. The original collection and all his papers are destined for the Library of Congress, Washington DC. Until then, he says,

> I still have them for my own use and I get a number of requests for them by scholars from time to time. The material has helped me also to produce articles in journals about aspects of local history, about people in Hong Kong and their social life, and development of communities. Some of these articles have been collected together in two published volumes which are very much quoted in studies on Hong Kong.

One of those articles is a fascinating case study of Ng Akew, a kept or 'protected' woman (to use a euphemism of the day) of a foreigner. She had several children with her protector, a ship's captain and opium smuggler from Salem, Massachusetts:

> I probably first got a clue to Ng Akew when I was going through the early newspapers of Hong Kong because there was a case reported in 1849 in which she was involved. It had to do with a pirate seizing some chests of opium that belonged to her.
>
> I kept finding her name in various records. She owned land. I was going systematically through the deed records, copying abstracts for forty-five years or so after 1842. In doing so I came across where her protector had given land to her in trust. Then I looked at her protector who was fairly prominent among the small number of foreign traders in Hong Kong at the time. This was just before a woman had come out from England to marry him as a 'mail-order bride'. As some Ng Akew's children were split up when her protector married, a man from Australia was able to come to Hong Kong twenty years later and pose as one of her sons. For a while Ng Akew was completely duped because her son had been taken from her when very young. Then Ng Akew went bankrupt and the bankruptcy proceedings appeared in the newspapers. There was a list of what was auctioned off in her estate which gave us a glimpse into the kind of lifestyle she had. So these were largely the sources I had for building up the story of this very enterprising, interesting, and unusual woman who exemplified the Eurasian context which developed in Hong Kong.

It takes a certain kind of mind to collect and make sense of data in that way. Carl Smith (pictured) compares it to 'looking at a tree or a shrub in a great forest, perhaps getting lost for a while, and then beginning to see what this tree or that shrub had in relation to its neighbours, and suddenly seeing the whole ecological picture'.

His research even survived redundancy: 'I happened to be in the US on furlough in 1970 when I was told that I was no longer needed to teach in Hong Kong.' But the University Theological Division, which had by then replaced the Seminary, was prepared to provide him with housing. 'So I came back under those conditions. I had somewhere to live but no salary and plenty of time.' Despite a small income from a family legacy, he had to learn to live in considerably reduced circumstances: 'For one thing I didn't return to the States for fifteen years after I became redundant.'

But, he says, his life has worked out, enriched as it is by what he calls his hobby and his joy, as well as by the many friends he has made through it. He has not stopped retrieving Hong Kong's past, and his work for the past thirty years has continued to be informed by a consistent engagement with the life of ordinary people 'and how they adapted or did not adapt to a colonial situation and the reasons for it':

I've always been left-wing in my thinking, and therefore I
wondered, what about labour in Hong Kong? what about the
mui tsai [bonded maidservants] and their plight? What about
the Chinese who were shot going over Sha Tin during the 1925
strike? I also had doubts about the way criminals were dealt
with here, with the judges and lawyers operating through
interpreters and what this meant for the Chinese appearing in
court. This wonderful British justice is wonderful in its own
way but like American justice it isn't always justice because it
was too slanted in certain directions.

All these things interested me. I tried as much as I could to
see them in the context of the Chinese. I know one could not
actually see it that way, but I tried. I tried to stand in the
Chinese's footsteps.

<hr>

Stacy Mosher's first job in Hong Kong was also as a teacher although,
as she claims with typical modesty, she was to prove hopeless at it
and unsuited to mission life. But tutoring in English at least gave
her a moderate income and time 'to gain some perspective on what
to do with my life'. In fact her year at the Lutheran Mission in
Kowloon provided her 'with an ideal introduction to Hong Kong,
pulling me so deep into its textures that I was unable to untangle
myself at the end of my one-year contract, and ended up staying for
nearly eighteen'.

When she arrived in Hong Kong, she was 'a graduate school
drop-out, a typical example of the aimless flotsam and jetsam of
the West that bobbed up on the shores of Victoria Harbour in the
1980s'. With little idea of what to expect, 'I generally accepted and
adapted to what I found with neither disappointment nor
amazement.' But having grown up in rural Michigan, Hong Kong's
cityscape and vibrancy entranced her from the start:

> The great advantage of my year at the mission was that it obliged
> me to work closely with ordinary Hong Kong people and to
> learn Cantonese. In addition, the modest pay forced me to live
> simply and more like local people. As a result I was saved from

the insular life that proves so alienating for many expatriates in Hong Kong.

In order to save money, I took the ferry and bus rather than the Mass Transit Railway, and for shorter trips I walked. Many of my fondest memories of Hong Kong resulted from early bumbling attempts to find my way around. I remember wandering into the San Po Kong street market, with its circus-like tarpaulins and crowds and a fat, bald man holding up eggs and shouting, 'One dollah!' I remember a ride on the number seven bus from the Star Ferry at night, noticing the multicoloured lights of Temple Street from the top deck, jumping off and discovering street operas, stalls of fortune-tellers and T-shirts and exotic snacks. More than once I ended up walking home from Yau Ma Tei to Broadcast Drive, dropping into bed and falling asleep fully clothed, weary with exhaustion and delight.

My year at the mission was to set the pattern for my life in Hong Kong, in that I contributed little but gained much. Learning Cantonese and basic written Chinese gave me a great advantage in future employment, as few expatriates ever progressed beyond '*Jo san*'.

As well as her mastery of Cantonese, Stacy Mosher's modest requirements for remuneration also endeared her to employers who were willing to gamble on youth and enthusiasm over experience. From teaching through a series of part-time jobs such as film dubbing and copywriting, she became a reporter for a television station, ATV.

At that time, in 1984, ATV paid very poorly, and the station was willing to shape the raw material of my writing skills and basic Cantonese in on-the-job training. Nowadays, of course, ATV would never entertain an application from a person of my limited credentials. As with the mission, I gained much more from my employment at ATV than did my employers or the viewing public, subjected to nightly displays of my lamentable ignorance. Working as a journalist was like taking a crash course in every aspect of Hong Kong life. During my years at ATV, and subsequently at TVB and as a print journalist, I met all sorts of people from the 'great and the good' to the poor and lowly, not to mention a few genuine scoundrels. I visited the Governor's mansion and hillside squatter huts. What better time to be a journalist than during the 1980s and early 1990s, observing close at hand the amazing political transformations, the cycles of hopes and despair, that gripped the territory?

As my career developed I benefited often from lucky timing, and came to appreciate the Chinese term for 'crisis'—the opportunity presented by danger. Hong Kong was in a state of flux in the approach to 1997. The advantage was to risk-takers and also to people such as myself who were happy to ride the flow.

In 1988 she married a Chinese journalist and publisher, Jin Zhong. Editor of the independent political monthly, *Open Magazine*, he had arrived in Hong Kong from China just a year before she came from the US. Neither of them anticipated the great crisis Hong Kong was to face shortly after:

> On a weekend trip to Macau in the spring of 1989, in a tatty room of the Hotel Sentral, we watched the televised funeral of former Chinese Premier Hu Yaobang. When the massive public demonstrations began in Hong Kong in late May, I attended nearly all of them, ostensibly as a journalist, but quickly pulled in as a participant. It is said that as many as a million people took part in marches and rallies in late May and early June. I pity those who missed the experience of being swallowed up in that vast organism, of being united with strangers of every age, class, and complexion in waves of defiance and sorrow. Looking back, I feel that to have been one of a million at that time was the pinnacle of my experience in Hong Kong.
>
> Perhaps it was inevitable that things must deteriorate. It has always been fashionable to refer to Hong Kong people as practical and politically apathetic. These labels fail to recognize the agonizing choices Hong Kong people faced in the run-up to 1997, when virtually every life decision necessarily involved a betrayal of some kind. June 4th brought ordinary Hong Kong people the closest many would come to heroism. Less recognized is the courage it takes to forge ahead after turning one's back on

hope. This is the historical strength of the Chinese. It is not one that I share.

The Chinese capacity for endurance even when hope is vain has prompted both admiration and criticism. But after Tiananmen, more than 60,000 Hong Kong people had no doubt that survival meant putting geographical and political distance between themselves and China. Through the early 1990s, emigration increased and confidence in the future seeped away. It was an alternately exhilarating and dispiriting time for writers reporting on the controversies of the day. For Stacy Mosher, interest in the political process began to wane; instead, she

> developed a fascination with the seamy underpinnings of society. This interest gave me a sense of direction I'd previously lacked, and after considerable initial resistance I was accepted into the Independent Commission Against Corruption as an investigator in 1995.

She had indeed penetrated deep into the very textures of the place. Looking back on her eighteen years, she says:

> I will always think of Hong Kong as a state of mind. More than any other place I've known, its identity seems defined by the collective consciousness of its inhabitants. It was my good fortune to have been part of that collective consciousness during the golden period when Hong Kong was no longer a colony and not yet an SAR—when it was a 'territory' in which the native-born had recently become the majority, and had come to think of themselves first and foremost as 'Hong Kong people'.

8
The Quality of Life

Expatriates arriving to live and work in Hong Kong used to come with certain assumptions. As English was the official *lingua franca*, they reckoned on a rather British flavour to the cultural life of the territory, and generally speaking their expectations were justified. But like the Jardines executive who couldn't find enough to fill his forty-eight page booklet on *The Artistic and Cultural Life in Hong Kong*, most thought Hong Kong merely provincial and its denizens philistine. The place had no culture.

Of course they meant European culture, which was a rather unreasonable thing to expect in an Eastern city. Still, the world was becoming smaller and more Westernized by the day, and it was not as if Hong Kong, with its affluent population of several million, couldn't afford or support a wider offering of the arts. The territory had been importing culture since 1973, when an arts festival providing a month-long programme of performances by repertory companies, dance troupes, and symphony orchestras from abroad was established. But the rest of the year was a 'cultural desert', a complaint much heard among expatriates in those days. Hong Kong didn't even have a quality cinema for cineastes, only a film club which showed its selections on an occasional basis.

It wasn't until the 1980s that a more cosmopolitan cultural and entertainment scene emerged. Deng Xiaoping might have been indirectly responsible for this transformation—he was responsible for so much else in Hong Kong after all. Certainly it was the unveiling of his Open Door policy in 1978 that allowed Hong Kong to reinvent itself as a service and financial centre for China and the rest of the region. Spectacularly rich rewards attended this conversion, and, as the territory boomed, more multinational businesses set up shop here. What ensued was pivotal: yuppies arrived on the scene, a different breed of expatriates—not serving the Empire or lording it in the traditional hongs, but a transient army of mercenaries, drawn by opportunism and the prospect of deals, and ready to spend the money and bonuses they earned on enjoying themselves.

Hong Kong was quick to accommodate these new consumers, and in doing so began to acquire a sophistication and gloss in the popular perception just at the point when independent travel became a mandatory rite of passage for middle-class students in the Western world, and South-East Asia replaced India as the backpacker's Nirvana. No longer was the city a sinkhole of the East, the place where you could mingle with the *demi-monde* of the likes of Suzie Wong and buy a twenty-four-hour tailored suit that fell apart in twenty-four days. Its attractions became more diverse and generic— in tropical Asia, Hong Kong was the city most similar to London, Sydney, or New York. It was where communications were reliable and things worked; for visitors it was a welcome antidote to the disorder and backwardness of the rest of the region.

And so more people came—travellers and backpackers who stopped off for a temporary job to replenish their dwindling cash or a break before tackling more arduous destinations in their Lonely Planet guides. They arrived with none of the social preconceptions of their predecessors. Actually they even introduced a touch of bohemianism, for they didn't think it was letting the expatriate side down if they went around on the local buses or served drinks in a Tsim Sha Tsui bar.

But a film club showing classic movies in a school hall emphatically wasn't their style. And so they imposed their own, aided and abetted by overseas Chinese and returnees, the sons and daughters of locals who had acquired their university degrees and Western tastes in London or Los Angeles, and were as dedicated to pursuing fun as their expatriate counterparts.

Their style is perhaps best epitomized by an entertainment quarter that sprang up around a street whose Chinese name translates as Orchid-Osmanthus Lane, found just above Queen's Road on the fringe of the central business district and some of the most expensive real estate in the world. The street is far better known, though, by its phonetic transliteration, Lan Kwai Fong, a name that has gathered to itself the resonance of a design brand or label, as nightspots in

Singapore, Beijing, and Shanghai called 'Lan Kwai Fong' attest. Lan Kwai Fong spells bars, restaurants, and clubs of the sort you might find in New York or London; Lan Kwai Fong betokens pleasure, sophistication, and the *dernier cri*; Lan Kwai Fong is about gilded youth and the good life; Lan Kwai Fong stands for Hong Kong's International Style.

The area used to be a hang-out for expatriates until the returnees started going there. Ted Pulling, an American fund manager, noticed the change: 'With the growth and rivalry of American investment banks there's been a huge hiring of Asians from the US to come to Hong Kong. Maybe they're providing the bridge between expatriates and locals. It's amazing how Asian Lan Kwai Fong has become in recent years. In the old, old days it was just expatriates who went there. Now it's a much healthier mix of people—this has certainly been a good development in Hong Kong.'

A truly cosmopolitan city that offered something for everyone would have a great diversity of toilers in the cultural and entertainment field. We asked a few of them to tell us their stories.

The phenomenon of Lan Kwai Fong is invariably associated with entrepreneur Allan Zeman, who owns many of the properties in the area. Originally from New York, he lost his father when he was nine and spent most of his school years in Montreal, Canada, where he moved with his widowed mother after his father's death. When he left high school at sixteen he decided to work for a year or so before going to university 'to see what that was all about'. Answering an advertisement in a newspaper, he 'wound up in the fashion industry by accident'. It was a job in the shipping room of a lingerie company:

All the salesmen used to come in chewing on their big fat cigars and ask me, 'How much did we ship today, sonny?' so that they could get their commission cheques.

I decided that selling was the job for me and joined the largest dress company in Canada at the time as a salesman by stretching the truth a bit and telling them I was twenty-four years old when I was actually seventeen.

I did very well, and at nineteen I decided to go into business on my own. The company which employed me put up the money and became a partner. Domestic production was difficult at the time because of the unions so I decided to start doing imports, and that's what brought me to Hong Kong about thirty years ago.

For a very young man like Allan Zeman, Hong Kong was 'like an enchanted isle':

It was full of energy, hustle and bustle, people everywhere, pandemonium, but a very wonderful place. Obviously it didn't have the sophistication we have today. There were signs in the streets which said 'No spitting', men were walking in Tsim Sha Tsui around the Peninsula Hotel in pyjama bottoms, women wore *cheong sam*. . . . The very British, rich expats with their short pants and their pipes spoke a language that was foreign to me; I had to listen very closely to understand what they were saying.

Hong Kong was intriguing for another reason—a very low tax regime: 'I happened to ask someone what the tax rate was. At the time it was fifteen per cent. So I figured maybe I'd move to Hong Kong for a few years and put away some money.' Those few years have turned into thirty.

His company, Colby and Staton, the name derived from a shelf company that he bought, began trading from a tiny office in Shell House on Queen's Road, Central. Its main business was sourcing fashion garments from the region for importers in North America and Europe. Zeman fitted into his new surroundings very well:

What I loved about Hong Kong was its international business climate, different to a place like Canada where the business was really local and you were dealing with Canadians. Suddenly I was living amongst people who were English, German, French, Chinese, Japanese.

Colby kept growing (today we have 155 offices around the world), sourcing not just fashion but also hard goods—furniture and almost all the things you'd see in a department store. We exported products all over the world. With all that I learnt one thing—to be successful doing business in different countries, I had to adapt my ways to fit in with their cultures. There's no point trying to change the culture to fit into *your* way of doing business, because the culture is much older than you.

In the late 1970s, less by design than chance, he diversified into a completely new sector:

We had a lot of expats working for us, and buyers used to come from the US and Europe. Everybody was always complaining that the only place to get a good Western meal in Hong Kong was in a hotel.

Also at that time I had an American designer working for me. I'd spent a number of years training her. Then she wanted to go back to the US. When I asked her why she wanted to leave, she said, 'I miss my boyfriend.'

'Well, what does he do?' I asked her.

It turned out that he ran a restaurant in San Francisco. Now in those days there were not that many qualified expats working here, it was difficult to get people to come to Hong Kong, so rather than lose her, I said, 'Why don't you bring him out here, and we'll start a restaurant?' And that was actually the birth of Lan Kwai Fong.

My designer's boyfriend flew out here, looked at different areas, and came to me with the space where California Restaurant is today, in Lan Kwai Fong. It was occupied by an old Chinese supermarket. The area had some flower shops, warehouses selling Swatow lace tablecloths, and there were a number of residential tenants. It was a little network of steep narrow streets, and it had a certain charm. A restaurant, 1997, had already opened there, and so had Disco, Disco. Lan Kwai Fong was also only a block from Queen's Road, the heart of Central at the time. I thought if I could get people to walk one block up, that space wasn't a bad idea. So when he came to me with this supermarket, I said, 'Let's take it.'

I decided to call the restaurant California. The expats in Hong Kong were all from different backgrounds, so I tried to come up with a name that Americans and Europeans as well as local Chinese would recognize and feel comfortable with. California the state had a certain mystique—you had the Beach Boys, sun, sex, girls. I thought the name had connotations that would appeal to everyone, and I was right.

From California, which opened in 1981, I slowly started to buy up property around it. I saw the potential for introducing more American and European cuisine. Hong Kong was getting quite international. California was serving hamburgers. I saw many Americans going into China on business and suffering withdrawal symptoms there. I still remember a woman calling me from the Kowloon–Canton train station—before checking into her hotel she wanted to come to California for a burger! I heard that kind of story all the time. I realized there was a need for a place like Lan Kwai Fong. Every major city had a similar area—New York has Soho, Montreal has a place called Crescent Street.

California's decor was based on a 1950s concept, and to get the American memorabilia we needed for it, rather than go to the US, we went to Tokyo because the Japanese were American crazy, the younger generation there was more American than the Americans, and we could find collections of Coca Cola and Pepsi signs and all that kind of thing.

I noticed that because Tokyo real estate was so expensive, in an office building you'd get off on the tenth floor and find restaurants and bars. You didn't have to be on the ground floor like in America. When I came back to Hong Kong, I thought, property prices were high here as well, so why couldn't it work in Hong Kong? And so when an office building became available in Lan Kwai Fong I bought it. I named it California Entertainment Building. I moved all the tenants out of the podium levels and I slowly converted those into restaurant spaces, and by putting restaurants on different levels I created critical mass. Also I could get higher rental for restaurants than for offices, and so I slowly started to increase the value of the building. From that I started to buy up more buildings as they became available. Nobody knew what I was doing at the time. I was being Chinese amongst the Chinese, getting in right under their noses!

Lan Kwai Fong became very famous; the name itself is now synonymous with entertainment around Asia and even around the world. Tourists came and more and more expats were hanging out there. And when many of the Chinese who'd emigrated to North America and Australia came back after getting their passports, well versed in Western culture, suddenly I found a new market.

The other thing Lan Kwai Fong did—we were the first to introduce Halloween in Hong Kong. It used to be the expats who dressed up and the Chinese who came and watched. Today it's the reverse, the Chinese kids dress up and come and have a good time in Lan Kwai Fong on Halloween night. Hong Kong itself went through a cultural change—it began to loosen up.

———◦◇◦———

For a long time support for cultural institutions was an expatriate preserve. Dig up some early lists of the Ladies Hospitality Committee of the Arts Festival, for instance, or the organizing committee of the annual Ballet Ball ('the number one social event'), and you will see few Chinese names on them. But where civic-minded expatriate ladies led, many local *tai tais* followed (*tai tai* is Chinese for Mrs, madame, or lady), according to New Zealander Karen Penlington, who covered the social scene for magazines and the *South China Morning Post* on and off from 1979 to 1993.

A zealous party-goer even when she wasn't working, Karen Penlington attended some of the most glamorous functions in the late 1980s and early 1990s, 'when Hong Kong was booming and people were feeling flush'. The Bela Vista Balls at Macao, for example, 'were brilliant'.

They would become more lavish as time went on. Ted Marr, an Australian lawyer who was involved in their organization, told a journalist that 'In 1985 a small group of Hooray Henrys from Hong Kong decided to throw a party in the hotel, which was then in a run-down state, but still charming.' When the Bela Vista closed for renovation in 1991, Marr and 500 revellers, many in specially-designed 1930s-style evening dress, converged on the Peace Hotel in Shanghai. Since then members of Hong Kong's most dedicated *beau monde* have gathered to party in Russia, Africa, and Cuba. For the Handover, a ten-day party started in Beijing, moved on to Shanghai, and culminated in Hong Kong. They were great fun, says Karen Penlington, but we shall probably never see their like again, 'though that's not a reflection on expats in general. It's just that the same crowd has been going to all those balls, and we're getting older and more staid, going to bed earlier, and we don't get quite so legless any more.'

In those days, what's more, 'money was no object and you were limited only by your imagination. Today money is still no object but nobody's doing anything fun.' Perhaps that's because expatriates have become less prominent on the social scene. When she first started in journalism, people she approached with her camera for her social pages were mostly expatriates, and they could be divided into three groups: those who didn't want to appear in the press, those who didn't object, and those who actively courted publicity. Most Chinese, on the other hand, would categorically refuse to be photographed for publication. But 'now it's completely different. When I began doing my column in the *Sunday Post* [1989], I could feel as I walked into a room the local socialites inching towards me!'

Today, the pages of Chinese-language tabloids and magazines such as *Hong Kong Tatler* are crammed with snaps of local celebrities—usually the very rich—during the 'season', which is always kicked off by a number of lavish charity balls:

> A mark of being socially accepted, admired even, was to be on a ball committee. If you were on a committee, you were in, you were part of the social fabric. And because the balls were organized to raise money for charity, you could bring royalty out from the UK or get a movie star to come, and if you were on the committee you could hobnob with all those people.

> Gradually more and more locals wanted to be part of it. But what took over was the using of the event socially, in terms of photographs, to establish that you'd arrived. The actual event itself is really immaterial—you give a bit of money to the charity concerned, of course, but the important thing is you were seen with your trophy wife, that she's in the latest Dior or Valentino or whatever, with jewels and furs, and that she's fabulous looking. That's how the *nouveaux riches* did it—by paying for a table and being seen in the photographs published afterwards.

M at the Fringe occupies a very cool and enticing space. High ceilings framed by cornices in dull gold combine with sage, burnt orange, and ochre colour-washed walls to evoke a sense both of faded grandeur and of eccentricity. Europe is suggested in a number of details—the fresco on a wall, a bucket-sized vase of flowers, old-fashioned cutlery, a Mozart string quartet being played on the music system. Immaculate white cloths on discreetly spaced tables and unobtrusive service add to its aura of being not so much a restaurant as a salon in an old house to which one has been invited for a festive dinner.

The restauranteur behind M, Australian Michelle Garnaut (pictured), has a vivid memory of the Lan Kwai Fong phenomenon because she was there working as a chef:

I came through Hong Kong in 1984 with a boyfriend and another couple to get a travel visa for China. Travel to China was the thing to do at that time. I had no expectations and certainly no intention of staying.

On our first night in Hong Kong we went out to eat and struck up a conversation with people at the next table. They were South Africans who came to Hong Kong on holiday ten years before but had stayed on. I was amazed that anybody would want to stay. I thought Hong Kong filthy and noisy and expensive.

My boyfriend and I ended up at a place on the corner of Jordan and Nathan roads called Sky Guesthouse. Only after five weeks did I realize that it was a rent-by-the-hour place! By this time I'd got a job.

I had been trained as a cook in Australia. At first everybody told me it would be very difficult for me to get a job as a cook. A foreign woman in the kitchen? You don't speak Chinese? Impossible! The chef at the American Club said there were only two restaurants which might employ me. One was California, the other was '97, both in Lan Kwai Fong.

California served hamburgers, but the menu at '97 looked more interesting. So I went along there and was taken on as second chef.

On my first Friday night the restaurant was packed, as I could see from a little chefs' office we had which overlooked it. I remember thinking, 'There's something strange here,' and then realizing that there were hardly any Chinese people in the room except for one or two women with expatriate men.

She also noticed that there were several pretentious Western restaurants in Hong Kong but a dearth of 'really modern, international-standard' ones:

There was Asian food, there were hamburgers, in the clubs you got basically English food, and there were fancy restaurants in hotels where waiters wore white gloves. I was cooking food nobody else was cooking at the time. Of course I was just as much of a fashion victim, doing things like spinach salad with strawberry vinaigrette and fresh beansprouts! But some people loved it and came all the time, so I established a loyal clientele.

It wasn't just diners who gravitated to Lan Kwai Fong. In Michelle Garnaut's recollection, it also became a magnet for 'an influx of young independent people who happened to be passing through, and the one place where they could get a job was Lan Kwai Fong.' She thinks they had a lot to do with what Lan Kwai Fong became:

> As foreigners, we were all a bit radical. I remember walking down the street with orange hair and dressed in a mini-skirt and getting stared at. We were young, international, and we were a very different class to the expatriates who were already here. For one thing we were paid absolutely nothing, and every three months you had to spend money to go on holiday somewhere to renew your visa.
>
> Coming in on the cusp of the signing of the Sino-British Joint Declaration, we also saw a change in the mentality of the Hong Kong Chinese. A lot of people who'd emigrated to the West were coming back with different ideas. Those crazy independent expatriates who influenced the entertainment scene then—it would never have worked if the young Chinese didn't join in, because there was nothing like a big enough expat population to support it.

But she tried to avoid employing expatriates when she opened her own restaurant, M at the Fringe, in 1989:

> Running a business I realized that I had to have people I could depend on who would be serious about their jobs because it was their livelihood. This meant local people. Of course I'd always have an expat head chef, and generally a white person on the floor because that's what customers expect to see in a Western restaurant. If I go to a Chinese restaurant in Italy and can't see a Chinese face, I'd say, no, no, no!
>
> In the early 1990s you had to pay local employees more than foreigners. Over that period you saw a strange reversal—the Chinese were calling expatriates 'white trash'! When I first came here the few local people who trickled into '97 were clearly not very comfortable and would never drink wine. But by the early 1990s you could see their growing confidence when trying Western food.

They were ready for a palpably contemporary Western restaurant when M opened, and it was an instant hit: 'M was based on a new idea, the idea of a restaurant being in a building with a soul. The restaurant I wanted to open wasn't going to be about showing off, or a fancy wine list, or having fawning, over-attentive waiters at the table rushing to flick a lighter in your face as soon as you took out a cigarette. And it couldn't be at the bottom of an office building—just *couldn't*!'

She thought others would share her aversion to crossing 'horrible, desolate' acres of marble to go to a restaurant. And fake décor—such as red and white checked tablecloths to suggest an Italian trattoria—makes her cringe. 'We did land searches of practically every old building between Pok Fu Lam and Causeway Bay. At that time there were lots of old buildings in Wan Chai, but our plan turned out to be unrealistic. Anything that was available to buy was fifty million dollars.'

The location she finally chose was a serendipitous discovery. Not only was the Fringe Club, a stone's throw from Lan Kwai Fong, located in a historical building, but it had space for a restaurant upstairs, and M's association with an independent, avant-garde arts organization gave it an appealing quirkiness too. All of these factors were ingredients in the restaurant's success, but 'I come from Melbourne, a glorious food city. One of the great things about Australia is that it has truly fabulous local ingredients and people from a lot of different cultures who'd taken their cuisines and adapted them. I've been cooking since 1979 and I'm serious about food. So most of all, the restaurant is about good European food.'

In 1981 Keith Statham arrived to take up his appointment as the first resident director of the Hong Kong Arts Festival:

Before me, Hong Kong Arts Festival directors lived in London! How they measured the feel of local tastes is another question . . . . Of course the reason for launching the festival in the first place was nothing to do with the arts. It was to attract more tourists, so the prime movers were the Hong Kong Tourist Association and British Airways—which is why previous festival programmes had included so many second-rate artists from the UK.

As I had no clear brief, I set about trying to make the festival one of international standard. From my experience in the British music and theatre business, I had excellent contacts among the top international artist managers, performing company directors, or their agents in Europe, the US, and Australia. . . . In some cases I was able to bring world-class performers to Hong Kong because I had close personal relations with the artists themselves. For example I knew Neville Marriner and James Galway when they were orchestral musicians.

If there ever was a time when support for the Arts Festival came only from 'Peak-dwellers who never went to anything else in the rest of the year', local audiences now turned out in force for major international theatre companies, orchestras, and instrumentalists. Participation by mainland performing groups from the mid-1980s coaxed out others who had hitherto dismissed the festival as essentially a gweilo event. Whatever its success as a tourist draw, the Arts Festival is now firmly entrenched as an annual cultural feast for the people of Hong Kong, both expatriate and local. But its significance goes beyond entertainment: 'I think it not only set standards for local artists but also had a huge influence on the quality of what the Urban Council promoted throughout the rest of the year,' says Keith Statham.

Like Michelle Garnaut, Lindsey McAlister came to Hong Kong as a backpacking traveller. 'I was working for the Arts Council in England and came to a point where I really wanted to do something different,' she says, 'so I decided to travel for a year with my then partner.' It was 1986, and their stop after China was Hong Kong. 'After being in Hong Kong for about two hours I knew that I was going to be here for the rest of my life. I had a tremendously strong feeling about Hong Kong, and everything I do is based on my gut reaction. It has been such a *true* reaction because everything I wanted to do has happened.'

With no plan in mind, nor any useful skills, she fell back upon teaching English 'for $23 an hour in some dump in Yau Ma Tei'. She also managed to find some freelance work such as choreographing fashion shows, and after a year 'we had a flat and my partner started a photography company'. From the very beginning, it was clear to her that there was

> a huge potential for the arts. Young people were involved in all sorts of artistic activities—dance classes, drama classes, lots of visual art—but the problem was it was all very prescriptive. I watched an art class in action once, where children were being taught to draw a chicken. Everybody would draw a circle, then the teacher would draw a smaller circle for the head, and the children would follow suit, then everybody would draw the beak in exactly the same way, and so on.
>
> Although parents were interested in their children being involved in the arts, there was always a competitive edge. Expectations revolved around coming first in class, or being the best, or winning a prize, or getting a certificate.

All this is contrary to Lindsey McAlister's beliefs: 'I'm passionate about community arts, the right of children to have artistic experience in their lives, and for the child not to be judged. Participating and giving a response is the most important thing. I tell the kids: you can't be wrong in the arts; you can only be right. The realization of this is highly positive and great for their self-confidence.'

She took her credo to an English-medium school in Quarry Bay, where she was artist-in-residence for a year, and to various arts consultancy projects that ensued. First there was a dance company called Scrambled Legs, with the accent on creative movement; next she founded a youth theatre company. But she was frustrated because her efforts touched so few: 'I wanted to do community arts projects but because I didn't have Cantonese it was very difficult.' To anyone who would listen, however, she continually proclaimed her idea of inaugurating a youth arts festival for Hong Kong:

> I kept saying to people that what Hong Kong needed was a forum for the young to create work and share it on a larger scale. And people went, 'Yeah, yeah'.

Then I got pregnant. My son Sam, who's nine, and the Youth Arts Festival are exactly the same age. When Sam was born, I suddenly realized, 'Actually, *I'm* the person who should be making the Youth Arts Festival happen!' And I had to do it even if it meant taking a few risks. So I persuaded my partner to accompany me to the bank, and we took out a huge overdraft. You could say that in the first year, the Youth Arts Festival was sponsored by me and my partner!

At the eleventh hour we got a phone call, as I knew we would, from somebody I'd been pestering and pestering. A group of businessmen, who had formed 'Business for Art', obviously thought there was a germ of something exciting about the Youth Arts Festival. They knew that I was underwriting it, and they also knew I didn't have any money. So at the last minute they came in with the necessary sponsorship.

The festival was a great success in so far as we actually managed to get something off the ground. It was an eight-day event and about twenty predominantly English-language medium schools were involved. We had workshops, an outdoor event in Southorn Playground, and fabulous publicity. Obviously people were quite captivated by the idea. That was year one, 1993.

The minute it finished, I went back to Business for Art and said, 'Right, I want to do it again.' And this time they not only agreed but they also offered to pay me. During the following year I saw lots of other sponsors and we did get bits of money from all over the place. And I tried to motivate more schools to participate. Year two went very well.

Year three was interesting in that there was a big turnaround. All of a sudden the Chinese schools got it. It was as if they had wanted to wait and see what it was all about. The head teachers hadn't been sure about this mad white woman who'd come round being really loud and pushy and over the top! Now we had 200 schools wanting to sign up.

Every year, she and her team initiate a range of projects, be it dance, drama, music, or art, in which all those who audition are found a part. As she explains, 'We don't want kids to feel rejected'. They also create a large exhibition project and a performing arts

project. One year they took the musical *Grease* and, by 'chopping it down, changing it about, making it bilingual', transformed it into something more relevant to Hong Kong children. Lindsey McAlister is justly proud of what the Youth Arts Festival offers them:

> We are in our ninth year, and we have 800,000 kids involved in our programme, which is now in two parts: the month-long festival in November and, because there is so much interest, so much demand, we've had to create a year-round line-up of events as well. . . . Compared with our shoestring budget in the early days, we now need eight to ten million dollars a year to function. We get it: we don't have any government support; it's all corporate sponsorship. Part of my passion is getting money out of these people. I'm a very boring person actually as I'm totally consumed by what I do. But I've got the best job in the world.

◇◇◇

Apart from Japan, Hong Kong is by far the best place in Asia to hear live music. And the musical fare has afforded ever greater variety in recent years, thanks to performers who now include Hong Kong on their tour circuit. Jazz composer and pianist Allen Youngblood even stayed on. As music director of the Foreign Correspondents' Club and a chain of European restaurants in Hong Kong, he and his group have regular gigs around town. And what with playing at other venues, teaching, and studio work, besides organizing a jazz festival in the Philippines, he is, he says, always thinking about going back to the US but 'just can't seem to get away!'

Allen Youngblood began studying classical music at the age of five, but discovered his path when he was in tenth grade:

> We generally had mid-term exams. I used to study with the radio on. One night it was so late that my station went off the air. Fiddling with the dial I came upon a jazz programme. It was broadcasting the music of John Coltrane. I can't say I fully understood what he was playing but I liked it, I liked the feel of it.
>
> This was in the 1960s, and a lot of stuff was going on then. There was still the Cold War, there were the Vietnam War, the civil rights movement, riots in the streets! Growing up then, we were very aware of all that. The music of people like John Coltrane, Miles Davis, and others fit in perfectly with what was happening at the time. It was not just protesting against war but also reflecting upheavals in society.

That late-night epiphany led to active musical experimentation on the piano and trumpet, Youngblood's preferred instruments. After university in Springfield, Ohio, he even joined a group and toured. He also taught in a school in St Croix in the Virgin Islands. By the early 1980s he had settled in Seattle, simultaneously serving on an artist-in-residence programme in North Carolina:

> As an artist in residence, you're basically in a college during term, so that's nine months when you can schedule pretty much what you want, because you're not there to teach, you're there as a professional artist. You can do exchanges with other artists, you do workshops, you give talks, but one of the things you have to do is leave some lasting contribution in the community.
>
> John Coltrane happens to be born in a town, Hamlet, in North Carolina, and Dizzy Gillespie was born only seven miles away, right across the border in South Carolina. Hamlet was a town of about 5,000 people; the area was rural, with a lot of rednecks! It had all these statues of rebel soldiers, but I thought there was no reason why in John Coltrane's home town there shouldn't be a memorial to him. So I decided to hold a jazz festival there, and it was launched in 1988.

In Seattle he had a friend who booked artists for acts in Asian venues, like JJ's, a nightclub in the Grand Hyatt Hotel in Hong Kong:

> One day in 1992 he calls me up, 'We need a six-piece band to go to Hong Kong,' he said. Hong Kong? It meant nothing to me, just Bruce Lee and cheap stuff! But that was actually one time when I didn't have anything to do while waiting for the summer jazz festival circuit to start. So I accepted the gig. It was for three months with a three-month option at JJ's.

On first impression, Hong Kong was definitely not a city he would have wanted to linger in—'It was hot, and it wasn't cheap!'— and he soon had the same litany of complaints as other newcomers: 'the stink, air pollution, density of people in the streets, the spitting, and of course the rudeness and staring'. It took him time to adjust, but 'then I realized people weren't being rude to *me* (if you want to call it rudeness). It isn't a thing about you being black, it's just the way it is.'

Three months have turned into nine years, during which he has played in other places in Asia including Vietnam and Singapore, and been courted by the local recording and film industry: 'We were able to fit right into this town doing TV commercials, studio work, recording Canto-pop. There are a lot of jobs for musicians in Hong Kong; the doors just kept on opening.'

But there are those who think Canto-pop is syrupy teenage music, and Allen Youngblood is one of that number. And since he is not fond of such music, he is doing less and less studio work:

> These days I'm music director for several places and my duties there are to line up the music calendar, help promote special events, and play, of course. . . . I find the audiences pretty mixed. A lot of Hong Kong people have been abroad and come back with minds expanded. Canto-pop may be king here but people are finding room for other types of music.
>
> In the States I didn't really play in clubs. It was usually concert performances. I'd never played in a restaurant to which families come. That's a chance for young people to be exposed, first to seeing somebody play music for real, and secondly to jazz. Normally there's no reason for a young person to know

anything about jazz, let alone like it. But playing in a venue which kids can come to, I find them standing right up close, mesmerized by the drummer, or guitarist, or bass player, and tapping their little feet. You can tell they're having a good time, and that makes me feel good.

———⋙○✦○⋘———

One of the most conspicuous recent changes in central Hong Kong is the appearance of art galleries among the dingy old shops of Lan Kwai Fong and its nearby 'antiques street', Hollywood Road. Art Scene China is a relative newcomer, but the owner of this gallery, Sami Wafa, has already established a reputation among Chinese painters for promoting creative rather than commercial contemporary work. 'I have my own inner standard,' he says. 'In a way being less commercial is more interesting, although at the same time you don't make as much money.'

His idealism is overlaid with a sophistication born of an international upbringing: 'I'm part Palestinian, part Jew, part Kurd, part Turk, part Armenian, maybe even part Greek. Originally from Lebanon, I've lived in many countries. I went to high school in Washington DC and university in Boston.' The circumstances that brought him to Hong Kong were conventional enough, however—he was offered a job with a bank. Halfway through his four years working there, he 'became fascinated by Asian culture and considered learning Chinese. I started a Hong Kong University course in my spare time but, working for a bank, I often stayed late at the office and fell very far behind. So I gave up on the course and got a tutor.'

Even so, progress was frustratingly slow; in the end he quit his job and went up to Beijing. There, by a combination of chance and effort, he began meeting and promoting Chinese artists:

> Modern Chinese art has existed for only twenty years. I've read quotes by Chairman Mao about art being for the masses, art serving political purposes, and that kind of thing. Creative art had no place in society. But now that people are allowed to, they are anxious to express themselves. And this is exciting.
>
> The first Chinese artist I met was just by chance. It was on the last day of a show at the Zhongguo Meishu Guan, the National Gallery of Art, in 1998. Some artists were there to remove their paintings. The work of one of the exhibiting artists struck me as very interesting, and I asked if he was around. No, I was told, but he was expected soon. So I decided to wait for him.
>
> The artist, Du Xinjian, did turn up. He's from Shandong but had studied at the Central Academy of Fine Art in Beijing. His wife was apparently learning English, so later when I couldn't communicate in Mandarin, she was able to translate. We kept meeting to have tea from then on, and became friends.

Du Xinjian is a very philosophical person and at the same time very modest. I was lucky to meet him. I thought he deserved to be promoted; I also thought there would be many other good artists like him in China.

Artists tend to hang around in the same circles and I got to know more and more of them. Then I came up with the idea of an online gallery to display their work worldwide. My first website, www.aschina.com, was as comprehensive as I could make it. Not only did I incorporate the full portfolio of each artist—between ten and twenty paintings per artist—but I also included reviews and introductions by the artists themselves, explaining their work, which for me were particularly interesting.

I wouldn't put every artist that I met on the website, only those I thought were creative or expressive or special in some way. I gradually built up a repertoire of artists. The website drew a lot of interest, especially from Europe and America. And although I set out only to promote Chinese art, I thought I might as well try and sell some of it.

All the same, not everyone would buy a painting without seeing it in the flesh. Sami Wafa's next move was to open a gallery in Hong Kong:

For a city of seven million, Hong Kong has very few galleries compared to a Western city of similar size. Most of our customers are Westerners. Local Hong Kong people do come in, but generally it's the younger ones or art students who like this gallery. Some of the art students tell me, 'I want to be a painter, but my parents won't let me as painters don't make money.' The older Hong Kongers tend to like photo-realistic oil paintings, especially of pretty girls in *cheong sam*. Paintings like that sell very well in Hong Kong, but I refuse to deal with artists who basically paint the same work over and over again.

I'm taking a risk in this gallery by trying to show something more challenging. I don't know if that is always appreciated in Hong Kong but I hope as time goes on, with greater exposure to creative art, more and more people will come to like it.

When it comes to the quality of life, food for the soul is as necessary as food for the body. Most people are agreed that art and heritage as enshrined in a museum have a part to play in the realm of the spirit. Museums are centres of culture at the heart of a community; they stimulate creativity and intellect and educate our taste. Hong Kong is not a world city in the mode of London or New York, but that is not to say it does not try to express its consequence and cultural sophistication in such enduring symbols as a raft of museums, concert halls, and theatres (although it has yet to open an opera house, the *sine qua non*, it seems, of a metropolis).

To some observers, though, the city planners have not always evinced a coherent policy where museums are concerned. Anthony Hardy, a connoisseur and adviser to the Hong Kong Museum of Art, states:

> We have on the one hand outstanding collections of every form of Chinese art, assembled by members of the venerable Min Chiu Society and other individual collectors. On the other hand we have adequate but hardly outstanding museum buildings which generally lack the ability to buy or attract on loan the high quality Chinese art which one sees in museums in America, England, Japan, and France. This is partially due to the fact that they are either government-owned museums which have very small acquisition budgets, or museums attached to universities which do not benefit from a historical culture of private endowment. . . . There is also no attractive tax scheme to help bring in donations of art works or cash from the Hong Kong public.
>
> It is also, in my opinion, a problem of museum governance. Very few governments have the know-how, ability, or dedication to operate successful museums. The system of civil servants establishing policy and being responsible for the running of the main museums in Hong Kong seems to preclude the appointment of truly inspired, experienced museum directors of international standard. Just as the appointment of an internationally renowned architect such as Pei or Gehry or Foster to design a new museum will attract visitors to that museum from all over the world, so the governance of a museum through an inspired and

internationally acclaimed director will in time raise the quality of the museum's own collections, long-term loans, and special exhibitions. Such a director will make better and more effective use of the academic and professional skill of the museum's staff and of the Friends and supporters of the museum.

A combination of both of these is what makes a museum great. You see such examples in Europe and America but that status has long eluded us in Hong Kong.

As one of a clutch of expatriates in Hong Kong who cherish and collect various forms of Chinese art, Anthony Hardy has been an eminent figure on the local cultural scene for many years. He came to Hong Kong to join a shipping company, Wallem, in 1961. Wallem was founded by a Norwegian who had made his way to Shanghai in 1897. With those connections, it was perhaps inevitable that Hardy should have bought his first painting related to China trade because it depicted a harbour scene 'strewn with sailing ships of many nationalities, Hong Kong island, its Peak, and the expanding Victoria city spreading along its coastline'. He stumbled upon it in a shop window in New York some thirty years ago, walking past an antique store called the Incurable Collector. By the early 1980s,

> I was beginning to make moves into collecting archaic Chinese bronzes of the Shang dynasty and the Western Zhou, principally ritual vessels. . . . One's taste does, I suppose, change over a period of time but my interest in archaic Chinese bronzes has been disciplined and unwavering. I have maintained all along that the late Shang period, when the capital was at Anyang, represented the highest point of bronze design and casting skills.

This collection of bronzes may one day be seen in the Hong Kong Museum of Art, and in time other collectors could similarly make their treasures available on long-term loan for public show. There is also talk, Anthony Hardy writes, of 'a new museum being built on reclaimed land bordering on the scenic Hong Kong harbour as the next step towards reaching the sort of leading position in the display of top Chinese art which several of us *aficionados* are pushing for and trying to help achieve'.

9
Fish Climbing Up a Tree

From 1841 to the Second World War a great many expatriates to Hong Kong came tinged in the colours of the imperialist. This fact had profound repercussions on how they and the Chinese related to each other. Racial attitudes, in particular, were intensified by a sense of mastery on the one part and subjugation on the other, as they were throughout the British Empire.

At the beginning, mutual incomprehension and distrust kept the races apart. As far as the Europeans were concerned, the crafty Chinese lived in filthy conditions and had unspeakable habits. They saw slyness in every flicker of the slanted eyes, shuddered at every noisy clearing of the throat, and were repelled when spitting ensued, as it inevitably did. The Chinese even 'made urinals of places never intended as such', claimed a correspondent writing to the Sanitary Board in 1899. It didn't help that apart from Hong Kong's indigenous fishermen and farmers, who numbered a few thousand, the first stampede of immigrants from the Chinese Mainland was from the lower orders of society. Coolies and prostitutes jostled with small-time traders and artisans to service the needs of the new settlement, increasing the population by as much as ten times within two years.

For their part the Chinese found the Europeans unattractively hirsute and smelly, and suspected them of vile designs. During the bubonic plague of 1894, they went to great lengths to prevent their sick from being moved to hospital, for a rumour went round that the wicked foreigners were planning to ship the patients to England to be pulverized into medicine for the royal family. And if the foreigners were not vile, they were certainly overbearing and abusive. The Victorian traveller Isabella Bird noted that 'Foreigners have misused and do misuse the Chinese. You cannot be two minutes in a Hong Kong street without seeing Europeans striking coolies with their canes and umbrellas.' Lord Redesdale, diplomat and traveller who published his impressions of China in 1900, was more trenchant: 'The Europeans hate the Chinese, and the latter return the compliment with interest.'

Physical segregation by confining the natives in their own quarter was ever a contrivance of the British colonialist—it vastly reduced the risk of reciprocal contamination. Hong Kong had its own 'Chinatown', created when the colonial authorities moved native inhabitants out of the central district of Victoria to Tai Ping

Shan in the west in 1844. The possibility of corralling them in Kowloon was contemplated too. Writing to the Colonial Office after the peninsula was ceded in 1860, Governor Sir Hercules Robinson confessed that his 'constant thought has been . . . how best to prevent a large Chinese population establishing themselves at Kowloon, and . . . how best to keep them to themselves and preserve the European and American community from the injury and inconvenience of intermixture with them'.

Fear of the encroaching natives was expressed by a prescient correspondent to a local paper in 1877:

> The Chinese will eventually buy us up, lock, stock and barrel. At a handsome premium, it might not be so calamitous an arrangement after all. The wave of Chinese building operations seems to be slowly advancing nearer and nearer to the Clock Tower [in Pedder Street], and the latest site fixed upon for Chinese houses is the premises facing Queen's Road now occupied by Mr Armstrong, the Government Auctioneer. It may be regretted, on various grounds, that the peculiarly foreign quarter

should be thus encroached upon but it appears to be the inevitable tendency.

Discriminatory legislation was passed from time to time to keep the Chinese at arm's length. The European District Reservation Ordinance of 1888, for example, required all new buildings in the area between Wellington Street and Caine Road, the upper levels of the town, to be constructed in European style. This didn't exactly forbid the Chinese from living there; indeed in self-justification it claimed that the Chinese themselves, being 'insensible to the conditions inseparable from extreme density of population', probably preferred segregation. It was discriminatory nonetheless. In 1902, to ensure that 'people of clean habits' might be safe from mosquitoes and malaria, 20,000 acres of the Kowloon peninsula were similarly set aside for Europeans.

Herding the Chinese together was not enough. They had to be discouraged from being 'at large in the City of Victoria' after dark. This was achieved by a curfew requiring those who must venture out between the hours of eight o'clock at night and sunrise to obtain a night pass and carry a lantern. Offenders were arrested and locked up.

Keeping the riff-raff under control sometimes called for brutal means. Criminals who were not imprisoned or deported were publicly flogged. The gaol being often crowded, a whipping with the cat-o'-nine-tails was retribution both summary and economical. All this implied a sense of racial superiority which provoked an anonymous resident to write bitterly to the press in 1878:

> That we Chinese in this Colony are despised individually, collectively, and socially, and that we are ignored as a community (except in a few instances) there cannot be the least doubt. Individually we have imposed on us certain burdens peculiar to our nationality and we receive uncivility and indignity even at the hands of the police, to whom we contribute to pay largely for our protection. In European society we particularly have no status. To correspond socially with Europeans with whom we are daily brought into contact, to be admitted as favoured guests at their dinner table, to have the privilege of counting them as

personal friends, are things which no Chinese, however ambitious he may be in other respects, would ever aspire to obtain. As a political body we are unknown. We are unrepresented, and it would be easier to find a fish climbing up a tree, as our adage says, than to see a Chinese Justice of the Peace, or a Chinese member of the Legislative or Executive Council in Hongkong.

Governor John Pope Hennessy was appalled by such inequalities. He thought public floggings a disgrace and suspended them. Upon investigating the gaol, he uncovered yet more ignominy which he could only remove by dismissing its drunken warders and pardoning some of the prisoners. Soon he was suspected of wishing to abolish the night pass and lantern system, having apparently called it 'a monstrous piece of class legislation'. None of this endeared him to the foreign merchants who believed only that his pro-Chinese and over-liberal attitude was encouraging crime and damaging British interests.

In 1879 Hong Kong residents were alarmed by several sensational cases of barefaced robbery, burglary, and murder. These clearly presaged a crime wave which would be attributable entirely to the leniency of the Governor—so the foreign community thought. The merchants, led by Jardines taipan William Keswick, decided to take matters into their own hands and hold a meeting to discuss 'public security'. What happened that day was the first significant racial confrontation in Hong Kong.

As advertised, the meeting was held at the City Hall. When the Europeans turned up at the appointed hour, they found the place packed with Chinese. One of them was Ng Choy, who had recently been admitted to the Bar and was to be appointed to the Legislative Council by Hennessy in 1880, the first Chinese to be so honoured.

The fact that there were educated men and rich merchants among the Chinese was lost on the outnumbered Europeans in the slanging match that broke out. 'Damned Chinamen, turn them out!' they shouted, and 'Let us have the meeting elsewhere to prevent the Chinese coming.' Appropriately, the meeting was reconvened at a place dear to British hearts—the cricket ground. Forming themselves into a tight circle there, the foreign merchants continued their discussion, ignoring Ng Choy when he suggested summoning an interpreter so that the other Chinese would understand what was being said. Thus snubbed, Ng Choy led his group off the pitch, leaving the meeting to pass its several resolutions, one of which asserted, 'what is needed is firm and unfettered administration. Flogging in public is the only means of deterrent. It should be reinstated.' In the event floggiing was not reinstated, although the night pass and lantern rule remained in force.

———◦◦◇◦◦———

The writer James Pope-Hennessy described the administration of his grandfather as forming 'a watershed in the history of Hong Kong'. Sir John Pope Hennessy, he said, was the first Governor to treat the 'native races' as 'human beings with rights equal to those of the Europeans'.

Ironically, the concept of human rights was alien to traditional China. Chinese culture emphasized virtues such as benevolence, loyalty, observance of ritual, and honour, all of which were consonant with a social order based on duty and obligation rather than individual rights. The idea that human rights could only be safeguarded by democratic government and the rule of law was equally exotic. In Hong Kong, however, the rule of law was embedded by 150 years of British administration, and today there is widespread agreement that 'The English legal system was the best thing that Britain brought to Hong Kong.' The quote is from

Marjorie Chui, the first Chinese woman on the Bench in Hong Kong. Appointed to the judiciary in 1976, she retired as a magistrate in 1993, and in a book about her career, which fell victim to what she regards as institutionalized discrimination against Chinese, she recounts the many occasions on which justice was administered erratically: 'There were wrongful and unfair prosecutions. There was detention without trial. People who should not be in prison were, while people who should be in prison were not. That such things happened could not remain a secret, but those in a position to correct the injustice merely closed ranks and mind.'

Lam Ping-chun was an eighteen-year-old illegal immigrant from mainland China. Caught only three days after obtaining work in a garment factory in 1988, and with an identity card belonging to another person, he was handcuffed and bundled off in a police van. He pleaded guilty before Marjorie Chui and begged to be repatriated to China.

Under guidelines laid down by the Court of Appeal, magistrates could pass a sentence of up to fifteen months in such cases. But this harsh sentence was prescriptive, not set in stone, as Chui knew, and its purpose was to deter others from sneaking across the border. Lam Ping-chun was not a criminal, only a pitiable youngster who had fled from poverty to the bright lights and plenty of Hong Kong. The burden of the charge was his unlawful presence in Hong Kong, so Chui passed a sentence of fifteen months but suspended it for three years. She said she couldn't in all good conscience send him to prison.

The Crown appealed against this sentence on the grounds that it was 'manifestly inadequate'. The Court of Appeal concurred, Chui's ruling was struck down, and the boy was clapped in gaol.

In another case two English deserters, also boys of eighteen, were charged with robbery. Stationed in the Army in Hong Kong, they had taken French leave, hailed a taxi, and then proceeded to help themselves to the driver's money. One of them had pinned the driver to his seat from behind. When they leapt out of the taxi at a housing estate, the driver raised the alarm and the boys were quickly apprehended. The driver got his money back.

Brought before Marjorie Chui, the two soldiers pleaded guilty, but as neither probation nor a spell in a disciplinary centre was available, she fell back on two alternative forms of punishment— the imposition of a fine or a term of imprisonment, which in a robbery case could not be suspended. In her view a fine was inappropriate. That left imprisonment, a course she was as reluctant to take as she had been in Lam Ping-chun's case. The law, she reasoned, did not allow a minor, particularly a first offender, to be imprisoned unless there was no other method of dealing with him. In the end she bound the soldiers over to be of good behaviour and returned them to the Army. She considered this better than sending them to prison where they might come under the corrupting influence of criminals.

The Crown did not appeal against this sentence. Reflecting on the fifteen months being served by Lam Ping-chun, she said only one conclusion could be drawn: 'A double standard was applied by the Crown: one for Chinese and another for English.'

She was equally bitter about the patronage, in terms of perks and promotions, enjoyed by expatriate lawyers in government service. That is of course a charge one might level at all institutions operating under a colonial system, which tends to favour its own however inept they prove to be. One horrifying specimen of those who dispensed justice under this system in 1980s Hong Kong is described by the author Jan Morris who observed a magistrate— 'nationality immaterial'—at work:

> sitting as he does alone upon his bench, hearing cases involving simple Chinese in a language he does not understand, he has long since perfected his techniques of brief authority. He bullies defendants mercilessly—'Shut up, don't you open your mouth and blurt out.' He bludgeons witnesses—'I'll ask you the question ten times, 100 times, 1,000 times if necessary, until it sticks into your thick skull.' He testily proclaims his own importance—'This is a court of law, not a fish market, and I am presiding over this court. Do you understand that? Do you hear me? I am not speaking German or Greek to you.' And when at last he fines some miserable prostitute, or sends a bewildered

hawker off to the cells, he does so without a flicker of regret, without a hint of understanding, only a petulant exertion of his own supremacy.

⊂─○⟨◇⟩○⊃──

The English legal system may be colonialism's best import into Hong Kong, but some still see it as a Pandora's box: what is valuable may equally well turn out to be a curse. A number of irreconcilable factors are at play here. English remains predominantly the language of the law although its use in a court where most of the protagonists are Chinese is both incongruous and cumbersome. However, translation and codification of statutes and case law, not to mention training in the use of Chinese, have been painfully slow, and there is a sneaking suspicion that one may end up throwing the baby out with the bath-water, for a maladroit handling of the semantic issue will severely erode Hong Kong's credentials as a world-class financial and service centre. The British being excessively legalistic, their law is best interpreted, argued, and applied in English. Quite apart from the language's richness of vocabulary and versatility, specific meanings have adhered to words and phrases as a result of several centuries of judicial review and usage. On the other hand Chinese, while opulently expressive in certain ways, is frustratingly imprecise in other areas where superfine shades of distinction need to be drawn. Some lawyers go so far as to argue that the English language is almost indivisible from common law, so that any attempt to codify or translate it into Chinese would simply result in a pale and unworkable imitation of the original.

Despite the vast inducement in terms of employment, income, technology, and culture to learn English, the language is not as deeply rooted in Hong Kong as more than 150 years of British colonial rule would lead one to expect. It's not surprising, therefore, that the government legal department and the judiciary were stuffed with expatriates, the majority of them from Britain, Australia, and New Zealand. They remained two of the last government branches to be localized, although there was an unseemly rush to do so in the countdown to 1997. The mass exodus of expatriate government lawyers hired on contract terms shook morale but did not make a significant difference to the composition of the upper echelons. In the year that Hong Kong reverted to Chinese sovereignty, more than half of the judges were still expatriate. The likes of Marjorie Chui would argue that this smacked of favouritism. 'Although more than 90 per cent of the population in the colony was Chinese,' she writes, 'English was the language of the law throughout the period of colonial rule. This was because the Bench was overwhelmingly expatriate.' But how could a legal system based on English common law be best practised if not in the language in which the original is couched? Hiring Chinese instead of expatriates and dropping English as the legal language are not the same thing. Actually, highly qualified local lawyers sporting British public school accents and Jermyn Street ties may be found in abundance in Hong Kong, and many of them function much better in English than Chinese.

If nothing else, the slow progress to legal bilingualism has kept open the rich seam of opportunities for English-speaking expatriate lawyers which may still be mined for years to come. And given the connections between English common law and the legal system of the United States, Hong Kong harbours many American attorneys, as the presence of several international law firms testifies.

—◇—

Most expatriate judges would have lived on the Peak. Residence in the clouds has always implied social and economic pre-eminence, but there was a time when the scheme of social calibrations was more precise, a man's exact position in society being 'not infrequently determined by the altitude of his house'. Rising over a thousand feet above the heat and humidity of the town, the Peak with its lower temperatures and glorious views endowed it with all the charms of a hill-station.

Just as the European District Reservation banished upstart Chinese merchants to the fringes of Victoria, so did a 1904 ordinance keep the cool and sparsely inhabited Peak safe for expatriates.

Delineating a reservation above the 788-foot contour and west of
an imaginary north-south line drawn on the map of Hong Kong
island, this ordinance made it unlawful 'for any owner, lessee, tenant
or occupier of any land or building within the Peak District to let
such land or building or any part thereof for the purpose of residence
by any but non-Chinese, or to permit any but non-Chinese to reside
on or in such land or building'. These restrictions did not apply to
native servants living in their employers' houses, of course.

Mount Cameron, Mount Gough, and Mount Kellet all fell
within the reservation's sweep. There bungalows and villas had
mushroomed since a funicular railway was completed in 1888, many
of them endowed with names that summoned up much-loved homes
or places left behind: The Neuk, for instance, or Ardsheal, or
Ligoniel. A whiff of homesickness also hung about the wicket gates
that opened on to rustic porches, the plots of grass passing for lawns,
and the pale silk curtains that billowed at the windows. The very
architectural mode of the grander houses could transport one, with
little imagination, to temperate climes. Mountain Lodge (pictured),

all turrets and pepper-pot chimneys, which served as the Governor's
summer residence until it was demolished in 1945, resembled a
castle in the baronial style, straight from some hilltop of Scotland
or Wales. This contrived world of Britishness, in tone much like an
affluent suburb undisturbed by the traffic and clamour of the town,
prevailed until the outbreak of the Second World War. Living there

as a child between 1912 and 1921, Michael Wright was carried up to school in a sedan chair and freewheeled down to his house at Coombe Road on his scooter, sometimes alongside a boy who rode home on a donkey.

Ligoniel belonged to Francis Henry May, who as acting Governor pushed through the Peak District Reservation Ordinance in 1904. It could be said that he had a vested interest in the Peak remaining exclusive. To mollify local sensitivities a clause was incorporated whereby 'it shall be lawful for the Governor-General in Council to exempt any Chinese from this Ordinance'. The exemption was famously granted only once, to the Eurasian millionaire Ho Tung, who was to be the only person of Chinese blood to live in his own house on the Peak before World War II. When approval was bestowed in 1906, Ho Tung acquired not one but three houses—two for his large family and one for himself. Nonetheless, the family's high social standing, buttressed by wealth, remained precarious. In her autobiography, Ho Tung's daughter Jean described afternoon walks with her sister Grace and their English governess Miss Hecht, who would

> meet other governesses and, sitting at some shaded seat, they would knit and chat whilst we played with the other children at hopscotch or some other game. This was the highlight of a normal day except, on occasion and without any apparent reason, the others might suddenly refuse to play with us because we were Chinese, or they might tell us that we should not be living on the Peak. Racial discrimination had extended even to the children and children can be so cruel.

Equally, if the Ho Tung children had tried to attend the Peak School, a short walk away from their home, they would undoubtedly have been rebuffed. In a dispatch from Government House to the Secretary of State for the Colonies, Sir Henry May speculated that 'if Mr Ho Tung exercised his right [to send his children to the Peak School], many if not all the European children at the School would be withdrawn'.

Eurasians were tangible products of colonialism. In early Hong Kong their status was indeterminate at best. Neither fish nor fowl, they hovered between Caucasians for whom they symbolized shameful liaisons with native women, and the Chinese community which, holding strict ideas about kinship and lineage, scorned anyone who couldn't emblazon his father's name on an ancestral tablet. Han Suyin, the writer, articulated this undercurrent of censure when she said that the very word 'Eurasian' evoked in some minds a sensation of moral laxity. But being Eurasian, she argued, 'is not being born of East and of West. It is a state of mind. A state of mind created by false values, prejudice, ignorance, and the evils of colonialism.'

One of the most acerbic observers of pre-War Hong Kong snobbishness was the American writer Emily Hahn, whose books and pieces in the *New Yorker* have been intermittently in print since they were written in the 1940s. She too had a story or two to tell about Eurasians. It is in the crowded dining room of the Hong Kong Hotel that Lieutenant MacBean, who 'simply reeked of the military', first mentions the affair of Captain Osgood and Miss Barbara Bartholomew to her. Osgood is in MacBean's regiment, and Osgood is smitten with Miss Bartholomew. But as far as MacBean is concerned, marriage for his fellow officer is out of the question: 'My dear *girl*', he explains to Hahn, 'the woman's Eurasian!'

When Hahn points out that newspapers announced marriages between British soldiers and Chinese girls every day, MacBean retorts, 'Oh, *privates*! Osgood's a captain. It's simply not done. You see, an officer has a duty to his men. Particularly in wartime. If Osgood should do a thing like this, his men would cease to respect him, d'you see?' But being at war saves Captain Osgood, and instead of having to resign for conduct unbecoming an officer and a gentleman, he is absolved by his colonel, who is far more concerned about losing a good officer in an emergency than making an example of him.

In the early days Eurasians, being locally born, could claim to be Hong Kong's only true indigenes. Almost all the rest of the inhabitants were sojourners who had either flocked from nearby

Guangdong or come from overseas. They made for an overwhelmingly masculine society. For various supplies and provisioning services the foreigners tended to look to the Tanka boat people, original settlers who were generally despised by the Cantonese and who were less scrupulous about associating with non-Chinese. Tanka women made themselves available to assuage other needs too, thus bringing into existence a crop of Eurasian offspring.

Ho Tung's mother was not a Tanka, but it was as a result of her becoming the mistress of a European trader that a dynasty of successful Eurasians was founded. Cohabiting with a foreigner, she would have been known in the language of bureaucrats as a 'protected woman'. An official publication defined such a woman as one who 'resides in a house rented by her protector, who lives generally in another part of town . . . [and] lives with her protector not for love, but simply for a stipulated sum payable monthly, coupled with the understanding that the offspring of such a liaison are not recognized by the father beyond making such allowance or settlement for the children's maintenance and education as his means may afford'. He might do this by establishing a trust or settling property on her, so it's no wonder her conduct was described in common parlance as *kow see tow*, 'seeking for a master'. And like servants of the day, she would speak to her 'master' in pidgin, the once ubiquitous idiom of interracial communication on the China coast.

A large number of protected women clustered in decent obscurity in a twilight zone behind the business district, bang in the middle between 'Chinatown' on the west and the European settlement on the east. That this was not considered too terrible a fate is suggested in a report by John Smale, the Chief Justice, in 1880: 'No one can walk through some of the bye-streets in this Colony without seeing well dressed Chinese girls in great numbers whose occupations are self proclaimed or pass those streets, or go into the schools in this Colony, without counting beautiful children by the hundred whose Eurasian origin is self-declared.'

However, Smale's concern with Eurasians went somewhat deeper than their numerousness. If the government looked into the

condition of these people, he urged, it would find that 'in the great
majority of cases the women have sunk into misery, [while] of the
children, the girls that have survived have been sold to the profession
of their mothers, and that if boys, they have been lost sight of or
have been sunk into the condition of the mean whites of the late
slave-holding states of America'.

There was worse; for so lucrative did pimping prove that girls
were kidnapped and sold to brothels or to foreigners as kept women.
Here was moral laxity indeed! And the illegitimate issue of all this
promiscuity, with their distinctive Eurasian features, must have
lived with the painful awareness of many a curled lip, averted look,
or wounding remark. Needless to say, many of them chose to deny
their mixed pedigree and to melt into the larger Chinese population.
It would have been far worse a fate to stay a perennial outsider, cast
adrift in a social no-man's-land and forever ambivalent. Ho Tung,
later Sir Robert Ho Tung, adopted this course for himself, discarding
Western dress for the elegant ensemble of a Chinese gentleman,
and deploying his energies into patriotic causes such as the
reunification of China.

Eurasian families might have adopted a Chinese mode of
existence by force of circumstance, but as they grew richer they did
at least ensure a competent degree of bilingualism in the younger
generation. The family of the Reverend Guy Shea, for instance, saw
to it that he had a classical Chinese education as well as an English
one. Eurasians in the early days, he said, 'had a Chinese upbringing
. . . and when they married they married Chinese style . . . they
would have ancestral altars in their homes, and they could generally
read and write both Chinese and English'. Their linguistic edge
was a striking asset when it came to commerce, in which they
excelled, so that Eurasian families were quickly numbered among
the most prosperous in the colony.

But they didn't often marry Chinese, as Reverend Shea explains:

> The higher-class Chinese wouldn't think of marrying them
> because of their European blood. Then there was the same
> problem, of course, in reverse with the Europeans, who wouldn't
> marry Eurasians either because of the Chinese blood. . . . So the

end result was that the Eurasians married within their own community. And that's why the old Eurasians of Hong Kong are interrelated—all tangled up together . . .

Ho Tung had married the daughter of a Jardines agent, Hector Coll Maclean, and Maclean's Eurasian mistress, and he was to arouse anxieties over the blurring of racial distinctions more than once. An invisible *cordon sanitaire* around the Peak, as we saw, once kept the encroaching natives from defiling the exalted colonialists. How this cordon was gradually breached, in what we might call the 'battle for the Peak', serves rather well as a metaphor for race relations in Hong Kong.

Ho Tung had won the first round by gaining permission to live on the Peak, but he was defeated in the second. The latter episode was trivial enough, but it was pursued all the way to Whitehall with a thoroughness which demonstrates how keenly racial segregation was defended. A house on the Peak, The Eyrie, was the battleground; its owner Sir Francis Piggott, Ho Tung, and the Governor Sir Frederick Lugard were the protagonists. What happened was this: in 1907, Sir Francis, the notoriously troublesome Chief Justice, having agreed to rent his house to Ho Tung while he went on leave, applied to the Governor for exemption from the Peak Reservation Ordinance on the grounds that his would-be tenant was not strictly Chinese. His application was denied. It did not help his cause that his house overlooked Mountain Lodge, the gubernatorial summer residence. Instead of letting the matter drop, however, Sir Francis made an enormous fuss, even going so far as to take his grievance to the Secretary of State for the Colonies, Lord Crewe.

Justifying his decision to the Secretary of State, Sir Frederick refers to the proposed tenant as 'an illegitimate half-caste whose wives and concubines numbered four'. This was not quite accurate. Ho Tung had taken a concubine when his wife proved barren. Later he married a third time, to his first wife's cousin, who bore him ten children. This multiplicity of wives and offspring was, it seems, the stumbling block, and Sir Francis Piggott knew it:

> the true reason, or at least the most important reason, why the exemption had been refused was that he [Ho Tung] was a 'real Chinaman' in his habits, had four wives, many children and lived in Chinese fashion, and that it was impossible that such a family could be allowed to occupy a house so close to Mountain Lodge.

The Eyrie remained unlet, but Chinese resentment continued to simmer until erupting again in 1917. Sir Francis Piggott had been well aware that the Peak Reservation Ordinance's discretionary exemption was nothing if not ambiguous. He correctly surmised that the government had originally 'intended to make the Peak absolutely exclusive, but . . . in order to appease the hostility of the Chinese to it, [the ordinance] had been whittled down to its present form, the original intention of excluding Chinese from the Peak absolutely abandoned.' He didn't notice, however, that careless drafting had left a loophole. While the ordinance precluded Chinese from leasing or building or living on the Peak, it did not specifically ban them from buying property there. And this was precisely what the increasingly more prosperous Chinese were able to do in the intervening years, driving up rents to such levels that the Europeans feared they were being elbowed out. Chinese couldn't live on the Peak because of the ordinance, but nor could many Europeans, it seemed, because they weren't rich enough. In an attempt to shut the stable door after the horse had bolted, the government then tried to bring a bill before the Legislative Council to amend the ordinance and close the loophole.

Here was an issue crying out for a war of words in the newspapers! Man-kam Lo, a bright lawyer educated in England (who was to marry Sir Robert Ho Tung's daughter Victoria the following year), launched the first salvo with characteristic eloquence. Such a bill, he protested in the columns of the *Hongkong Daily Press*, was wrong in principle and contrary to all ideas of fairness and justice. The government had advanced two arguments: one, that the bill was purely to amend a

slip in the existing ordinance; and two, that since the Chinese as a whole did not object to the original ordinance, they could not properly object to a reasonable amendment of it. Lo begged to disagree. The Chinese were indeed opposed to the ordinance, just as those who had heard about the bill were opposed to the bill. 'Moreover, it seems to me that the question is not so much whether or not the Chinese did oppose the Ordinance; it is a question of right or wrong; and I submit, with due humility, that two wrongs cannot make one right.'

Lo's letter provoked a riposte the next day. A correspondent who signed himself 'S. L.' wrote thus to the editor:

I must crave a little more of your valuable space in which to attempt to set further a few reasons why Asiatics should not be allowed to reside in, or own houses on, May Road and upwards . . . does Mr Lo recognize who made Hongkong the lovely isle that it is? Who made it a safe refuge for thousands of our neighbours, wealthy and poor; amongst them some who would not dare to return to their own country? Who allowed thousands of Chinese to pour into the island when Southern China was in rebellion and oust the Portuguese and unwealthy Britishers from their houses? Who allowed the Chinese to purchase many houses in Hongkong at this time (the title deeds of which are safe for all time) and raise rents to meet their ideas of interest on invested capital?

Can Mr Lo picture Hongkong under Chinese rule? Can he see the hillsides completely denuded of trees and grass, cut down and uprooted for fuel? Can he picture the filthy streets and lack of sanitation which would obtain? Would the Chinese then consider their invested wealth as safe as it is at present? Surely, then, those who have made Hongkong what it is should be allowed to make one little ordinance for their own comfort . . .

One would, perhaps, not have such a rooted objection to living amongst Asiatics if they observed more of the ordinary decencies of life, as understood by Europeans, and also followed some simple rules of hygiene. At almost any hour of the afternoon, along one of the prettiest middle-level roads one sees filthy garbage pails without lids standing outside imposing gateways, and where can one walk without the Chinese clearing their throats and expectorating all over the paths and roads? We do not want our children to grow up in this atmosphere.

———◇———

Man-kam Lo did not carry the day and a more unambiguously worded Peak District (Residence) bill was passed unopposed by Chinese members of the Legislative Council in 1918. The affront to Chinese pride was not forgotten, however, and was specifically referred to by Sir Man-kam Lo (as he had then become) when the ordinance was repealed twenty-eight years later, but at least Hong Kong was spared the fate of some colonies where ethnic conflicts were resolved with violence. The territory experienced sporadic anti-British and anti-government demonstrations, yes, but these were squabbles rather than wars when compared to the experience of India, say, or Kenya.

If the road to equality has been less bumpy in Hong Kong than elsewhere, it may be because European condescension has been well matched by Chinese conviction of cultural superiority. 'It is not too much to say,' writes historian James Hayes about Hong Kong society in the post-War years, 'that each tended to look down on the other.' Clearly neither wished to be more closely acquainted. Realization that both sides wished to be separate and exclusive may help to restore the perspective a little.

Finding greater comfort interacting in one's own language and with one's own kind is natural. All the same, Han chauvinism can manifest itself in racial bigotry as obdurate as that of any imperialist. Take the soubriquet 'gweilo' or 'fan gweilo', with its sense of demonic man, derived from the fact that the first Westerners in China were seen by most Chinese as fiendish invaders and enemies. While used nowadays generally as a convenient way of denoting somebody as white rather than, say, English, Canadian, or German, it is still occasionally a term of abuse and mockery. Equally, a mingling of the races through miscegenation can still collide with age-old Chinese prejudices. For years the common Chinese term for the offspring of interracial unions—*zazhong*, meaning hybrid or crossbreed—was also derogatory, carrying the same connotations as 'bastard' or 'son of a bitch'. Eurasians were said by Chinese to be 'sons of the foreign devil' and to have sprung from 'tainted families'. The one saving grace was to have been born of Chinese fathers and to have adopted 'proper Chinese family names which can be traced two or three thousand years back'. As a Chinese correspondent to the *Hongkong Daily Press* in 1902 explained, there were

> two kinds of Eurasians, one who are born of Chinese fathers and European or Eurasian mothers and the other who are born of European fathers and Chinese or Eurasian mothers. For better reference I will classify the former as A and the latter as B. According to Chinese social laws and customs Eurasians of Class A, if their fathers had their names entered in the ancestral register, have as much right to be called Chinese as pure-born Chinese themselves; but those of Class B are no more Chinese than they are Europeans.

There would be no stigma, it seems, if you denied one of your parents. Sir Robert Ho Tung certainly went to great lengths to avoid it, inventing a genealogy for himself by way of an impressive inscription on the headstone of a fictitious grave. Etched on it were resounding words which translate as: 'Conferred by imperial mandate, senior mandarin, deceased father Sze-man, noble gentleman of the house of Ho'. Transforming his father Charles Henry Maurice Bosman into Ho Sze-man was one way of placating the likes of the correspondent quoted above.

———◦◦◇◦◦———

The War went a long way towards discrediting racism and snobbery in Hong Kong. For how could the belief in white supremacy be upheld after the humiliating loss of the colony to the Japanese? And as British colonies gained independence one after the other, the imperial ethos gradually withered away. Of course, remaining a colony until 1997, Hong Kong was a significant exception to the imperial retreat. This fact alone enabled British expatriates to continue holding sway in government and commerce for several decades after the War, so that even in the sunset of Empire there remained in the territory a 'very "colonial" society', with 'a small expatriate élite holding itself apart from, and considering itself superior to, the mass of the native population'. That was certainly the conclusion drawn by James Hayes who, on arrival in Hong Kong as a cadet in the Overseas Civil Service in 1956, tuned his acute historian's antennae to his social surroundings. The expatriate community, he wrote,

> revolved around the Governor, his senior civil servants (who were British almost to a man), the taipans, the consular corps and the senior officers of the Armed Services which were then present in considerable numbers on account of the still recent change of government in China (1949) and the uneasy peace following the end of the Korean war in 1953. These various parties were continuously entertaining each other, and were consequently well acquainted. This charmed circle included the rich Chinese. . . . At this exalted level *who* was Chinese, Indian, Portuguese, Eurasian did not matter any more. Success created a genial social milieu in which genuine friendships existed within the cosmopolitan group possessing wealth and power.

All the same, those friendships rarely extended to intermarriage, which was 'not welcomed by either side, and was seldom found in executive and professional business circles'. According to Michael Wright, 'Chinese families by and large disapproved of mixed marriages, looking upon them with suspicion, same way as the Europeans.' He remembers the difficulties faced by H. K. Kwan, whose marriage to an Englishwoman he had met in the Astoria Dance Hall in London's Charing Cross Road produced Nancy Kwan, the movie actress who memorably played the tart with the heart in the film *The World of Suzie Wong*. In fact the stereotype of the Wan Chai bar girl on the lookout for a good catch and snaring some stupid besotted rich foreigner was quite tenacious, pandering as it did to existing prejudice and snobbery. No well brought-up girl, it was felt, would marry outside her caste or race. Those who did must therefore be suspected of low origins and loose morals. Prattling tongues had a condescending name for those obliging Chinese girls who doubled as bedmates and informal language teachers: they called them 'sleeping dictionaries'.

So it was a brave foreigner who married a Chinese or Eurasian girl in the 1950s. Not only did he risk the contempt of his peers, but it was commonly believed that such a marriage 'could somehow reduce both [his] standing and [his] career prospects'. Vandeleur Grayburn had said as much to his staff when he was Chief Manager of the Hongkong and Shanghai Bank in the 1930s. They were informed that he looked 'with disfavour on most marriages to non-British women', while 'Foreign, native, half-caste are definitely taboo'. James Hayes detected the same tinge of censure when he first arrived in Hong Kong. Not that there were any rules on the subject—certainly no such code existed in the Civil Service—but 'in the banks and the big European "hongs", the "rules" were probably more of a reality, and the consequences more severe. . . . In this regard, the views of the senior men's wives were thought to be a powerful factor.'

Nearly twenty years later he found himself facing just this kind of disapproval:

> I recall being strongly advised by a European lady against my second marriage to a Chinese female colleague in the Administrative Service. Perhaps because her family had been Hong Kong residents since the later nineteenth century, and despite having spent a lifetime teaching Chinese girls in a prestigious secondary college, she spoke of them in very disparaging terms, in a way that blended fear, dislike, and scorn in almost equal proportions. I was a close friend, otherwise I do not think she would have allowed herself these comments; but they were very revealing.

Sensitivities over race die hard, not least among the victims. Peter A. Hall, a Eurasian himself, was commissioned by Hong Kong University Press to write a book on Eurasian families. In 1990, just before he left Hong Kong on retirement, he heard from his publisher that the manuscript, provisionally entitled *In the Web*, required revisions 'so as not to upset certain well-known Eurasian families in Hong Kong'. These he refused to make, but 'in order to cover myself, I spoke to a few well-known Eurasian friends of mine who might have been concerned about some aspects of my book'. *In the Web* had traced some of the most prominent Eurasian families back to their original European ancestors. 'This was probably the touchiest of all the matters I had to deal with,' writes Peter Hall. 'Many of the persons I spoke to were now either Chinese or Caucasian, certainly not Eurasian.' One may safely assume that in almost all cases the European men never actually married the Chinese women by whom they had children, and the reverberations of illegitimacy were still felt generations later. Sir Robert Ho Tung would have understood this touchiness. Greatly to Peter Hall's credit, when Hong Kong University Press decided to relinquish the project, he published *In the Web* himself.

Born into one of the Eurasian families mentioned in that book, the Reverend Guy Shea once expressed the misery of half-castes through poetic imagery. Written in Chinese while he was up at Oxford in 1955, his poem (reproduced here in English translation) touchingly evokes the ambivalence of the mouse-like animal with membranous wings:

> The bat is like a rat and a bird
> During the day it lives among the ancient temple
> By night it enters the forest.
> Who knows the bitterness of the bat
> Within the body of a mouse,
> It has the heart of a bird?

Nowadays, judging by quite visible evidence around Hong Kong, mixed marriages and the fruits thereof are more common than ever. By their locutions, the new generations of Eurasians reveal themselves as not just home-grown but to have come from the United States, Canada, Britain, or the Antipodes. Migrating to Hong Kong to work, they may also retrieve something of their roots. For Veronica Needa, a home-grown Eurasian, this became a compelling quest: 'Tracking our personal journeys, mapping out our place, claiming our space in the world, facing who we are, becomes an urgent call. We cast our nets into the ocean of our ancestry and haul in old skeletons and hidden bounty.'

How many Eurasians, though, still experience the kind of conflict Guy Shea wrote about? Mixed doesn't have to mean mixed-up any more. However exotic the concoction of their genes, for Eurasians today 'facing who they are' has less to do with race than with cultural identity. Since Hong Kong's educated class inhabits a sort of hybrid cultural zone, more Westernized than strictly Chinese, few Eurasians take the Ho Tung route, preferring instead to go with the current rather than against it. As long as intermarriage between a foreign man and an Asian woman, not vice versa, remains the more popular pairing, children will by and large be brought up to the Western way of life and become more assured in that culture. Above all they will grow up with their fathers' language as their primary tongue, not their mothers' (although it's not unknown for a third language—English—to be adopted by some Eurasian children raised in Hong Kong, for instance in a family where the mother is, say, Japanese, and the father Dutch). And the mother of a Eurasian child will tacitly acquiesce in all this, will not insist on imposing her own customs and persuasions, not just because she is mindful of the Chinese saying 'A woman follows her husband no matter what his lot', but also because it is easier and seems more natural to someone who has probably adopted elements of her husband's culture already.

Veronica Needa thinks that would be a great pity. She feels not only that there were deeper issues at play in her own upbringing, but also that they needed to be fathomed and articulated. A second-generation Eurasian, she was born in Hong Kong in 1956 to parents who were themselves Eurasians. Although she was speaking Cantonese fluently by the age of five,

> my mother wanted me to grow up like a little English girl, partly because for her being caught in two worlds was problematic and she didn't want to give that predicament to me. So she put me into the English Schools Foundation, first Glenealy Junior and then Island School.
>
> That was a tremendous boon, because I learnt to speak good English, but the bane is that at a subconscious level I absorbed *her* pain and my father's pain. They never spoke about their past. But, you know, kids don't miss a thing. Maybe I made it bigger than it was, but I had a sense of their not being acceptable.

Whether the exclusion was real or only perceived, Veronica Needa didn't find it easy being Eurasian in Hong Kong. In an article she wrote for the *South China Morning Post* she recalls that as a child she used to have

> such a pang in my heart when some of my friends would say, with unequivocal clarity, that they were 'Chinese' and not 'British' or 'Hong Kong' when we talked about our birthplace. . . .
>
> Then, I did not have such a clear sense of belonging or allegiance, and I was envious. I could not say I was Chinese, neither could I say I was English. I was Hong Kong British, I

suppose—and I was unsure what that meant to me. I did go away to England eventually, and have found my feet there. It took me a while though, because my Chineseness became even less visible there. The way the genes got jiggled between my Eurasian mother and father, I came out looking more occidental than oriental. You cannot see the Chineseness very clearly in my face. But it's there, inside, somewhere. And I struggled with a sense of being lost for a long time.

England meant university and acting school at the Bristol Old Vic. Somehow, though, she felt compelled to 'find my own way back into my Chineseness'. It took a long time, but she did find it—through studying Peking opera (in Wales of all places) and through her involvement in Yellow Earth Theatre, a company she co-founded with other British-East Asian thespians and producers in London. They all shared the idea, she explained, of trying to discover a way of amalgamating and integrating their Eastern and Western heritages. In 1998 she presented a one-woman play, *Face*, at a festival in Hong Kong. It has since been performed again in both English and Cantonese. Through a series of vignettes about her parents, her childhood, and other Eurasians in Hong Kong, the play charts her recovery of the East–West dichotomy which is her heritage, and her unfolding sense of self. 'Every bit of angst I had, every bit of confusion', she said, has fed her creativity. But retrieving her past is only part of it. It is time, she suggests in her newspaper piece, 'to put some things on record, before the stories fade away, and before the history books are entirely rewritten. The stories of our fascinating, multi-generational, mixed-race, mixed cultural experience are a fabulous legacy for Hong Kong to claim and own.'

10
Trailing Spouses and Single Women

The very first expatriate woman in Hong Kong was probably the American missionary Henrietta Shuck. Since then they have come in all kinds. If they are single, they tend to be professional women, a number of them engaged in the 'care industry' as doctors, teachers, or missionaries. But the majority are wives, ordinary women who behave almost exactly as they would in Edinburgh, Wisconsin, or Brisbane. They look after the home and shop at the supermarket—or send their amah to do so. Every now and then they may give a dinner party or go to one. If they are mothers, they fuss about school runs, or swimming lessons, or little Sophie's nasty cough, just as they do at home. In their spare time they meet friends for lunch, play tennis or bridge, help out at school bazaars, or do voluntary work for a local charity. The foreign posting is generally something that happens to their husbands, and only by extension to them. They are sometimes called, rather unflatteringly, 'trailing spouses'. This tag is assumed to fit all, even those who have their own careers. Nicci Button, who had been a studio manager for BBC Radio, found Hong Kong 'very chauvinist. . . . At dinner parties I was never asked what I did for a living, but what my husband did. It was assumed that a wife did not work.'

On the surface, Hong Kong is very far from the 'hardship posting' of Henrietta Shuck's day. She, poor lady, died of complications after childbirth in November 1844, a casualty of early Hong Kong's primitive medical facilities. Today's expatriate women not only enjoy all the essentials of life, they are able to indulge in its luxuries too. Some of them may even allow their heads to be a tiny bit turned by the higher disposable income, by suddenly becoming a big fish in a small pond, and having servants to order around for the first time in their lives. Social life is

transformed by the existence of domestic help. Expatriate dinner parties, for one thing, would be less polished affairs without Filipino or Thai amahs to cook and serve. Of course, many a newcomer begins by feeling conscience-stricken about having servants and tries to treat her amah as a friend or one of the family, despite such advice from old Hong Kong hands as: 'Make sure you draw the line early; remember you are the employer; have her call you ma'am.' But not only is the newcomer horrified to be addressed as 'ma'am', she is also careful to refer to her employee by the less feudal term 'helper'. Karen Pittar, who suffered agonies of indecision wondering whether she should offer her maid a cup of tea when she was making one for herself, found her footing 'six months down the track. . . . I now keep things on more of an employer/employee basis when it comes to important issues and my helper is more relaxed about the smaller things. She is happy to call me Karen and even seems pleased when I sometimes make tea for the two of us.'

Such initial misgivings aside, most expatriate women come to appreciate the freedom gained when housework can be delegated to others, whether it is one part-time maid to clean and iron or a whole bevy of live-in staff as at Government House. Lavender Patten says: 'It's surprising how quickly you can get used to having all your meals produced for you (particularly when they are delicious) and all those tedious domestic chores done for you.' Many women would echo those sentiments.

However, if asked how they felt about living in Hong Kong not all of them would honestly and categorically tell you they loved it. Their homemaking instinct baulks at living in company-rented flats, and the sheer unfamiliarity of their surroundings, not to mention the difficulties of communication, can turn the simplest domestic chore into an obstacle course. One expatriate woman, while conceding that 'there are always annoyances in everyday life,' says what irritated her were the little things: 'you phone up for someone to come and mend your air-conditioner, you give your name, then you're asked, "how you spell?" And as for the rude taxi drivers!' Another oft-heard complaint is that you can never find *everything* you need for a dinner party at one supermarket, which is good news for the delicatessens and speciality stores that put a premium on rocket lettuce or fresh pappardelle or whatever happens to be in vogue at any given moment.

Joan Barst, a New Yorker, took a long time to get settled in 1995 after a stint in Tokyo. Having previously made occasional visits to Hong Kong from Japan, she thought that she was 'coming here with a concept of what it would be like'. She was to find her expectations overthrown:

> It was an isolating experience, strangely enough. . . . When I come to a new place I like to explore the city and get my land legs, and figure out how I'm going to approach it. It took me some time. I started first by joining the American Women's Association [AWA] and the YWCA; that seemed like the right answer at the time. I got to meet some people although I still felt outside it all.
>
> I went to a coffee morning at the AWA. They had hostesses, women who looked after new people. Then I went on a trip and met a girl with whom I became very friendly, and she told me about the Friends of the Chinese University Art Gallery. In their newsletter they used to publish all the activities going on including those in other organizations, so I got involved.
>
> In Tokyo almost every foreigner takes language classes. In fact it's bad form not to . . . there's peer pressure, and I had friends—husbands and wives—who had private lessons together before the husbands went to work in the mornings. They even took

competency exams in Japanese. A lot of people became skilled in the language (which I might add is easier than Cantonese). There's a lot of interaction within the community. You had to speak a bit of Japanese. I learnt some just through shopping.

In Hong Kong very few expatriates feel a compulsion to study Cantonese. I tried. I found that for my particular lifestyle, as much as I wanted to use Cantonese I really didn't have many opportunities to do so. If you don't use it you lose it, and it wasn't really that firmly implanted anyway! So there's the difficulty of the language, plus the pretence that English is widely spoken by local people because of the history here. When I go back to the States and I talk to people, if they can even figure out where Hong Kong is (usually I get 'oh, Hong Kong—is that in Japan?'), if they even have a concept of what Hong Kong is, they'd say to me, 'Oh well, you have no problem there because they speak English, don't they?' But I don't think there is a high level of English spoken here.

Adjusting to unfamiliar surroundings often involves coping with high-rise living. 'One thing I found difficult was that we'd come from a large house and were put into quite a small flat' is a recurrent comment. In contrast, Janet Kaye moved to Hong Kong from Penang in 1964 and was charmed by Stanley, where she and her husband rented a 'leave flat', which is temporary furnished accommodation, sub-let by leaseholders who have gone on a long holiday. She remembers celebrating her daughter's first birthday on the terrace with a cake—although she failed to muster a candle. But she says

> Hong Kong didn't feel Asian in the way Malaysia did. In Hong Kong everyone wore business suits and there was air-conditioning. In Penang we had mosquito nets and ceiling fans. For a time I worked for a real estate company showing apartments to newcomers. Traumatized Americans would say, 'Oh my God, where are the family rooms, the yard where my boys can play basketball?'

Anne Dickson-Leach was fortunate enough to be accommodated in a house with a garden when she came with her husband in 1951.

'Number One Barker Road, opposite the Colonial Secretary's residence, was a lovely house. It has Chinese owners now. They carved a swimming pool out of the rock—rather dramatic! I'm told the pool alone cost two million dollars. I shall always remember our first evening. All the azaleas were coming out at the time. And the lights of Hong Kong, which I could see from our house, were wonderful.' However, nobody had warned her about the bane of Peak living: the damp spring mists which would suddenly descend and blot out everything: 'Shortly after we arrived I was taking the children down to Central to buy swimmers. When I saw that we were all in mist I said, "You had better put your macs on." So there we were, marching into Lane Crawford [a department store] in boots and macs when it was sunny outside!'

Mr and Mrs Dickson-Leach, like other expatriates attached to the hongs or the government, were not required to find or rent their accommodation. Until it started selling them off in the late 1990s, the government owned entire blocks and allocated flats in them according to a points system based on the prospective tenant's grade and length of service. Similarly, the hongs provided staff flats and furnished them down to the last lightbulb and teaspoon, thus relieving expatriates changing postings every two or three years from any concern with fixtures and fittings. As Sisse McCall explains:

> How different it all was—you were put into a Jardines flat, a Bank flat, or a Swires flat, and so on. You could walk in and see exactly which company had employed the tenant because the basic furniture was the same. Nowadays it's designer this, designer that—everyone wants their flat lavishly made over. We lived with the basic furniture provided by the company, and then you got what they called a chair cover allowance which barely covered a chair in actual fact.

The musical-chairs procedure of allocating flats played havoc with those who liked to garden. Eager to plant some favourite flowers around her house in Shek O, an expatriate woman was vexed when the gardener ignored her instructions, only to be told, 'Missee come, missee go. But I stay.' In the government, a coveted perk that came with seniority was the right to keep your flat from tour to tour. Until you rose to such dizzy heights, however, 'every time you went on leave you had to pack everything away and give up your flat. Then when you came back you had to wait in a hotel, in a queue, to get another one.' But the wife of one expatriate civil servant, Anne Sorby (pictured), did stay long enough in a government ground-floor flat to make a garden, although she had trouble with the inhospitable terrain:

> The ground in Hong Kong is decomposed granite. We used to go and get earth from gardens around buildings that were being demolished, before it was buried by rubble. We'd take our buckets, dig out the soil, bring it back and put it in a big trench we'd managed to hack out. In order to make the soil more fertile we dug another trench and got some Jockey Club manure. But you weren't allowed to put that straight on; you had to bury it for ninety days so that it wouldn't be breeding disease. After the required period of interment we could then put it in the flower beds.

Not for nothing was their Peak apartment block dubbed 'The House of the Four Winds'. Strong gusts, especially during the typhoon season, meant that when she planted a tree it had to be anchored with ropes. It flourished nevertheless, having grown very big when she revisited the garden some fifteen years after leaving Hong Kong for good in 1973. Another feature of the garden also remained in place:

There was a rather boring patch in the garden which we hadn't known what to do with. My sister-in-law Marigold lived in Mid-levels. There had been a terrific storm and a lot of stuff had been washed down just by their flat, including a huge rock. She rang me and said, 'I think I've got the ideal thing for your garden.' So we went down and there was this enormous, heavy rock in a rather attractive shape, and with the help of some workmen and wooden rollers we managed to move it into position. And that was my birthday present.

About a week later we were invited to a dinner party and there were lots of wealthy Chinese ladies there wearing wonderful jewellery. We were chatting away and I told them I'd just had my birthday and my husband gave me a very nice present. 'Oh, what did he give you?' they asked. I said he gave me a huge rock. This made them all nod approvingly, because of course they thought I meant a big diamond! They were speechless with amazement when I explained what sort of rock it was.

The rock was still there in 1989 when I visited, looking splendid.

It is only natural to want to be at home in one's surroundings, although endeavours to recreate the familiar can sometimes be pathetic and absurd. When writing about expatriate women in the Far East, what Somerset Maugham said about them comes constantly to mind. In one of his sketches he pokes gentle fun at an Englishwoman in China whose efforts to turn an old temple into something resembling 'a nice place in England, Cheltenham, say, or Tunbridge Wells' succeed in obliterating all that is beautiful in the original. Considering the thick red columns oppressive, she covers them 'with a very nice paper which did not look Chinese at all'. The walls, too, are transformed by a nice pink stripe which 'might have come from Sandersons . . . it made the place look more cheerful at once.'

All this was decades ago and, although you can still sometimes find yourself stepping into a flat filled with the furnishings usually found in a middle-class house in the West, changes have crept in since Maugham's day. Collecting South-East Asian or Chinese antiques has become a fashionable expatriate activity and the décor

is more likely to be sprinkled with oriental touches. That means you can sink into large deep sofas covered in a Sanderson fabric and put your wine glass down on a Ming-style coffee-table. Or find two Chinese folding screens, all dull gold and black lacquer, flanking a *faux* fireplace. Blue-and-white china, whether Qianlong-period or the rougher sort picked up in a market, is scattered among the silver photograph frames. And atop a Ningpo cabinet reposes an antique wooden Buddha encrusted with gold leaf—'Oh, just a cheap old thing I found in Bangkok.'

———◦◇◦———

There is an established lifestyle for newly arrived expatriate wives to emulate. As they come from a self-selected élite (they are mostly middle-class, married to men whose professional qualifications and experience command not only the overseas job in the first place but also the financial package that makes moving to Hong Kong worthwhile), there is a striking affinity of interests between them. For years, like the colonial types who inhabit Somerset Maugham's stories, expatriates 'played tennis if there were people to play with, went to the club at sundown if there was a club in the vicinity, drank in moderation, and played bridge. They had their little tiffs, their little jealousies, their little flirtations, their little celebrations.'

One American woman says, 'The society is so small you are always coming into contact with the same people.' This makes for an effortless social life—effortless because there is a pool of middle-class women like oneself, with similar interests and preoccupations, and it is easy to make friends quickly. In a society of transients one has no time to stand on ceremony. Husband's job, background, ages of children, whether you play bridge or tennis, and which club memberships you have can be reviewed within the first ten minutes of being introduced. As mothers have found time and again, social connections are immediately established through having children at the same school or with the same extracurricular activities. Nonetheless, some find such a homogeneous society and its compulsive sociability boring and uncongenial. To paraphrase an observation made by an English writer, Hong Kong is notoriously a good place for expatriate men whose highest idea of wit is a joke about being drunk and expatriate women whose only outlet for intelligence is a game of bridge.

Everyday life can also be lonely. Thousands of miles away from her family and friends, with a husband who works long hours, the expatriate wife can feel out of touch and disorientated. Her body may lodge in Hong Kong but her mind wanders the distant, greener pastures of her homeland. If she hasn't been educated beyond school level, she tends to possess neither the curiosity nor the intellectual resources to learn about the new culture and people among whom she finds herself. Employing a maid and perhaps a driver, she has hours in the day when there is nothing to do. Every evening, her husband returns from the office to find her seated in the immaculate sitting-room, barely rumpling the perfectly plumped cushions on her designer sofa, the Filipino amah hovering with the dinner in a state of near-readiness, and the children already bathed and only waiting for a goodnight kiss before being bundled off to bed. He may well wonder why his wife is peevish and discontented. But then it is easier for the men, whose main preoccupation on arriving at his overseas posting is to get on with his new job. An American wife claimed her husband was initially able to adjust to Hong Kong more readily than she did, 'because he went right into the work situation', which was in a large investment bank. 'The Hong Kong office afforded him a lot of latitude. I think he enjoyed that.'

Expatriation can sometimes put marriages under such strain that they break down, especially when husbands are able easily to find solace outside the home. Gilbert Rodway, a lawyer, handled many divorces during his time in Hong Kong: 'When I arrived [in the 1970s], there was not a great deal of divorce. . . . but in the twenty plus years that I was there, the number of divorce petitions filed annually increased by many times.' This statistic applied not only to Chinese couples but expatriate ones too. At first expatriates 'didn't want to air their grievances in public, and usually waited till they were posted home before they got divorced', but gradually, in line with the general trend, divorce became more prevalent: 'drunkenness and domestic violence often forced wives into taking proceedings in Hong Kong. Airline pilots' affairs with stewardesses (particularly in Cathay) also provided a lot of work.'

Infidelity, alienation, tedium, and loneliness are compounded by separation from children, although the habit of dispatching offspring, especially sons, at the tender age of eight or nine to boarding-schools 'back home' is mainly confined to the British middle class. For them, the private school (which they call 'public school') is almost synonymous with a fine academic education, the injection of sound character, and a dependable launch-pad to university and a glittering career. The early separation, tearful mothers say, is a sacrifice they make for their children's sakes. Expatriates claim to be under greater pressure because when they themselves make frequent moves it is all the more important to contrive a measure of stability for their children by keeping them at the same boarding schools.

Heart-rending though such separations are, relatively inexpensive jet travel unites today's expatriates with their children more often than in the past. One Hong Kong boy sent away to school in the late 1920s did not see his parents again for five years, and he was not an exception. Now, a familiar sight at Hong Kong airport around the end of term is of mild pandemonium when one of the 'lollipop expresses', as the flights are jocularly called, comes in. Disgorged into the arrivals hall, children clutching tennis rackets and teddy bears are matched with parents by the airline minder one by one, like so many pieces of luggage waiting to be claimed. Equally often, mothers fly to be with their children at half-terms and holidays, taking advantage of special-offer air fares specifically designed to tap this burgeoning market as commuting by plane becomes increasingly commonplace. That some mothers still have pangs of guilt and worry is affirmed by one who said, 'I am afraid these children have no cosy home with the stew bubbling on the stove to stumble into when they are in trouble.'

Ease of commuting has led to another phenomenon among some expatriates, which is relocating the family home back to their own country while continuing to work in Hong Kong. In some cases they have been forced by prohibitive rents to give up their spacious flats in Hong Kong, perhaps as a result of losing their jobs with the expatriate package; in others where the choice is between husband and children, the women have opted for the latter. It is then the husbands who commute, so that the epithet 'astronaut', used before 1997 to describe Chinese seekers of foreign passports who spent a great deal of time flying to visit wives and children sent on ahead to establish residence in North America or Australia, has been dusted down and reapplied, this time to expatriates. Not surprisingly, 'astronauts' pass an inordinate amount of time in their clubs, postponing the moment when they must return, alone, to their dismal service apartment and a microwaved dinner. They are wryly depicted by one of their number as WANKERs (Wife Away, No Kids, Eating Rubbish).

───────◁○◆○▷───────

Departed expatriates love dwelling on the violence of Hong Kong weather, and in the domestic sphere this usually meant too much water or too little. Those who remember the early 1960s speak of being at the mercy of the elements and enduring one natural disaster after another. Noreen Lightbody says the worst typhoon she ever knew was in 1962, when 'the garden was swept clean—there was not a leaf left. Next door, the cookboy lost the top of a finger which got caught in a slammed door. Strong winds took all the tiles off our roof. Rain was pouring in, the water was flowing down the stairs, and we were sweeping it out of the front door.'

The other extreme was acute water shortage and rationing, when domestic taps were supplied for four hours every four days and standpipes in public areas were open for an hour or two each day. As Noreen recalls:

> We filled all the baths with this rather dirty brown water. I had two children in nappies then so it wasn't very easy. But at least we could store water in baths. People dependent on standpipes must have been desperate. You used the water for washing and kept it for flushing. I remember being so economical that I spat my toothpaste into a potted plant! Friends in England thought we led a cocktail-party life; admittedly the photographs we sent back were always of people with glasses in hand or lolling on a junk in the sunshine. But there were lots of less enjoyable excitements as well!

A few years earlier Anne Sorby's son was nearly born in a typhoon. There had been a power cut. Her husband, Terence, then working under the Colonial Secretary, Claude Burgess, was supposed to be going to the office to do an emergency fill-in:

Claude Burgess, a wonderful boss, who was technically on local leave, rang up my husband and said, 'I hear Anne is just about to have the baby. You're not to come down to the office. I'll take your place and you stay with Anne.'

I was busily mopping up the floor because lots of windows were broken and horizontal rain was pouring in. Terence said, 'For heaven's sake, go into the back room and lie down, but don't have that baby!' Our doctor friend was prepared to be at the other end of the telephone to give my husband instructions on what to do if necessary, because he couldn't get out of his flat either.

Luckily I managed to hold off until I was able to go to Queen Mary Hospital the next day. I had the baby almost straight away on a tablecloth, all the hospital linen having been totally wrecked. Because of broken windows the clean sheets were soaking wet. There were masses of women giving birth at the same time—the place was crawling with babies. I don't know if it had something to do with the atmospheric pressure but there was definitely an unusually large number of babies.

The natural world intruded in other ways. Through the Hong Kong year the housewife wages routine war on cockroaches, mosquitoes, a multitude of insects, and perhaps rats. At many a coffee morning, agitated voices can be heard reciting encounters with nasty tropical creatures that lurk behind skirting boards or in the undergrowth. In a recent issue of the American Women's Association magazine, a newcomer to Hong Kong describes herself staring in disbelief at a page in the *Settling Into Hong Kong* guidebook, where it said, 'In the case of a snake in the house or garden, call 999 and ask for the snake-catcher.' Coming face to face with a king cobra was an experience Noreen Lightbody has never forgotten:

I was having lunch at home on the enclosed verandah and our dog started barking. It was barking at a snake with its hood up. I quickly got the dog into the house and shut the inside doors to the verandah. Then I rang the Peak police. The policeman who came up clearly didn't believe me. He said, 'Where's the snake?' And I ended up having to go in search of it—he wasn't leading the way! Some of the verandah chairs were piled up on top of each other and eventually I found the cobra curled up on a rattan chair asleep. The policeman had to believe me then. Off he went to get the snake-catcher. An hour later a great big police van came up and a little man in a white singlet, black trousers, and flip-flops came out of it with a sack. He just put his hand down, picked up the snake—even held it up for me to see—and then dropped it into the sack.

Driving up to Mid-levels from the airport—where she had a whiff of the infamous stink from the Kai Tak nullah—Nicci Button found to her surprise that 'Hong Kong was green and lush. I couldn't believe the beauty of the hillside going up to the Peak. I had seen postcards of views of Central from the Peak, but was not prepared for how stunning the vista was.' It was 1979, her husband's company had asked if they would move to Hong Kong, and Nicci had arrived for a preview. She thought the sight of the city from where they were staying in May Road breathtakingly impressive:

Directly below was the Ladies Recreation Club with its swimming pools and tennis courts and then beyond was Central, the harbour and the hills of Kowloon. . . . From the back of the flat was the view of the hillside with all its wild vegetation and roaring waterfall. White sulphur crested cockatoos would suddenly rise from the trees with tremendous squawking and fly across the valley. A few had escaped from the Botanical Gardens below apparently years before and then had bred and formed quite a colony.

A British television programme about Triads, in which the camera took viewers into 'decaying tenement blocks and balconies dripping with washing and tangles of greenery, and banyan trees projecting above them' suggested to Carolyn Watts that 'there was probably rather a wonderful natural world' in Hong Kong behind the 'facade of tall airy forests of skyscrapers'. Her intuition proved absolutely correct when she got here. Arriving one wet, unruly, rain-swept night in 1984, she ran into the beginnings of a typhoon and found it a thrilling experience:

Someone—a friend of a friend—came to the airport in his car, and suddenly there I was, standing in a multi-storey carpark dripping with sweat, as twisting sheets of rain sheered the unfamiliar world outside. Life, I felt at once, was here. The sense of having dropped into another dimension was borne in on me quite physically by the air. In London air simply isn't there; in Hong Kong it has a dense, humid, perpetual presence—you wade through it in your daily life, steaming and sweating. It smells of fuel, soy sauce, and joss and never in three years ceased to fill me with a primal joy.

I remember intensely, and physically, that first dramatic, surreal drive from the airport through the sluicing rain, when my heart pounded and I felt I'd tumbled on to the set of *Blade Runner*. On all sides slender, umbrella'd figures bent into the wind, struggling through dark canyons of tenements lit in places by vast neon signs; and between the buildings old and new, odd primitive outcrops of rock, concreted over against landslips, with shrubs pushing up between the cracks, and bursts of blossom against shiny wet leaves.

It wasn't just the vehement weather that filled her with passion. She had arrived as an eager journalist, and soon got a badly paid but exciting job on the *Hong Kong Standard*. Reporting on life around the territory, she was not only enthralled by what she saw but also became aware of a 'seismic shift' in herself. What happened in Hong Kong, she said in retrospect,

> was partly a strong emotional engagement with the sensory world, one that gave me a fuller vocabulary of feeling. Above all it was a visual awakening, a sudden sense that the vocabulary of light and colour and form was more important to me than words, to which I'd long been academically or professionally tied. What caused this seismic shift was partly the nature of the new place, as much the man-made stuff as the marriage of land and sea or the beating of rain on banana palms. Colour was the most influential element of all. Every culture has its favourite set of hues, and the spectrum loved by the Chinese spoke to me as nothing in Japan, or Africa, or Europe had ever done. I relished the sea-green doors and walls, the pink and yellow facades of housing blocks, the reds and golds of temples, the festive rainbow flags, the neon glow in every shopping street.

But another reason I responded so strongly to the city was that suddenly I felt as if I'd lost the power of speech. I couldn't understand what was being said around me on the street; nor could I read a word of the noisy galaxy of overhead signs—whose characters to me were bold, intricate, and utterly silent patterns. And my whole shift from words and reason to sight and feeling was pushed along by the fact that Chinese culture itself is such an insistently visual one.

In real terms what this all meant was that I bought my first camera and carried it everywhere I went. And with the new Nikon came a rapid disengagement from the world of newspapers and words.

Within eighteen months Carolyn Watts had left journalism to run the photo department of a travel-book publisher, and by the time she left Hong Kong 'the visual awakening had run so deep that I was starting to think in terms of working as an artist and photographer. Which, ten years after I left the territory, is pretty much what I'm doing now.'

—⊙◇⊙—

The nursing, medical, and educational services as well as various missions were responsible for bringing the first single expatriate women to Hong Kong. If these eminently respectable ladies were not provided with housing, they could lodge at the Helena May Institute, a reincarnation of the Young Women's Christian Association and the Hong Kong Benevolent Society, which was established in 1916 specifically as a hostel for independent working women from Britain. It was a decorous residence, its doors firmly closed to the odd adventuress or courtesan who also made her way to Hong Kong in the early twentieth century. American and European prostitutes were able, however, to find a convenient perch in and around the Lyndhurst Terrace end of Hollywood Road, above the central business district.

There are fewer takers for the Helena May among the type of expatriate women who have come to the fore in recent years—the highly qualified unattached professional brought in to fill jobs previously monopolized by men. She can afford not to live in a hostel, and she happily pays for domestic help. Of course the ready-made social network provided by club, children, and husbands' colleagues, which a married expatriate woman takes for granted, is missing. On the other hand she may find a warm reception among other singles like herself, except that it tends to be a rather transient group. This was what struck Deborah Glass, an Australian lawyer who had worked for an international bank in Switzerland, when she took up a senior job with the Futures and Securities Commission in Hong Kong in 1989:

> Everyone was just passing through. Expats were all on short-term contracts, even the ones who'd been there for twenty years. Even the locals seemed to be passing through, on their way to Canada or Australia. People were always coming or going, and that meant they did not have fixed, closed social groups but were willing to open up to the latest 'FOBs'—those 'fresh off the boat'.

That, she said, suited her fine. In her first year or so she revelled in the contrast Hong Kong posed to clean, tidy, and clockwork-efficient Switzerland:

> I was twenty-nine, not ready to get married but hoping to meet interesting people. I hung out with other late twenties or thirty-something expatriates in a crowd sprinkled with overseas Chinese in the bars of Lan Kwai Fong and on junk trips to the Frog and Toad on Lantau, trying to develop a taste for Tsingtao beer and a style in slick conversation.
>
> But the novelty of this kind of Hong Kong living began to wear off. There were too few women like me—with my job I was acquiring a certain power and responsibility, and this was hard to put away in the bars and on the junks. The Hong Kong singles world was a small incestuous fishpond in which women were pretty and unimportant, and my new male friends seemed much more taken with the many charming Cathay air hostesses in our midst. I tried for a while to separate my job and social life but it didn't work.

She was not the first foreigner to find herself competing with the Hong Kong version of the 'dumb blonde'—a compliant 'China doll'. As she herself acknowledged, 'there were some humiliating moments':

> One night I went to a ball with a chap who proceeded to spend the evening with his hand up the skirt of some pretty Chinese girl at the same table. At least I had my revenge. He'd given me the keys to his Porsche and apartment to put in my handbag, and when I went over to tell him I was leaving, neither of us remembered the keys. He apparently came round and knocked on my door in the wee hours in search of them, but I had the air-conditioner on full blast and never heard a thing. He had to doss down somewhere else for the night and rescue his beloved car in the morning.

Coming to terms with all the isolating differences of language and lifestyles must involve an attempt at marking out some boundaries. For one's own comfort, it is usually necessary to traverse the cultural chasm, at least partly, and then to settle for a *modus vivendi* that lies somewhere between perpetual estrangement and total assimilation. Many expatriates, Deborah Glass among them, had the chasm narrowed for them through the mediation of overseas-educated Chinese:

> In all this time I was not oblivious to living on the edge of China. I had arrived in Hong Kong as the Tiananmen demonstrations were gathering strength, and within a few weeks of my arrival I watched a million silent mourners march through the streets of Central. My friends of the time weren't exclusively the Lan Kwai Fong set. I had Chinese friends from work, mainly a network of overseas-educated women with whose husbands I had nothing in common—it seemed neither did they—and with whom I would spend happy evenings over dumplings and karaoke while their menfolk played pool.

But acquisition of the one tool that might unlock the mysteries of Chinese thought and culture and close the chasm eluded her:

> I struggled to learn Cantonese, never getting much beyond the basic stage, although my ability to eavesdrop in lifts earnt me a

respect far beyond my due. I found it a depressingly difficult language, all the more so as there was so little encouragement to learn. My attempts to practise in the street very often led to blank looks or snickers, presumably as I came up with one of Cantonese's many swearwords that is just a semi-quaver away from a common expression.

What comes out of all this, for those with the confidence to acquiesce to a compromise, is a perfectly agreeable way of living between the two worlds:

> There was a limit to my localizing. I didn't particularly like the Cantonese lifestyle, the endless multi-course ceremonial eating, the crowds, the noise, the frantic gambling and passion for a brand-name bargain. I would get off the crowded ferry to Lantau, get on the crowded bus to one of the villages, and leave the crowds behind in the village restaurants while I shouldered a picnic lunch and headed out along the trails.
>
> So I had friends in both camps, and drifted between the two, neither attempting to become a true Hong Konger nor immersing myself in the expat scene. The Securities and Futures Commission was, sensibly, localized, so my job did not come with the old government perks of housing, travel, and education for kids, much better anyway for a single girl like me, and much more conducive to harmonious relationships at work. So for years I nested in a large old flat in unfashionable Pok Fu Lam, where I had a glorious view of the Lamma Channel over the cemetery next to which most Chinese would not like to live, and battled the biannual rent hikes of my greedy landlord living in Canada. I crewed on a yacht in Aberdeen in summer, hiked the hills of Lantau and the New Territories in winter, and fled to Europe for a few weeks every August.
>
> But like almost everyone I met in Hong Kong I was always just about to leave. I knew I did not want to stay there forever, that despite my terrific job Hong Kong was not my home, and that I wanted eventually to settle down in the kind of relationship that seemed unattainable in Hong Kong.

Her last assumption turned out to be mistaken. She had given up all hope of Hong Kong romance when she met Jonathan Mirsky,

East Asia Editor for *The Times* of London:

> He was very smart, very funny, very famous and much older than me, and quite unlike anyone I had ever met before. We met at the dinner party of a mutual Chinese friend and he talked to me all evening. I made him laugh, and for the first time in years a man called up his hostess and asked for my phone number.
>
> I knew almost nothing of his world, nor he of mine, but soon I found myself dining with the Pattens, with royalty, and with politicians, and becoming immersed in the hotbed of debate on China and democracy that was the legacy of the last Governor of Hong Kong. I had been quite a big fish in my own small pond, but now I felt very inconspicuous, a minnow among sharks.

But gradually their worlds came together. Deborah Glass and Jonathan Mirsky were married in November 1997 and left Hong Kong for London the following January.

———◦✧◦———

Carolyn Watts's emotional engagement with the physical reality of Hong Kong was immediate, as we saw. She was to acquire a new subjectivity to its denizens almost as quickly. Within days of moving to Hong Kong she encountered a Cantonese photographer with whom she soon began an affair. There couldn't be a more intense connection with the place than falling in love with a local Chinese.

She was given his name by a friend who had lived in Hong Kong a decade earlier. When she rang him, he was 'cordial and polite', and it was ages before she realized

> how hard it must be to give time to the endless stream of Westerners who came for a year or two, then left. Nice, eager people, who wanted something from Hong Kong they only vaguely intuited and would take years to understand.
>
> We met for lunch in the dark-at-midday dining-room of the Foreign Correspondents' Club. He bounded towards me, wonderfully slender with a beaming smile. I'd already spotted how handsome Chinese men were, with their elegant limbs and expressive hands, and he was certainly no exception.

We talked about studying and working in the States, and
how he'd finally come home on a wave of optimism that brought
back a whole generation of middle-class exiles. Now, a few years
on, they, like the territory, were doing well. I felt suddenly
ignorant and provincial, my past small and dull. I'd never really
thought about the enormity, the diversity, of the Chinese
diaspora. But he was patient and friendly, and had a bright energy
and sense of humour I came to enjoy in many Hong Kong friends.

A few days later I sat on his sister's boat, bumping through
the green spray of Hong Kong harbour. Suddenly he emerged
from below deck in a pair of totally unfashionable swimming
shorts, and I realized I'd fallen in love with a place and a person
all at once, and both had qualities I hadn't met before.

We spent our first night together in another typhoon, in
his flat high above Mid-levels. Wild blue-black clouds over the
horizon had wiped out the mountains behind Kowloon; rain
beat down the grey-green waves. I felt extraordinary exhilaration
at the heat, the humidity, and the totalness of the weather. I
also felt incredibly protective and fond of my new friend as he
made us tea in his endearingly modest flat—just wood floors,
white walls, and a painting of the Buddha by the window.

During our time together I made plenty of mental
comparisons between English and Hong Kong men. By some
happy twist of fate, Chinese culture seemed to produce exactly
the kind of men I liked: gentle, sensitive, and perceptive;
aesthetically aware; even fond of flowers and trees. Such agreeably
non-macho traits often went hand in hand with a fiery,
sometimes bloody-minded, sense of purpose and career. The
combination was perfect.

One of the delights of dating someone who 'belongs' is being
invited to share the ordinary rhythms of local life. I still miss
breakfasts of rice porridge and dough sticks in small, sea-green
cafés, as I miss a certain dizzying walk over the crest of Hong
Kong island which led through a beautiful tunnel of trees.

One evening we went up some backstreet stairs to a modest,
dimly lit restaurant, where quiet diners chose sleepy fish from a
bubbling tank. There was nothing visibly élite about the place,
but it felt somehow special and the food was good. Months later,
after we had split up, I found my way back there, hoping to

impress an important business guest. For half an hour no waiter approached our table, so I went and stood hopefully by the fish. Finally, after a bit of whispering in one corner, a fellow diner came over and suggested kindly that perhaps my friend and I should leave. As we marched back down into the hot Wan Chai night, tears of exclusion burned my eyes. Only years later did I discover it was in fact a private club.

⸻⸻◦◆◦⸻⸻

While some expatriate women find time hanging too much on their hands because they never have to lift a finger towards housekeeping, an enterprising number ferret out rewarding outlets for their energy, the most worthy of which must be philanthropy and voluntary service. Their enthusiasm, some discovered, was often a source of wonder to many local Chinese, who tended to view 'doing something for nothing' with scepticism. Those at the receiving end were also suspicious. This was Martha McGinnis's experience working as a volunteer for the Society for Promotion of Hospice Care when it was planning to establish Hong Kong's first hospice, the Bradbury, in 1990: 'Even though a Home Care programme had started, the Chinese nurses were very reluctant to let volunteers assist them, and that continued to be a problem.'

At first the volunteers made themselves most useful in fundraising: 'we had small projects like selling roses on Valentine's Day or Christmas cards, which was a lot of work for not much money. But it did bring us volunteers together and that was almost as important as the money generated.' What Martha McGinnis also found inspiring was people's dedication and selflessness. Contrary to assumptions about a different cultural attitude to voluntary service and charity work, some of the most generous fundraisers and donors were Chinese:

> Although expatriates were always the backbone of the volunteers, our Chinese ladies were invaluable. There was an official dinner and one of them, Cecilia Wong, found herself sitting at the same table as the Bradbury administrator. She asked him, 'What is it

at the Hospice that the patients like most?' He told her, 'The bath, but not many of them can take advantage of it because it takes so long for the water to be pumped in and out.'

Cecilia said, 'Oh, you need a more powerful pump then. What would that cost?' When she heard the sum, US$15,000, she said, 'Well, go ahead and order it. I will have the money by Monday.' This was Friday evening. She hosted a mahjong party on Sunday and raised the whole amount!

One of McGinnis's team was another American, Pat Youngberg, who became the volunteer co-ordinator at Bradbury Hospice:

It took a while for me to be accepted by the patients and their families, and even longer for me to be accepted by the staff. Language was a problem and whenever possible I would need someone who spoke English and Chinese to help me. I learnt a few words and used lots of hand signals and charades! I used to say the language I spoke was 'body English'.

When no drivers were available I would sometimes pick up patients myself and bring them to day care at the Bradbury. One Saturday I agreed to take a patient home to spend a final weekend with his grandson. Along with my Chinese friend Nancy to do the translating, we set off. The patient lived in a squatter village outside Sheung Shui in the New Territories. He didn't know the way by car but he knew how to get there by bus. We finally followed the bus route home. Nancy and I expected to leave after delivering our patient, but we were invited by his son and grandson to share tea and cookies with the family. On Monday I returned by myself to pick up the old gentleman. He had tears in his eyes when we left his home.

Voluntary organizations depend crucially on patrons to help elevate their profile and advertise their respectability. Before 1997 their choice of patron usually fell on the Governor's wife. Like her predecessors, Lavender Patten received a number of requests for her patronage from such organizations after she arrived in Hong Kong:

I understood that Natasha [Lady Wilson] had been patron of about 48 organizations. She had tried to drop one—the Ladies' Bowls Association, I think—and had caused a lot of resentment, so it seemed a good idea to accept most of them but say that I would be restricted in what I could do for each of them, so as not to raise expectations. By the time I left I was patron of about 65 organizations. I wanted to concentrate on matters I knew about and was most interested in—domestic violence, child abuse, and family law. I had early meetings with, for example, Priscilla Lui of Against Child Abuse. She explained how Chinese people had always considered that family problems should remain dealt with in the family so there had been little reporting of such abuses until recently.

A successful way of promoting charity events which the Pattens initiated was to hold them in the ballroom at Government House: 'It was very good for the charities because they found it easier to sell their tickets at a good price—everyone wanted to spend an evening at Government House—and it was good for us to be seen to be using the house not just for ourselves but for the benefit of the community.'

There has always been an abundance of gimmicks for soliciting donations to charity, but not many have equalled the annual sedan-chair race for amusement and fun. Its prime mover, Joyce Smith, came to Hong Kong as a nurse in 1967. The Matilda Hospital that she joined was opened in 1907 for expatriates who did not qualify for medical care in a government or military hospital. Patients included merchant seamen and passengers from the liners that called at Hong Kong. Standing on top of Mount Kellet and just below Victoria Peak, the hospital was known for having the maternity ward with the best views in the world.

On the first Saturday in October each year, the roads around Mount Kellet take on a carnival air. Joyce Smith explained how it all started:

In 1975 there was a meeting to discuss ways of raising the hospital's profile and letting the general public know of its existence. Several of us suggested holding a fête to raise money not for the hospital but for needy Hong Kong charities. One of the doctors asked how we would get people to come. Clearly we needed a different attraction.

At that time I had just discovered how, in the early days, patients came to the hospital from the Peak tram terminus in a sedan chair. So I suggested a sedan-chair race. Everyone thought I was mad but told me to go ahead and plan it. The hospital carpenter made four chairs to a copy of my cardboard design. I invited a team each from Jardines, Dodwells, Hongkong Bank, and the Chartered Bank to run from the Peak tram terminus to the Matilda gates dressed in coolie costumes. This they did and raised in sponsorship about $80,000 for charity. The competitors and onlookers thoroughly enjoyed the event and the seeds were sown! Fifty-six teams competed in the year 2000, all bedecked in weird and wonderful costumes. The best decorated chair was in the form of an oven, several athletes were dressed as waiters taking spectators' orders whilst the others were chefs frying eggs as they ran. A total of HK$1.8 million was raised.

11

A Small World

Some expatriate families can be fairly described as having been 'made in Hong Kong'—expatriates meet, marry, and have babies together here—and others are unmade and remade, as in the case, for example, of a husband who trades in his wife for a younger, Asian, model. Quite a few couples go so far as to adopt children locally or from the mainland of China. The family of Rupert and Martin (who wish to remain anonymous) was made in Hong Kong, but in a rather singular way.

Rupert, a Mandarin-speaking Jewish banker and painter from New York, and Martin, an Anglo-Yugoslav musician from London, are the last people you would expect to be adopting Chinese babies. Yet they are 'papa' and 'daddy' to Marcy and Lori, girls of four and two. They had arrived in Hong Kong in 1996 but were packing up for a move to Tokyo, where Rupert was taking up a new posting, in the summer of 2000.

Although their time in Hong Kong had been relatively short, the sojourn was, as Rupert characterizes it, 'transformational'. The course of this change started with an invitation to a party soon after the pair had arrived in the territory. Two 'straight' couples who had adopted Chinese children were among the guests, and their stories made Rupert wistful. Although he had long wanted to be a parent, and had been involved in what he describes as 'all sorts of mad adventures' with female friends, he had been uneasy about the prospect of having a child with these women. What this period of experimentation did convey to him, though, was a clear understanding of 'the difference between men and women'. He realized 'that if I was going to become a father, it would have to be via the adoption route.' Adoption, however, was not that simple; in London, his posting prior to Hong Kong, 'the social services made the process so perilous even for the British that I had all but given up my dream. But now, at the party, it was recalled to life.'

As suggested by his friends, Rupert telephoned a Hong Kong adoption agency which arranged international adoptions, matching non-Chinese applicants with children in mainland China:

> By making that first call, I somehow felt that a baby would arrive by courier the very next day. I later learnt that this feeling was shared by all fantasizing adoptive parents. The social worker advised me that the process was not in fact sequential—that several activities had to be undertaken at the same time.
>
> I was instructed to approach my home government which, in the end, would be providing citizenship to the adopted child. I had instead been dwelling on the Chinese authorities, assuming that all power and potential headaches rested with the social services in Beijing. The US Immigration and Naturalization Service, as part of the screening process, immediately required a fingerprint check as well as police investigations at each place I'd lived.
>
> As it turned out, neither condition was easy to meet. The fingerprints were taken by a clerk on his very first day of employment and couldn't be read properly in Washington. It took three months for me to be told that the prints had to be retaken; and that very same clerk, who was now a seasoned veteran, managed to get them wrong again. The last impression was finally taken by an officer whose embarrassment ensured success. When it came to the investigation into criminal activities, it turned out that most police departments are loath to offer a clean bill of moral health based on the absence of a police record. Nevertheless I prevailed. Despite the frustration, I knew that incompetence and bureaucratic fiddle-faddle, though maddening, could ultimately be addressed. Then came the bombshell.

He received a letter from the adoption agency informing him that there would be an eight-month delay to his application but without citing a reason. What he didn't know was that with the reversion of Hong Kong's sovereignty to China that summer, the agency lost its franchise for handling further adoptions on the Mainland. Kept in the dark about all this, Rupert couldn't help but feel that his application was being singled out and derailed.

When the adoption agency offered him assurance but still no explanation, he came to a spirited decision, and so

> began an independent journey which ended with contacts amongst the highest echelon of officialdom in Beijing. Though keenly aware of truly being out of my depth—neither the study of Chinese classics nor an earlier stint in Beijing had prepared me for such drama—the last chance to become a father kept me going. In the end, making dear friends along the way, I was helped, but it was not until I flew out of Canton with Marcy in my arms that I could be sure the miracle was safe.

Throughout the process, Martin had to remain invisible as Rupert was applying as a single parent. Since unmarried heterosexual couples were largely ineligible to adopt jointly in America, there was little point in raising a similar, if not more, contentious scenario with the Chinese authorities. At times they did feel that they should be more political on behalf of gay couples who might want to adopt. But they could not put their application in jeopardy, and the benefits of any public action, they felt, paled when set against the prospect of parenthood. If that political message was to have meaning, they believed it would be reflected through their raising of a happy child.

Rupert's quest led to Hangzhou. He had wanted to adopt a child from Yunnan because the province had been the subject of his doctoral thesis, but few babies from China's ethnic minorities, who are exempt from the national one-child policy, ever come up for adoption. So he put down Hangzhou in the application; and if pressed for a reason, he would have said that the cities of Hangzhou and Suzhou were traditionally renowned for their lovely and refined women.

The orphanage in Hangzhou offered Marcy. She was twenty months old, a tiny, withdrawn, and hauntingly beautiful child. When Rupert first caught sight of her in a Chinese ministry office, she seemed swallowed up in one of those enormous brown couches found in all such places in China, clutching two packets of biscuits. Given the surname 'Hua' (meaning China) along with all the other children accepted into her orphanage that year, she has since been renamed after members of her new family, in English and Chinese.

All her names, together with the Chinese character for 'rat' (her birth sign) and staffs of music tracing a Scottish ditty (written for her by Martin) appear on the announcement of her adoption. This has been pasted into an album along with the visa granted by the US Consulate in Canton and her first airline ticket out of China. On another page is the first photograph sent by the orphanage of Marcy, her mouth slightly agape, with the dazed look of a malnourished child. Martin says she was quite simply starved; and for months after her adoption, she was obsessive about food—a dropped morsel invariably triggered hysterics.

For a Hong Kong-based American adopting in China, becoming a father is only the beginning of a marathon. From Hangzhou, Rupert made his way to Canton to apply for Marcy's US visa. He recalls staying at the White Swan Hotel there and finding 'dozens of newly created families, the sight of whom both touched and amused'. He himself took along his cousin, a larger-than-life grandmother of three, who briskly showed him the ropes of basic childcare:

> Ilene's no-nonsense attitude, practical nous, and long experience on the front line of parenting were the perfect antidotes to my own heightened emotional state. I remember her calmly soldiering on as Marcy screamed through what was likely her first hair wash in a bathtub and then her casual retreat to her own hotel room, leaving father and daughter completely alone on that very first night. So determined was I to impress her that, after a sleepless night spent hovering over the crib, I had my daughter fed, washed, and dressed well before Ilene knocked on our door the next morning.
>
> The vodka-and-tonics which Ilene and I shared each evening in Hangzhou and her pride of place in this extraordinary tale will also be long remembered.

Martin joined them in Canton. Although he had been worried about the prospect of fatherhood, he experienced 'a thunderbolt of emotion' when Marcy was unceremoniously thrust into his arms. They immediately set off together for the Fellini-like bird market of Canton, certainly the filthiest place I'd ever seen. I was terrified that Marcy would touch something and develop some frightful disease. Instead, I was treated to her first smiles as she became transfixed by a riot of coloured feathers and even more screaming than she had probably encountered in the orphanage.

For Rupert there was one more bureaucratic hurdle before the new family could settle back into life in Hong Kong. Since the baby was travelling on a Chinese passport, she would be permitted to stay in Hong Kong for only one week, and the Hong Kong government plays by stringent rules when it comes to Chinese immigrants in the SAR. The visa stamped in her Chinese passport assured eventual US citizenship, but the conventional naturalization process usually took eighteen months. Rupert was temporarily stumped: 'How could I return to Hong Kong to resume my duties with a daughter carrying a Chinese passport? The answer was declarative: I could not!' The conundrum was finally solved by the discovery of a fast-track process of expeditious naturalization usually used by American soldiers abroad for their new foreign brides.

Rupert took Marcy to Washington DC and was again to be terrorized by paper. The paper trail led them to an interview with the Immigration and Naturalization Service representative, a large black woman with quarter-inch dyed blonde hair. Rupert recalls the exquisite moment at the conclusion of their successful interview when Marcy reached over and gave this exotic woman a great big kiss!

Being only children themselves, Rupert and Martin wanted Marcy to have a sister, their choice of a second girl dictated as much by their own notion of a family as by China's one-child policy and abiding discrimination against females. Since the majority of Chinese couples want their one child to be a boy, it is invariably girls who are abandoned or given up for adoption. In any case Rupert and Martin felt that a boy with two fathers would prove more problematic, especially as athletics do not loom large in that household. This time Rupert requested a baby from the northern heartland of China, and Lori was adopted from Luoyang, the peony capital of the nation. A disarming and sunny child, Lori smiles so readily that it is easy to imagine the orphanage staff feeding her well but doing little else. In fact as a podgy fourteen-month-old, she seemed unaware that she even had arms and legs. Her parents did not grasp the sadness of her inability to sit up or even move until much later. The contrast between the two sisters couldn't have been more stark: Marcy, the dextrous scavenger; and Lori, the inert and jolly doll.

When application was made for a second child, Martin and Rupert could only guess at the complexities of sibling rivalry. Martin made the point that Marcy's simply hearing about a sister over a lengthy period of time just wasn't the same as seeing 'a bump growing in mummy's tummy'. To prepare her, the orphanage photograph of Lori—of a chubby child swaddled in myriad winter layers against a garishly painted landscape—was pasted in a little album and sent off with Marcy to nursery school. At about the same time, Marcy began lobbying for a pink bicycle. The fathers decided to cast Lori as the giver of the bike. As it happened, when Lori and the bike finally arrived, Marcy ignored the gift and made straight for her new sister—Rupert, Martin, Marcy, and Lori were a family at last.

⋙◦✧◦⋘

Liz Dewar is the single mother of two Chinese girls, four-year old Tamzin and Zoe, who is just under three. Her ties to Hong Kong go a long way back. In fact she insists that she is not an expatriate but a local: 'My great-great-grandfather, a Scottish seafarer, had settled in Shanghai where my family remained until 1937. The Japanese occupation forced my grandfather to relocate to Hong Kong, where subsequently I was born.'

If you were dyslexic and had left school with no academic qualifications, but if somebody harnessed your organization skills, courage, and innate feeling for form and space, you could succeed, as Liz Dewar has done spectacularly as an interior designer. She ran her own design company through the 1980s and most of the 1990s and is adamant that she couldn't have done it anywhere else but in Hong

Kong. She possesses one other considerable advantage: the ability to speak Cantonese. Someone who worked with her on an office fitting-out project saw how 'she could interpret designs made by expatriates for Chinese contractors who didn't speak a word of English'.

Her first office was located in the street where Wan Chai meets the more expensive Central district. She was advised to buy rather than rent her premises, and by exchanging ever larger spaces to accommodate her expanding business, she also made money from property and eventually built up a nest egg. She was to think of this nest egg as rather more than a pension fund when she became convinced that she wanted to adopt a child, for no-one can contemplate the prospect of being a single parent without the assurance of financial security. For Liz at that juncture of her life, a number of necessary conditions were already in place, not least of which were property investments in Hong Kong and Cornwall, the place where her parents live and where she has chosen to spend her retirement.

Adoption agencies in Hong Kong rank a single Caucasian applicant some way below the model parents they'd like to find for their children. It is said that adoption by single foreign parents is well nigh impossible except in China and Vietnam. Liz is neither married nor Chinese, and her best hope was to be offered a handicapped child. If one's preference is for a girl, the chances are further lessened. Orphanages in Hong Kong, she found, had a preponderance of boys because adopting Chinese couples, who trace family descent through sons, generally favour girls out of some deep-seated aversion to mixing bloodlines. Liz's case seemed impossible until she realized she could try and adopt in China.

On 14 May 1997 she was attending a seminar on 'The Office of the Future' at the Hong Kong Convention and Exhibition Centre. As she was about to sit down to lunch, she received a telephone message from her secretary. It seemed that the adoption agency was urgently trying to get in touch with her. When she rang and heard through all the noise that the authorities in Beijing had matched her with a little girl from Guangdong, a full year after she had applied, there was only one way she could give vent to her emotions—she burst into tears. Returning to her lunch companions, she announced that 'in the time I was absent from the table I had become a mother. We all drank to the news with mineral water. I can honestly say the rest of the day was a complete blank.'

Little Fu Xiaojian (Tamzin), then eleven months old, had been taken in by Sanshui Social Welfare Institute when she was found at two days old beside a village market about an hour's drive away. Sanshui is a town west of Canton in Guangdong province and there, on 17 June 1997, after formalities had been completed at the Guangdong Provincial Adoption Registry for Foreigners, Tamzin was handed over to Liz Dewar.

Like Rupert, Liz had to fly on to Beijing to start the process of applying for nationality papers for her adopted baby, which in her case began with getting a settlement visa chopped into Tamzin's Chinese passport by the British Embassy. Armed with this and a one-week visitor's visa for Hong Kong, mother and child returned home to all the excitements of the Handover. In early July Liz took three months off work to spend the summer in Cornwall. She didn't know then that it would end on a disquieting note:

> Through the summer we waited for the result of the British nationality papers, which we had sent to the UK from Hong Kong. As time went on, with no news I began to get a bit worried. The Hong Kong immigration rules were very clear: Tamzin would not be able to enter Hong Kong as a dependant without being accepted as a British citizen. My secretary in Hong Kong had been in contact with Hong Kong Immigration constantly, and we kept coming up against dead ends and brick

walls. Late in August Tamzin had been given a file number, which made me feel a little better as I then knew that her papers were in the UK system.

By September the holiday was coming to an end and still no permits appeared. 'We then heard that Hong Kong Immigration would give Tamzin a month-to-month visitor's visa while her British papers were being processed.' On 15 September they returned to Hong Kong, where three visa extensions were to take Tamzin's permit to stay to 22 December:

> A week before this date we had a reply from the UK. Tamzin had been turned down for British citizenship! I could not believe it and said to the officer on the other end of the phone, 'You must have the wrong file.' Panic hit; it was nearly six months to the day that we had the settlement chop stamped in Tamzin's People's Republic of China passport. I knew I had to get into the UK before that expired on 23 December.

Liz handed over all her work to her business partner, packed her bags, and got on the next flight to London. In the meantime a friend had made an appointment with an immigration lawyer there. The senior Dewars travelled up from Cornwall, 'and we all sat and listened to what we should have done six months ago. This was not going to be an easy thing to sort out. . . . I had visions of Tamzin being sent back to China and as she was now my daughter I would not let that happen.' Liz's predicament was complicated by the fact that, with three generations of Dewars born outside the United Kingdom, she was not entitled to pass on British nationality to her daughter under British immigration rules.

The lawyer estimated that redress would take about six months. This was too long for Liz to be absent from her business; but she also knew that she could not be away from Tamzin for that length of time either. Christmas, she recalls, was very fraught. In the end she decided to engage an English nanny to look after Tamzin:

> Tamzin and the nanny would live with my parents and I would commute—two weeks in Cornwall and two in Hong Kong. Tamzin settled down to a routine and I to jet lag.

In May the decision was overturned and Tamzin got her British citizenship . . . I had been through some scary situations in my life but none that drained me quite as much as this.

In the story she has written for Tamzin to read one day, Liz looks back on those uncertain days and counts her blessings:

Tamzin has just had her third birthday. She loves school and is learning to speak Cantonese. If anyone asks her where she comes from she answers 'China, but I am English.' China seems to get the blame on where she gets coughs, colds or any cuts or bruises. She talks to her friend Alex [a Chinese girl adopted at the same time as Tamzin by another single expatriate] and one day I overheard them talking about 'daddies'. Tamzin was insistent that her daddy was in China whereas Alex's daddy was at work. Both Jo-Anne [Alex's adoptive mother] and I will have to handle this problem in the near future. As single mums I am sure we will handle it in different ways, but handle it we will. In March of this year 1999 my paperwork for my second daughter, Zoe, was sent up to China to start the slow movement from one in-tray to the next. Most of my friends think I am mad to go through the whole thing again. Mad, yes, but Tamzin is my life and, although I would not have chosen to have spent the last two years as we have, I would live through it again to be the lucky mother of Tamzin.

Chinese by birth, American or European by adoption, Marcy, Lori, Tamzin, and Zoe are not run-of-the-mill expat kids. But whatever their future holds, chances are that as grown women with all the advantages of an East–West heritage, they will defy narrow definitions of nationality or culture. More likely than not, they will develop into adults who will be thought of as citizens of the world.

Not long ago, one of those round-robin messages that roam in cyberspace and periodically alight in electronic mailboxes appeared in mine. It consisted of a light-hearted attempt at defining the characteristics of 'an expat kid in Asia'. What was striking about this ephemera was how true it rang—every expatriate child would recognize some or most of the criteria:

YOU KNOW YOU'RE AN EXPAT KID IN ASIA WHEN
You can't answer the question, 'Where are you from?'
You flew before you could walk.
You have a passport, but no driver's licence.
You watch National Geographic specials and recognize someone.
You run into someone you know at every airport.
You have a time-zone map next to your telephone.
Your life story uses the phrase, 'Then we went to . . .' five times.
You speak with authority on the quality of airline travel.
You read the international section of newspapers before the
    comics.
You live at school, work in the tropics, and go home for vacation.
You don't know where home is.
You sort your friends by continent.
Someone brings up the name of a team, and you get the sport
    wrong.
Your second major at university is a foreign language you already
    speak.
You realize it's really a small world, after all.
You watch a movie set in a foreign country, and you know what
    the nationals are really saying into the camera.
Rain on a tile patio—or a corrugated metal roof—is one of the
    most wonderful sounds in the world.
You haggle with the checkout clerk for a lower price.

Your wardrobe can only handle two seasons: wet and dry.

Your high school memories include those days that school was cancelled due to tear gas (or riots, or demonstrations, or bomb threats, or the usual problems of corrupted countries).

You have a name in at least two different languages, and it's not the same one.

You think VISA is a something stamped in your passport, and not a plastic card you carry in your wallet.

You automatically take off your shoes as soon as you get home.

Your dorm room/apartment/living-room looks a little like a museum with all the exotic things you have around.

You won't eat Uncle Ben's rice because it doesn't stick together.

Half of your phone calls are unintelligible to those around you.

You go to Pizza Hut or Wendy's and you wonder why there's no chili sauce.

You know the geography of the rest of the world, but you don't know the geography of your own country.

You have best friends in five different countries.

You ask your room-mate when the maid service is scheduled to clean the room.

You're spoilt. You know it. You're very spoilt.

Andrew Eldon and Alexander Waller, two grown-up expat kids whose 'passport country', for want of a better term, is Britain, deny that they are spoilt, although they do find answering the question 'Where are you from?' not entirely straightforward.

ANDREW: Spoilt? No, I feel lucky, not spoilt. As for questions about where I'm from, they don't bother me—they're like water off a duck's back. My answer depends on where I am. In the UK it's usually easier to say I'm from England because I hold a British passport. That saves time as you don't have to do any explaining. When I'm here I say I've been here most of my life.

It has always been quite difficult to decide where I'm from, because my mum's half South American, my dad's English, and I've never lived in either of those places full-time. And we've moved around. I was born in Dubai and moved to Hong Kong one year after that. My dad works for the Hongkong Bank. We spent five and a half years here, then he was posted to Saudi Arabia. From there we moved back to Hong Kong for just over a year, then on to Malaysia for three and a half years, and now we've been back here for just over eight years now.

I went to school in England when I was eleven and later to university. I got back to Hong Kong in 1999 and am now living and working here for a windsurfing company as its head of multimedia.

ALEXANDER: I don't feel as if I come from any place at all—not that it matters. There're greater things around than mere tags of nationality or even race. I would probably say I'm British; somehow British sounds most comfortable. But there are people from our Hong Kong peer group, a bunch of blonde-haired, blue-eyed kids who, when asked that question in England, always go: 'We're from Hong Kong.'

I feel slightly different to that. I think of myself as quite rootless—or flexible, looking at the good side of it. I think I will be able to cope in any part of the world.

I was born in Birmingham in 1978. My parents moved to Hong Kong when I was four years old. I was at school here till I was eight, at which point I went to school in England. I spent a couple of years teaching English and working for a law firm and I'm currently studying law at University College, London.

ANDREW: There are pros and cons to growing up in a second country. The advantage is exposure to a lot of different things—culture, people, food, travel—and you get to do it all. The expat lifestyle tends to be a very good one. I remember as kids we used to be able to go out on a boat any weekend, waterskiing or just hanging out in the sun. Hong Kong is very safe; we were going out at night when we were fifteen or sixteen and there was never any problem. And after you've been away you always come back to a place where you have a lot of friends with whom you can do the same things together. Disadvantages? Probably leaving places. You build up a really close group of friends and then you have to uproot and go away. It's harder when you're younger. That's why I enjoyed school in the UK so much. It afforded a stable base. I still associate England with school and university; but I felt my life was elsewhere. In the end the pros and cons balance out—it's half a dozen of one and six of the other. I'm quite happy with the way things have worked out.

ALEXANDER: My entire expatriate life has been in Hong Kong, so I haven't had the problem of losing friends. Yes, as an expatriate you enjoy a higher quality of life than you would in England if your family had been based there. I like being able to go to the Ladies Recreation Club and sign chits on my parents' bill!

I also like having a wider world view, being alive to issues that affect Asia. In England, if I read something in the papers about Indonesia or Vietnam—I've never been to those places—I take an interest because I see those countries as part of my backyard.

But it's a mixed blessing. You have a comfortable way of life, and that means you grow up with higher aspirations. Unfortunately that also means that money becomes something of a necessary target when you think about what you're going to do with your life. If you were brought up in London you get to know a wider cross section of people. Okay, they might all have gone to private schools, but you would know people like teachers and people who haven't sold out in pursuit of money. I don't know anyone in the academic, cultural, or creative circles in Hong Kong, whereas I probably would if I were in England. And with the kind of role models around in Hong Kong you get pushed into one kind of mind frame and a willingness to emulate your parents or your parents' friends.

If particularly conscious of the alloyed pleasures of money and materialism, many of the present generation of expatriate youngsters in Hong Kong are also aware of 'a prevailing sense that the good life is going to end', that what they've known is already passing. Quite what this 'good life' consists of is more complex than at first appears, however. No doubt it has something to do with affluence and the glamour of jet travel, but much of it also relates to the evanescence of friendships formed in an expatriate context: 'Every time you come back, you wonder if it's going to be the last time. Slowly my friends drift away, because their parents are reaching retirement age and will leave Hong Kong.' This happens to every generation, of course, but the regret of those who grew up in the shadow of 1997 is more poignant, regardless of whether their parents had chosen to leave or stay on. Perhaps those presentiments came to them sharply on Handover night.

ANDREW: For the Handover, we were on the top floor of the Hongkong Bank headquarters building. My parents managed to get the function room for a private party. We got a fantastic view of the fireworks from there. My father—he was then Chief Executive Officer of the Bank—was at the official Handover ceremony so he couldn't be there and my mother hosted our party. There must have been about thirty people, including some who were our first friends in Hong Kong—a nice mix representing the time we spent here. I don't know what the Handover meant to me, but I feel a strong attachment to Hong Kong, it was undoubtedly a historically important occasion, and one can't but feel emotional seeing one era end and another come in.

ALEXANDER: I didn't feel any sense of loss; I didn't think my country was losing a colony or anything like that. But I tend to be almost illogically impressed by key moments in history. I liked being there when something important was happening. And it was the biggest day in Hong Kong's history, with a wider significance outside of just this city.

If Alexander Waller and Andrew Eldon had not become boarders in England, they might have entered one of the secondary schools run by the English Schools Foundation (ESF), set up in 1967 expressly as a result of many English-speaking parents' reluctance to send their children for education overseas.

Such educational provisions as there were in Hong Kong's early days as a colony consisted of a few village and missionary schools. As the population grew, voices began to be raised in support of government intervention in public education: it was time, many felt, that the domination of education by churchmen was brought to an end. In 1861 all this culminated in a decision to establish the Central School, a secular institution which would gather together boys of all nationalities under a Scottish headmaster at a site on Hong Kong island.

In 1900, an alumnus of this school, the Eurasian philanthropist Ho Tung (later Sir Robert Ho Tung), no doubt in gratitude for the fine training he received there, offered to fund a similar school in Kowloon. His only stipulation was that it should be open to all races. A site on Nathan Road was soon found and approved, but the establishment of the school proceeded in fits and starts, while the correspondence over its composition took up the best part of two years. The stumbling block, as the government's advisers had it, was Ho Tung's insistence on a 'mixed' intake which ran counter,

they claimed, to the latest educational theories. According to these, a school which admitted children of different races and languages was 'foredoomed to failure'.

Such theories were a plausible enough explanation for second thoughts, yet a faint question mark hangs over the government's candour. Actually it was perfectly well aware that English parents in Kowloon would never have countenanced their children mingling with Chinese girls and boys, so with some embarrassment, its officers approached Ho Tung with an alternative proposal. What was urgently needed in Kowloon, they said, was a school for *British* children, and since the Chinese were already catered for in an existing school that was by no means overcrowded, would Ho Tung allow his gift to be redirected?

Ho Tung was far from convinced, but the new school was ready and only waiting for his blessing, so there was nothing else to do but submit with good grace. All the same, he made his reservations known in a letter to the government in which he said he was yielding 'with much reluctance . . . [and] on the definite understanding that the Government, on their part, undertake to appoint for the new Yaumati school for Chinese, at least one properly qualified English master and to maintain the standard of education there on the same level as that in the Kowloon School for European children.'

Kowloon British School duly opened in 1902. Subsequently called Central British School, it eventually adopted the name King George the Fifth or King George V School and remained government-run until it was incorporated into the English Schools Foundation in 1981. For years it stood alone as the only non-Chinese secondary school in the colony, admitting not just British students but also Americans and Europeans who had no school of their own. Today, with a student body representing some forty nationalities, it has retained its international flavour although like other ESF schools it has had in recent years its European intake much diluted by the children of Hong Kong Chinese returning from sojourns in the West.

Unlike the government education officers who looked Ho Tung's gift horse in the mouth, expatriate teachers in Hong Kong invariably comment with approval on the racial mix of children that pass through their hands. Pauline Young, who came from Scotland to teach at Quarry Bay Primary School in 1959, opposite what was in those days Taikoo Dockyard, remembers the first Indian pupil admitted to that school as well as a number of Russian–Chinese children: 'There was this child. The mother spoke Chinese, the father Russian—I don't know how they communicated! And Nina spoke English, Russian, and Chinese, so when we had parents' evenings, she had to be there to translate for the teacher. You had those lovely mixes which perhaps you don't get so often nowadays.'

In Pauline Young's day, Quarry Bay and other primary schools, themselves bursting at the seams, annually produced eleven-year-olds who, if they didn't go to England, went to King George V. This involved them in a long daily journey across the harbour by ferry and then to the school by bus. Matters were not helped by the fact that after the Second World War the number of expatriate families in Hong Kong multiplied. Clearly there was a very good case for opening a secondary school for English-speaking children on the island. But education is a highly political issue, not least when the government was at pains to avoid being accused of favouritism, in this instance by continuing to provide disproportionate funding to expatriate rather than Chinese schools.

Free and compulsory education had not yet been instituted in the 1960s, and only one in five Chinese children who went to school at all had a place in a government school. The majority made do with aided or private schools where the fees were higher. English-speaking children, on the other hand, fared much better. Even though their schools, staffed by expatriate teachers, were necessarily more expensive to run, they paid the same fees as those attending Chinese-language government schools.

So the issue of an additional English secondary school would have been a racially controversial one had it not become subsumed into a wider debate about the government's role in the education of *all* children in Hong Kong. Out of this came a recommendation that the government should relinquish direct control of schools altogether; instead, it was to concern itself only in furnishing subventions. Teachers' salaries and other outlays in both English and Chinese aided schools were to be brought into line, with the higher costs of expatriate staffing passed on in increased fees. And so the English Schools Foundation was born—set up as a trust to receive grants of land and subventions from the government and to administer its first two schools, Beacon Hill offering primary education in Kowloon, and Island School providing secondary education on Hong Kong island. The latter opened to its first intake—237 children—in temporary premises at the old British Military Hospital on Bowen Road in September 1967, and has gone from strength to strength ever since. Eventually all the schools offering an English curriculum, including King George V, were gathered into EFS's sway.

Other international schools opened in the ensuing years, and today's expatriate children have a much wider choice of curriculum and medium of teaching than before; academies based on the French, Swiss–German, Australian, Canadian, Japanese, and Korean systems have seen to that. And if one wants one's child to slot back into the US curriculum on return, there is the Hong Kong International School (HKIS).

Arguably no school in Hong Kong is as well appointed and equipped. HKIS's 2,500 pupils, ranging from the very youngest in reception class to the pre-university twelfth-grader, are taught on

two campuses tucked between the hills and the sea on the southern shore of Hong Kong island. As they span more than forty nationalities, the school may fairly claim that it is itself a culturally diverse community. What's more, many of the students may have followed their parents to a number of postings abroad by the time they reach Hong Kong and are, at the tender age of fifteen or sixteen, already expatriates several times over. The present Head, Charles W. 'Chuck' Dull, puts it this way:

> The world is getting smaller every day. The young people who walk the hallways of this institution will live and work in a world where they interact with people of greatly diverse backgrounds. We have a unique opportunity to prepare the next generation to live wisely and ably in a world where moving across borders—literally and figuratively—is more common with each passing day.

Miltinnie Yih, a Chinese American, is Director of Community and Resource Development at the school. She has seen how expatriate institutions such as English-medium schools in Hong Kong have changed. Founded in 1966 by a group of businessmen with the support of the Lutheran Church Missouri Synod, HKIS was intended to offer 'an American-style education grounded in Christian faith'. Typically for an expatriate school, it has a debenture system: 'A company buys so many seats for their executives. That guarantees them a spot for their employees' children', she explains, 'If their employees can't have appropriate schooling for their children they won't come to Hong Kong.' But the school has become increasingly popular with Chinese families too. '60 per cent of the student body are US passport holders. That of course could mean many things. It could mean Chinese Americans or Hong Kong people who'd acquired passports recently. All along we've had local students; now we're having a little more.'

Thus the growth of HKIS has not only mirrored the expansion in the number of Americans coming to Hong Kong, but is also a reflection of the local population's increasing affluence and respect for American tertiary educational qualifications. Not surprisingly, HKIS is commonly perceived as an American school and the best

US college feeder in Hong Kong. It is a development that HKIS welcomes: 'We as a school see ourselves as a place with a tremendous opportunity to train and influence the future leaders of Hong Kong and Asia.' With this undertaking has come the awareness that it's time for today's expatriates to throw off the 'enclave mentality' of the past and assume a greater share of social responsibility in the wider community. Expatriates, Miltinnie Yih says, tend to have the best places, the best facilities, the best schools. In return, shouldn't they be giving something back to their host society? 'We have six learning goals, and one of them is "contributing to society". We teach our students that this is an important part of being educated and becoming global citizens.'

Becoming global citizens, however, sometimes exacts a price, according to Dr David C. Pollock, writer and sociology instructor in Intercultural Studies at Houghton College, New York. He travels widely talking to expatriates about the tremendous challenges as well as benefits facing what he calls a 'third-culture kid'. His own experience as an expatriate was gained when he went to teach in Kenya in the 1970s. Returning to the US in the early 1980s, he agreed to become director of Interaction, Inc., which was then involved in educational services for missionaries' children, on condition that the organization would make as its primary focus 'the support and care of international personnel and international mobile families'.

One of his first projects was to start a programme of re-entry seminars designed to help young Americans in 'international mobile families' who were aged fourteen and upwards not only to think through the issue of transition from one place to another and back again, 'but also to think about who they are, so that as they make some critical decisions of life in the next ten or fifteen years, they're making them in the light of who they are and who they have become because of their international experience.' He calls these people 'third-culture kids' and defines one as 'an individual who, having spent a significant part of the developmental years in a culture other than the parents' culture, develops a sense of relationship to all of the cultures, while not having full ownership in any. Elements from each culture are incorporated into the life experience, but the sense of belonging is in relationship to others of similar experience.'

The key word in this definition, Dr Pollock points out, is 'individual', and of course individual responses vary depending on personality and age. Children on the cusp of puberty, for example, could face a greater struggle adjusting to new countries than younger or older siblings because it is during the early teenage years that they begin to crystallize their sense of identity, and for them the pressures involved in living as a stranger in an alien place are compounded by the unfamiliar emotions and anxieties released on approaching adolescence. Dr Pollock sums it up this way: 'High mobility during that time can be confusing.' There are other potential traps. Observation of HKIS students over many years leads Miltinnie Yih to conclude that the expatriate experience can be more stressful for a child than for the parents:

> The fathers generally love being in Hong Kong—the business is so seductive, they can work for hours and not get involved in anything else. The expat wife who isn't working but employs a maid has lots of time on her hands for once, and lots of choices to make. Having lost her role, which is managing the home, she can get very involved in tennis or bridge and end up spending less time with her children.

Meanwhile the children are left to piece together for themselves all the new experiences they are encountering so that these might assume some coherence in their minds. One way of easing this transition, according to Dr Pollock, is to have started the process earlier, with parents involving children in any decisions well before the move, and preparing them for departure both physically and psychologically.

If the moves are frequent, children may begin to inure themselves against the pain of loss by keeping a constant guard against attachment and intimacy, a habit that may impede their forming close relationships later in adult life. The issue of relationships is particularly relevant, because third-culture kids, says Dr Pollock, find their rootedness not in geography but in relationship to others of similar experience. He tells of a conference organized for universities in Washington DC, where

> we had this auditorium filled with third-culture kids. Doors opened at 9 a.m. They came in, we had coffee and doughnuts and encouraged them to mill around. Within about ten minutes, when you stood back and listened it sounded like this was a class reunion! You'd hardly realize that these people had only just met each other. 'Singapore? Oh yes, I was there,' said one; and 'I went to second grade there, and you sat across the aisle from me,' said another. They always find they know somebody who knows somebody else who knows the guy they're talking to at that moment. So there was a sense that this was one huge family.

If third-culture kids find the world small, one reason is that, bending their adaptability and adroitness in reading social cues to every new society and culture they chance upon, international borders fade away. And they never lose an identification with the places they have been to and which they sense, if only inchoately, that they 'possess'. David Pollock gives the example of third-culture kids who might

> pick up a newspaper and see on the front page way down on the lower right-hand corner mention of one of the countries they'd lived in, and somehow the print jumps off the page. Then they mentally take a journey to another part of the world because not only do they see its name in print but they smell it, they taste

it, they're there. This interest grows out of a sense of ownership, of thinking, 'that's mine'.

Even if this sensitivity is no more than superficial, it is patently enriching. For every third-culture kid, the impact of expatriation continues beyond childhood and beyond the point of return, throwing up a chain of connections and contacts and endowing him with the lineaments of what is becoming a universal type of our times—the global citizen, whose knowledge of the world, to borrow a phrase of the writer G. K. Chesterton, has been acquired *in* the world and not in a closet.

12
Healthy Pleasures

On the face of it, there is nothing nostalgic about the floral emblem on Hong Kong's flag. It is a stylized *Bauhinia blakeana*, named after a Governor like so many things in the territory. Few people would make a connection between the emblem and a soldier who moved with his regiment to Hong Kong in 1847. But it was Captain John George Champion of the 95th Regiment of Foot who made one of the first systematic collections of the flora of Hong Kong. This included several entirely new species, details of which were later published in the *Kew Journal of Botany*. His discoveries are also remembered in the plants named after him, among which is the *Bauhinia Championii*, a white-flowering relative of the emblematic *Bauhinia blakeana*, found commonly in ravines, we are told, and on Victoria Peak, but not known from elsewhere.

There were others: notably the rare *Rhodoleia Championii*, of which there were only two trees on Hong Kong island, growing side by side; varieties of asters and camellias; and the *Rhododendron Championae* (pictured), which was named 'in compliment to his amiable and accomplished lady, whose partiality for plants equals that of her husband and who accompanied him on many of his botanizing excursions'.

An obsession with plants—hunting them, collecting them, ordering them botanically, or just growing them in a garden—provided one of the richest sources of pleasure and interest to early European and American expatriates. In the three years he spent in Hong Kong, Captain Champion must have passed many a blissful hour scrambling down ravines and climbing up peaks to collect more than 500 species. These, according to George Bentham in *Flora Hongkongensis* (1861), included the great majority of the dicotyledonous plants, orchids and ferns, which have hitherto been found in the vicinity of Victoria, in the rich watery or wooded valleys of the north-west from West Point to the Happy Valley, and thence up to the principal central peaks, Mounts Victoria, Gough, and Parker. He had also extended his herborizations to Chuck-Chew [Stanley] on the south coast, and to Saywan on the east, and perhaps to a few other distant points.

Captain Champion's field notes were exemplary, Bentham added, the specimens being documented by 'analytical sketches and descriptions made on the spot, and almost always by most valuable memoranda relating to precise station, to stature, colour, etc., which it were to be wished were less neglected by the majority of collectors'.

Apparently just as exemplary a soldier, Champion (he had been promoted to lieutenant colonel) gave his life in the Crimea in November 1854, dying of his wounds in the hospital at Scutari aged thirty-nine.

The field of botanic exploration widened considerably after Champion, with professional collectors venturing as far as they could into the interior of China. One of them, Robert Fortune, passing through Hong Kong in 1848, left a record of the fine garden at the waterfront villa built by Dent & Company, a merchant firm which, like Jardines, had recently moved from Canton to Hong Kong. It was a marvel, he thought, that within such a short time a barren island should have been transformed into a gracious town 'containing houses like palaces, and gardens, too, such as this, which enliven and beautify the whole, and add greatly to the recreation, comfort, and health of the inhabitants.'

Others shared Fortune's view that gardens provided healthy pleasure, and some felt that they could be a source of intellectual delight too. Sir John Davis (Governor, 1844–48), President of the local branch of the Royal Asiatic Society, once addressed its members on the claims of natural history and botany to being as worthy subjects of study as history or literature. He even suggested applying to the Colonial Office for the grant of a piece of land to create a botanical garden. Enthusiasts were not slow in coming forward, but Sir John's term ended before the scheme could be taken further. Later, prodded by the missionary Charles Gutzlaff, the plan was revived only to founder for lack of funds; the government was feeling pinched at the time, and more than a decade would pass before a public garden was laid out at its expense.

When finally authorized to act, the Surveyor General was unstinting in his exertions, displaying much gusto in the terracing and planting of the pleasure ground. No doubt Sir Hercules Robinson had something to do with this enthusiasm. The Governor 'has ever proved himself a zealous promoter of botanical research,' reads the dedication in *Flora Hongkongensis*, 'especially by the assistance and encouragement given to botanical travellers, as well as by the valuable contribution he has himself transmitted to the Royal Gardens at Kew.'

The Botanical Gardens opened to the public in 1864. Inside, flowers, orchids, ferns, trees, and shrubs, some of them imported from England and Australia, profusely burgeoned and bloomed, and to all this subtropical splendour was later added a bandstand, paid for by a donation from the Parsee community, and a menagerie. Performances by the regimental bands also served to 'enliven existence in this out-of-the-way and drowsy quarter of the globe' from time to time. Summer monotony was agreeably relieved by midnight concerts, when a snatch of Rossini's overture to *The Barber of Seville*, for example, or a selection of polkas and waltzes, all brought to a rousing finale by *God Save the Queen*, would be carried on a welcome breeze over a splashing fountain and the gay Chinese lanterns that illuminated the walks, to every corner of this verdant park.

Knowledge of the natural history of Hong Kong would have been inmeasurably more meagre without the likes of Captain Champion and his illustrious successors, a number of them serving officers like himself. Each one was indefatigable—once the collector had fixed his beady eye on his quarry, he went after it with tenacity, braving hot sun, wet mud, slippery screes, and tangled undergrowth

to find an insect, bird, or
flower of peculiar rarity. But
the entomologist,
ornithologist, or botanist did
more than just satisfy his own
curiosity; he was equally
concerned about the conserva-
tion of nature and the wildlife
in it. Habitats can be fragile, and
relentless urbanization and
development put them at further risk.
Studying and publicizing the increasingly
rarer species of flora and fauna help to galvanize public support for
their protection. A field guide to the birds of Hong Kong, for
example, was first published in 1946, and the Hong Kong Bird-
Watching Society, which has been vociferous on behalf of the Mai
Po Marshes, a feeding point for migratory birds, was founded in
1957. A majority of the people involved were British expatriates
working in Hong Kong for whom natural history was a hobby.

According to Dr Alistair Ballantine, medic and part-time
lepidopterist,

> At the end of the nineteenth, beginning of the twentieth century,
> an enormous amount of research into natural history was being
> done by essentially two groups of people, a professional group
> of naturalists and a second group of people who were really in
> the service of the British Empire—soldiers, sailors, and civil
> servants. The latter were just working as gifted amateurs, not
> qualified scientists. That's really what happened in Hong Kong.

Where entomology was concerned, the first person to publish
a preliminary list of the butterflies of Hong Kong, which included
118 species from the island and Kowloon, was J. J. Walker, chief
engineer on HMS *Penguin*, who visited Hong Kong between
December 1891 and May 1893. Then, Dr Ballantine continues,

> there was a man called J. C. Kershaw who wrote and illustrated
> a book on Hong Kong butterflies. After that there was a bit of a

gap till the end of the Second World War. Colonel John Eliot, another British soldier, was stationed in South-East Asia and became a world expert on the region's butterflies. In the early 1950s he used to travel all round the New Territories and collected specimens and wrote everything up in an academic and formal way. He retired from the Army and went on to work in the British Museum of Natural History. I remember when I first started collecting; each time I thought I'd caught something new I'd find that Eliot had got it in 1953!

He made an enormous contribution. And when asked how he set about his collecting, he was always quite candid. He used to say, 'I was a very idle soldier. There was a railway station quite near my office. I'd slip out of the back door in the afternoons, jump on the train, and go out to the New Territories.'

Colonel Eliot was followed by a handful of other amateur naturalists, including

a Major M. S. C. Marsh and a doctor called J. Carey-Hughes. There was also a government engineer called J. B. Pickford, and another character called Bill Palmer who was a keeper of government stores—the chap in the brown coat!

Carey-Hughes, Pickford, and Palmer were the three main collectors here at that time. They had a tremendous rivalry. The main collecting day obviously was Sunday and they would all go out, frequently independently. Then they'd have a frantic session in the evening ringing each other up to find out who'd got what and trying to outdo each other. I think Palmer used to do it all on public transport—he'd get on a bus and trudge around. The others had cars, but they never did much better than Palmer. Palmer wore very thick glasses but despite his poor sight he was very gifted and knew a lot about plants. He was doing a lot of the rearing and scientific work and they discovered fantastic numbers of butterflies.

Another group of dedicated naturalists, Mike and Frieda Bascombe and Gweneth Johnston, recently distilled over twenty years' experience in the territory into a definitive book, *The Butterflies of Hong Kong* (1999).

Most butterfly collectors were aided by Kadoorie Farm, says Ballantine: 'Kadoorie Farm is on a hill right next door to Tai Mo Shan and has a lot of wild natural vegetation and a lot of interesting introduced vegetation. You have very good access there; you can drive right up to the top of the peak, Kwun Yum Shan, and you can spot butterflies of high altitude, and you are allowed to collect and record there.'

Since it is vegetation that draws the butterflies, lepidopterists also become knowledgeable about flowers and plants, particularly caterpillar foodplants. That collectors invariably have an affinity with the great outdoors goes without saying. Andrew Russell, a former investment banker in Hong Kong, thought his Sundays well spent butterfly-hunting in the company of Ballantine partly because 'the biggest range of butterflies tends to be found in environments which have not been damaged such as forested areas in mountains, so the pursuit of them takes you to wild places often with wonderful scenery, even if you have to walk or climb a long way to get to them.'

Healthy pleasure the pursuit undoubtedly can be, and yet it is no less certain that discovering a new or very scarce species is a greater thrill. Alistair Ballantine even has a subspecies named after him, the *Allotinus substrigosus ballantinei*—'a rather boring brown butterfly, which had been the first female ever caught'. Equally exciting was the capture of an *arhopala*:

> There are hundreds and hundreds of different species of a family of butterflies called *arhopalas* in Asia. Beautiful shiny blue, they are very mysterious; they hide in dense forests and tend to go to the top of trees when the sun comes up. The species differ by a small amount in the spots underneath, and they are very difficult to identify. John Eliot is the world expert on them.
>
> I'd been up to northern Luzon in the Philippines with Tim Fisher who is a bird expert. He also studies butterflies. Tim and I went collecting and caught an *arhopala*. I brought it back to Hong Kong, and what I did in those days was to photograph anything that wasn't obvious and send the photographs to John Eliot. He'd identify the butterfly for me and if it was anything

interesting I would take the specimen back when I next went to England, and he'd dissect it to confirm whatever it was, and if it was important put it in the museum in London. Anyway, John wrote back when he received my photograph and said 'I don't know what this butterfly is; there's nothing like it in the museum. We just have to put a question mark against it.'

It's difficult to erect a new species just on one specimen; you really need more information than that. After all, it might just be an aberrant form of something else. Anyhow, I stuck the *arhopala* in my collection and forgot about it. But John did say, 'While you're at it, send a photograph to this young schoolteacher in Japan called Takanami who's brilliant.'

Japanese collectors are fantastic. So I sent a photograph to Takanami. He wrote back and said he didn't know what it was either. Then about ten years later Takanami caught two more himself. So once we'd got enough specimens we could claim to have found a new species. That was called after the island we caught it on, *Arhopala luzoniensis*. I think there are still only the three specimens of this butterfly. Mine's in the British Museum of Natural History.

————⊂o◈o⊂————

Nothing contributes more to healthy pleasure than vigorous sports, and even a torrid climate in the summer months is no bar to giving expression to the belief in *mens sana in corpore sano*. It was no accident that Hong Kong's first cricket ground was plonked in an accessible location at the heart of the city. Reporting to Parliament about his visit to China in 1898, just after an imperialist scramble had delivered spheres of influence to various European powers and a swathe of land behind Kowloon (the New Territories, on a ninety-nine year lease) to the British, Lord Charles Beresford recounted this anecdote:

When I was out there, the German admiral made a very curious remark to me. He said, 'You English are the most extraordinary people. Three ports have been taken from China. One is Port Arthur, taken by the Russians; another is Kiao-chau taken by

the Germans; and the third Weihaiwei taken by the British.
The Russians are working with very great activity to fortify
their fort, the Germans are working with great industry in
making a parade ground, and you are employed with great
industry in making a cricket ground.'

Cricket was energetically played in Hong Kong from the very
beginning. By 1851 there were enough enthusiasts to form a club
(the Hong Kong Cricket Club), whose members played matches

not only amongst themselves but also against the Army and Navy
and teams from the Treaty Ports. A random trawl through old
newspapers furnishes several reports of matches in early colonial
Hong Kong. Here is one played between 'Garrison' and 'Club' on 5
January 1877: the ground was rather heavy for running, reports
the correspondent, but the weather was all that could be desired;
the Garrison, who went first to the wickets, made forty-eight runs
while the Club, with seven wickets down, scored fifty-two.

Athletics had its heyday when the hongs organized meetings for
their supervisory staff—overseers at the dockyards, perhaps, or
mechanics at the sugar refinery. One fine day in January 1897,
members of the Taikoo Club competed in obstacle races, putting the
shot, the long jump, the hurdle race, throwing the hammer, and a
three-mile bicycle handicap race which was won, we are told, by Mr
A. McKirdy, overtaking one De Silva Netto who was going well

until thrown by a dog on the track. This cheerful scene included children, for whom 'there were swings, sweets, and cakes, and further along a spacious marquee was erected where liquid refreshments were dispensed to the gentlemen. . . . On all sides the familiar greeting 'A Guld New Year' was heard. . . . Sergeant Pickford donned his kilt for the occasion, and played some pipe music in fine style.'

Where else could one pursue outdoor sports so easily and convivially but at a club? It's true that the very first one to be established, the Hong Kong Club (founded 1846), was a centre for social intercourse only, but others soon opened to cater to more hearty interests. To name just a few, there were clubs for those who liked horse-racing (the Hong Kong Jockey Club, founded in 1884), golf (the Hong Kong Golf Club, founded in 1889), sailing (the Yacht Club, first formed in 1869, gaining permission to call itself 'Royal' and fly the Blue Ensign in 1894). And for lighter relief one could join a number of social and sports clubs where a friendly game of tennis might be played, the thud of bouncing balls in nice counterpoint to the gentler sound of tinkling teacups—at the Ladies Recreation Club, for example. Opened in 1884 after lobbying by a Mrs Coxon and eighteen other ladies, who asked the government for a plot of land where they could take exercise of 'the most health-giving and bracing kind', the Ladies Recreation Club initially had only European and American members but no Chinese.

It was not alone in observing an unwritten colour bar. Anne Baker, a Eurasian, states that her husband had to resign from the Royal Hong Kong Yacht Club and the Hong Kong Club in the 1950s after he married her. Michael Wright, a Public Works Department architect, remembers being called to a special meeting at the Hong Kong Club:

> Members were asked at that meeting to agree that locals should be encouraged to join. Of course the Club didn't have to change any rules; there was nothing in the rules to say that Chinese couldn't join. It had simply been understood that you didn't put a Chinese up for membership.
>
> One man, a Scandinavian working for a shipping company, got up to speak against admitting more Chinese. The fear was

that with the European population being a moving one and the Chinese population by and large a static one, after twenty, twenty-five years the Club would become 90 per cent Chinese and 10 per cent European.

Exclusivity was, of course, part of the clubs' charm. It was a relief for members to be cocooned in a familiar world with their own kind, however brief the respite. A British bequest, the Club with a capital C in its former Anglo-Indian guise, was said to enshrine the imperial way of life, at once aloof and select, yet totally dependent on a host of native servants for its upkeep. Many astonishing specimens were painstakingly constructed in imitation of an English cottage or a country pub—styles evocative of home for their pining expatriate members. There week-old newspapers from London could be eagerly scanned, and 'winter sweaters from Scotland' might be 'purchased by chits'. That reference to Scottish woollies for the rather balmy Hong Kong winter of 1999 was seen pinned on the door of the ladies cloakroom at the Shek O Country Club, which remains closest to the colonial prototype in both its ambience and membership.

Stunningly set on an outcrop of rock protruding into the South China Sea and overlooking the eastern approaches of the harbour, Shek O boasts a neat, deep-verandahed clubhouse, a swimming pool, some tennis courts, and a short golf course. All this, as well as twenty-two houses, was conjured out of 110 acres leased from the government in 1919. Nothing could be more exclusive, which was precisely what the original European residents and members had in mind when they developed the land. To a man, the householders either belonged to the oldest and grandest expatriate families in the colony, or headed the leading hongs. As a club publication had it, 'everybody who is anybody . . . maintains a home there'. It then rattled off a string of names—'names that spell power in this town'.

Still, Shek O's popularity has waxed and waned. Members couldn't always come to terms with its distance from the centre of things. Nor were residents of the adjoining houses fully persuaded that its charms exceeded those of the Peak. Sir John Masson, later taipan of Swire's in Hong Kong, said as much in his letter to Warren

Swire on 25 September 1936. He had spent May and June living at Shek O, he said, and returned there every weekend since, so it might interest Mr Swire to know that

> Even mitigated by fans, Shek O is far too hot for comfortable sleeping after 10th June. The necessity for mosquito nets keeps away air and the Waglan light is an interruption to a light sleeper . . . [In contrast] Nets are not required at all at 'Taikoo' [the Swire house on Peak Road] and Mount Kellet. . . .
>
> It is rather a horrible thought in some ways but cars now go everywhere on the Peak, hence 'Taikoo' to office is 12 minutes—against Shek O to office 30–35 minutes. Both prudent driving. . . . From the housewife's point of view the practical inaccessibility is greater than the difference in time would suggest. The Club Lorry goes into town 3 times a week and Lane Crawford [a department store] send out twice, but provisioning requires a certain degree of foresight which at times is a nuisance. . . .
>
> While a Saturday afternoon or Sunday at Shek O still remains, to my mind, the pleasantest and easiest form of entertaining, greatly appreciated, and infinitely preferred to Peak dinners (!), still one cannot altogether elude one's dinner conversations, and as every Shek O resident knows people will just not dine at Shek O. The drive back denies the soporific Peak resident 45–55 minutes of slumber, and I have heard it suggested that the over-delicate of their sex find the curves of the road induce car-sickness. Anyway I'm quite sure they dislike hiding slim ankles in mosquito-boots.

Today, despite making a point of attracting a multiracial membership, most clubs in Hong Kong have remained true to type. They are a home from home, but in some ways better than home, offering as they do all the facilities one could possibly desire, from sports to meals to changing rooms to providing a neutral ground for meeting friends. Ask any returned expatriate, and you'll find that one of the things they miss most acutely when they go home is the practical and social advantages of belonging to a club.

Outside of clubs, there remains another venue where national
identity is unaffectedly expressed, and that is at a stadium where
your country's team is playing a match. At Hong Kong's most
exuberant international tournament, however, xenophobia is not
much in evidence. In fact the annual Hong Kong Rugby Sevens is
neither cathartic nor nationalistic. If anything the event is known
for the sportsmanship of both its participants and its audience;
everyone cheers for the weaker teams and the star players, whichever
nation they represent. It is also unquestionably the most thoroughly
expatriate gathering of the year.

Since its establishment in 1976, certain features of the Hong
Kong Sevens have become traditional—the spectators' comical hats
and costumes, logo-emblazoned T-shirts, and painted faces; the
Mexican Waves; the plastic jugs of Foster's and San Miguel beer;
the carnival atmosphere; and above all the rapturous roars when a
favourite team scores a try.

A lot more energetic than spectator sports is the other annual
event, the Trailwalker, a sponsored hike in the hills that raises money
for charity. It is dubbed 'Trailwalker' because the hundred-kilometre
route, which hikers in teams of four must finish within forty-eight
hours, is the Maclehose Trail, aptly named for the Governor who
placed large tracts of rural land under protection as country parks
during his term of office. In the early 1980s it was traversed by
soldiers of the British Army out on exercise. From this grew the

annual Trailwalker, an event at first heavily dominated by expatriate teams and later becoming immensely popular with local participants as well. Large companies and banks usually field several teams, which all help to make it a highly successful fundraising affair. Until 1997 it was organized by the Queen's Gurkha Signals, who manned the nine checkpoints and whose own teams regularly took the shortest times to finish, covering the Trail generally in under fourteen hours.

Tracing a wriggly, not to say convoluted, line from east to west across the New Territories, the Trail is physically challenging for a hiker at the best of times. When he or she has to cover it in one go, walking through the night, it becomes a test of mental stamina as well. The walkers start at Pak Tam Chung in the Sai Kung Country Park on a Friday morning in late autumn (though such is the popularity of the event that a staggered starting time has now been introduced). If they complete by Saturday evening, stepping across the tape at Perowne Camp in Tuen Mun having had no sleep, they are considered to have done well.

Over the years, some aspects of the Trailwalker have become ritualized. Team supporters congregating at certain checkpoints to dispense soup, porridge, and first aid like to turn their gatherings into outdoor parties. An Englishwoman was once heard to remark at Kei Ling Ha, a pit stop: 'Oh, isn't this fun? Just like a point-to-point!' Others, such as a group of Morris dancers, dress up in traditional kit and deliberately finish last.

Veteran of six Trailwalkers, Esben Poulsson emphasizes the importance of teamwork:

> To put it simply you're only as fast as your slowest person. In lots of teams, the macho guys would run ahead, get to the checkpoint and then have to sit and wait for the other one or two. I always felt that this was pointless because it's dispiriting to both the fastest and the slowest. So I was very much into the idea that you have to go at the pace of the slowest guy. It's of course inconceivable that four people are at the same level of energy and enthusiasm at any one time.
>
> So if someone seems to be flagging a little, my strategy is to say, 'Why don't you take the lead for a while?' That achieves

two things. One, it exerts a little bit of mental pressure because he can feel the ones behind and maybe he'll step up the pace— it makes him try a little harder. But equally he wouldn't have the feeling that he was keeping the others waiting.

One starts gently walking along a road, as the first stage of the Trail loops round a reservoir and ends above a beautiful white beach. It is a section that tends to be covered too fast, leaving one in less than top form to tackle the first climb. This was certainly Poulsson's experience: 'My own view is that this is a long event and we should keep our powder dry for later. But I never made my view prevail, and I was always struggling up the first hills.'

Halfway through stage two the route winds inland and lovely views of the sea give way to vistas of tawny hills and valleys. By the end of stage three, Kei Ling Ha, the faster teams would be rushing to catch the last of the fading light. 'We would want to try to be on top of Ma On Shan [Saddle Mountain] before dark, which everybody thought was mad. But by that point I would be getting into my stride,' says Poulsson,

> I remember changing my shirt then. Getting a clean shirt was just the most wonderful thing. And then taking a little liquid, some soup perhaps, and maybe one of those awful power bars. Then the assault on Ma On Shan, getting up there just as dusk was falling, and looking out at the lush green hills, the sun going down, and a golden light all around. 'Right, boys,' I'd say to the others, 'now we're going to jog it!' Well, not so much jogging as shuffling. That's what we called it—a light jog across the fairly flat terrain after Ma On Shan and before getting into Gilwell's.

Gilwell is a boy scouts campsite and another checkpoint. One team supporter claims that her first sight of Gilwell's would be indelibly etched on her mind: 'In that eerie grey light of the evening, there were people stretched out with bleeding feet and legs, and people throwing up. It was a scene straight out of the Crimean War.' For Poulsson, Gilwell's was where

> you began dreading a few things—Needle Hill, for example. Needle Hill is a real killer because it's straight up. You get to

the top of it and then would be lying like dogs in a heap. The pain of going down, and then the long boring slog up Tai Mo Shan [Big Hat Mountain, at 3,130 feet Hong Kong's tallest peak]! By that time it was into the morning. You wouldn't be feeling very happy; in fact you're beginning to suffer. But you knew that after Tai Mo Shan somebody will be at the carpark checkpoint to dispense kindness and everything you needed including another clean shirt. And after that it was going to be a twenty-kilometre blast to the finish which was largely just a matter of getting it over with.

In 1992 it was to be rather more than a matter of getting it over with for him and his fellow walkers. In fact it turned out to be nothing less than a triumph, for they were the first civilian team to finish, completing the Trail in seventeen hours and forty-two minutes. As he tells it:

> I remember getting to the Rifle Range, which is at the end of stage six, and someone saying to us, 'Well, the Mass Transit Railway Corporation team are through, and the Swire team, and the Hongkong Bank team, and you're lying fourth.' It was the first time that any of us had focused on the possibility that we might be anywhere near the money! We always thought among ourselves that coming within the top twenty would be very good. The idea of getting remotely near the front was just inconceivable.
>
> Later we came upon the Mass Transit Railway team which had been way ahead—and they were just sitting down to a good picnic dinner. We couldn't believe that they would give up their lead for dinner! That spurred us on. A section later, we came upon the Hongkong Bank team, but there were only three of them. It turned out they'd lost a guy. So that left Swire's. And lo and behold there they were, and we were cruising right past them!
>
> We got to Route Twisk [start of stage nine] thinking 'Now we can have a pit stop and change our shirts,' whereupon the Swire team caught up with us. I remember saying to my team, 'Listen, are we in this race or not, boys? I mean, this is it. We stuff the pit stop, just fill our water bottles and let's be off.'

And we took off—furiously! Every time we looked over our shoulders we could see the Swire team's torchlights behind us. An hour or so passed and suddenly we didn't see the lights any more. The strain was beginning to make us all feel pretty washed out. But we told ourselves, 'We've only got ten kilometres to go, and we're going to win this damn thing.'

And we did. We came to the line. I remember Martin Spurrier standing with the tape. We said to each other, 'Come on, we've got to line up and go over together.' And bursting through this tape—it was just incredible!

You know that you're tired when you can't even face a beer. You don't have the taste for it, nor can you sleep because your body is in overdrive. You sort of dose for an hour, restlessly, and then you wake up. You just can't unwind.

⊃o⬦o⊂

Gale-force winds, towering waves, torn rigging, and split sails—all these strike fear and terror into the heart of anyone out on a sailing boat in a storm. But there are those who relish pitting their own physical frailty against the power and perils of the sea. When Esben Poulsson talks of sailing, the list of races won and lost turns into a tale of adventures, mishaps, and triumphs.

Family circumstances conspired to inculcate his love of sailing. Born of a Danish mother and Norwegian father, he remembers as a child of six or seven walking along the Sound in Cophenhagen and begging his father to let him take sailing lessons. But 'we weren't a sailing family at all', and the death of his father when he was a teenager put such an activity even further out of his reach. Then his life changed radically. In 1961 his widowed mother married a Canadian, Dick Sandwell, and he and his brother Andreas moved to Vancouver:

> My stepfather Dick Sandwell, an accomplished sailor and well-known yachtsman there, had a lovely forty-eight foot yawl called *Gabrielle II*, designed and built in Sweden, and his first move was to enrol us in sailing classes at the Royal Vancouver Yacht Club, as much as anything to improve our English which in my case was almost non-existent. I enjoyed those sailing classes as much as Andreas hated them.

For two more summers he went back to classes at the club, and on his fourteenth birthday his stepfather gave him a one-man dinghy, a Penguin, which he raced very actively whenever he could. Growing up in Vancouver he had ample opportunities to hone his sailing skills doing international races with his stepfather. And when he graduated from the British Columbia Institute of Technology it seemed perfectly logical that he should find his livelihood in a shipping company in Canada. But an old Norwegian friend told him 'this was a very bad idea. He said I should get out in the world, and arranged for me to interview with Wallem and Company, a long-established ship-owning, ship management, ship-broking, and ship agency business in Hong Kong.'

Needless to say, he set about looking for opportunities to sail straight after arrival in the territory in 1971. Hong Kong is inseparable from the sea that surrounds it, and Poulsson must have quickly realized how popular sailing was and what superb conditions existed for it. As hobbies go, few can be as absorbing or as expensive as sailing, but Hong Kong is never short of men rich enough to indulge in the sport. As Poulsson explains:

> Sailing in Hong Kong is excellent for two reasons. First, it's very easy to get to it; whether your boat is at the Yacht Club,

which is in the harbour, or at the Aberbeen Marina, or at Clearwater Bay—all of the marinas are easily accessible, and to get on your boat rarely takes more than an hour. Secondly, from September through January or February, when the north-east monsoon blows, you are almost guaranteed excellent winds so you can set very good courses. The only downside is that it's a bit limited, because with the border situation you've only got about thirty miles of coastline from Mirs Bay to the Soko Islands. For anchoring it can get a bit crowded. And it's too hot in the summer. But the winter months are first class. Hong Kong has had the benefit of many good sailors passing through.

Poulsson found that prominent among a number of well-known names on the yachting scene at the time was Hector Ross, former merchant seaman and a senior civil servant; another was

this ferocious albeit talented sailor, a solicitor named Bill Turnbull who had a boat called *Ceil II*. Bill had a bit of a reputation for . . . I wouldn't say volcanic—that might be overdoing it—but he certainly had a temper and he was a very competitive man. I rang him up completely out of the blue. I told him what I'd done, and he said, 'Well, anybody who wants to sail with me always gets one try. There's a race coming up and you can come and do it.'

It wasn't a particularly high standard of competition, and we won it. Bill said then that he would like me to crew for him again. And that was the beginning of a relationship that was to last for some time.

Since 1964 the China Sea Race (Hong Kong–Manila) has been run every other year over Easter, a time of great climatic variability, with monsoon winds dissipating and becoming quite unreliable by April. When Poulsson was transferred to Manila in 1972 for two years, it was a foregone conclusion that he would be involved. He participated three times, in 1972 on *Ceil II*, winning the inshore race in Hong Kong, the inshore race in Manila Bay, coming second in the China Sea Race itself, and winning the overall series as well. For the next China Sea Race

I chartered a boat called *Shenandoah* together with some Americans. The most memorable thing about that particular time was that we had to sail the boat up to Hong Kong. The trip actually took us seven long days of beating into the wind. We didn't have proper sails for the conditions which were absolutely horrendous. I was with two other guys both of whom were puking their guts out. Seven days later—we'd run out of everything except water—I remember walking into the Royal Hong Kong Yacht Club, long overdue, to a tremendous welcome. The Excelsior Hotel across the road had just opened. I remember negotiating my passage from the club, full of beer and totally lacking in sleep, stumbling through the tunnel [under the road], and finally falling into my bed at the Excelsior Hotel.

This heroes' welcome was nothing compared to the blaze of glory which greeted the Hong Kong team when it returned from the Admiral's Cup in 1977. The unofficial world championship of offshore sailing, the Admiral's Cup series is held every two years off the south coast of England, and is conducted in a team format with participating nations entering three yachts each. Great Britain, the USA, Germany, and Australia had consistently taken the prize since the inaugural race in 1957. 'It was a largely Corinthian event,' Poulsson explains, 'although the idea of bringing hotshot sailors on board to steer was not unknown.' At that time the series consisted of five races—three inshore in the Solent, one called the Channel Race to France and back, and a 630-mile run from Cowes on the Isle of Wight to Plymouth via the Fastnet Rock, with the two longer races counting more points.

Hong Kong had competed in 1975 with two of its three boats chartered and Bill Turnbull's *Ceil V* coming eighth. But Poulsson thought the territory could build its own challenger. He had come to know David Lieu, head of the Van Shipping Company and proprietor of a shipyard called Supercraft, who did not sail himself but owned Hong Kong's most luxurious motor yacht, *Van Triumph*. From a Shanghainese family, David Lieu had studied at the University of Newcastle-upon-Tyne, a leading academy of naval architecture and marine engineering. Poulsson knew that Lieu had a wonderful yard at Tsing Yi Island where he built very solid, high-quality motor boats. I used to go out there with him and he'd say, 'Sailing is boring.' One weekend we were out on his boat, motoring in the harbour, looking at becalmed sail boats, and for no particular reason I said to him, 'David, your yard could build an Admiral's Cup-style yacht, and it would be a great thing for the yard and a great thing for Hong Kong.'

He'd never heard of the Admiral's Cup. But he said, 'Come to my office tomorrow. I want to hear all about it.'

David Lieu hardly hesitated at all when he did hear about it the next day. And so began a frantic and exhilarating time for Esben Poulsson and Bill Turnbull, soon enlisted to bring his experience to bear on the enterprise. Turnbull was initially very negative. He said to build a boat like that in Hong Kong, where high humidity prevailed for most of the year, was technically too challenging. But by this time Lieu was determined. As discussions proceeded, it became clear to Poulsson that

> there were a number of alternatives. We could either get in the queue with one of the proven designers and naval architects and they probably wouldn't take us seriously, or we could do something radically different. It happened that Bill at that point had bought a share in a UK sail-making company, Miller and Whitworth, which was run by a former Olympic medallist and world champion called John Oakeley, arguably one of Britain's

greatest sailors at the time and was to be for many more years. Working for him was Ed Dubois, a long-haired, pimply twenty-three-year-old who had designed only one boat at that point. But this boat performed impressively in the UK national championship and put Ed on the map overnight.

I said design was important but surely the right crew was just as important? I thought we should try and get John Oakeley to be on the boat and bring along a couple of other hotshots.

It was a proud moment when the two-tonner *Vanguard* slipped into the water at Tsing Yi after a bottle of champagne was smashed across her bows. Denis Bray, the Secretary for Home Affairs, was to be navigator at the race, so his wife Marjorie was invited to launch the yacht. Poulsson sums up the significance of the occasion:

> No Admiral's Cup boat had ever been built in Hong Kong before, in fact no proper racing yacht in the true sense of the name had been built in Hong Kong. This was quite a big deal. We knew immediately that we had an exceptional boat. She had a deck-stepped mast and that meant we could change her rake at the top, allowing her to angle, which would give us a huge advantage when sailing close to the wind.

Vanguard was put to the test in a race in Hong Kong and performed beautifully. 'She absolutely annihilated everybody,' says Poulsson, 'but so she should. There was no boat like her in Hong Kong.' Meanwhile, several other owners had decided also to build. One was Chris Ostenfeld in partnership with Ernest da Lasala, who had commissioned a boat, *La Pantera*, in the UK; another was John Ma, one of the first Chinese sailors to be involved in ocean racing, with a boat built in the USA. Hector Ross built a boat in New Zealand, the *Uin Na Mara*. As Poulsson remembers it, there were

> four boats altogether, but only three could make it. So naturally there had to be trials. We wanted them in Hong Kong; the others preferred to hold them in Europe. There was an argument. In the end it was agreed they would be held in the UK and *Vanguard* was shipped over. She arrived on a Friday in May 1977, and literally the next day, John Oakeley wrote 'On Saturday

Vanguard won the Solent's points race against all British and French Admiral's Cup contenders, and was racing level with boats of a much higher rating.' This was tremendous news—unbelievable.

There were nine trial races and *Vanguard* won seven of them. So there was no question that we would be selected. But there was bad blood and argument over the selection for the third position. The final team was *Vanguard*, *La Pantera*, and John Ma's *White Rabbit*.

That year happened to be a light series. Nineteen nations took part, including Australia, Belgium, Brazil, France, Germany, Great Britain, Holland, Italy, and the USA.

Vanguard's crew consisted of the skipper, Bill Turnbull; John Oakeley the helmsman; Denis Bray the navigator; Esben Poulsson one of the two sail trimmers; Ed Dubois and three others. According to Poulsson, 'David Lieu came over for it, chartered a launch, followed every race, and was fully bitten. He loved it. Immediately after the end he said he wanted to do one more.'

In the opening race, Hong Kong came second behind Great Britain, less well in the second race, and sailed the third in boisterous winds, a performance reported in the London *Times*, August 4, 1977, under the headline, '*Vanguard* lives up to her name till Oakeley errs on final beat'. In the overall cup team results Hong Kong was placed third out of the nineteen competing nations, a dazzling feat in the circumstances.

Here is what the *Times* correspondent wrote about the third race:

> Oakeley . . . sailed an almost faultless race and must have been leading on handicap over most of the 20-mile course. At one time *Vanguard* was leading on elapsed time as well, an outstanding performance, considering the much larger yachts that were trailing in her wake.
>
> But one error by Oakeley, the only one he made, cost him his lead on the final beat and victory overall went to the United States boat, *Imp* (David Allen) . . .

By the time the 1979 race came around, Poulsson had moved to England, although at David Lieu's insistence he was still involved. In the spring of that year he was headhunted by Kleinwort Benson to set up a ship-broking company for them back in Hong Kong, but he was able to postpone his starting date until after the Admiral's Cup:

> David built a new, bigger, boat, *Vanguard II*. He also built a boat for Hector Ross. There were five trialists, and Hector Ross in *Uin Na Mara*, us in *Vanguard*, and Chris Ostenfeld with a new *La Pantera* made the team. The boats were shipped to England. Again nineteen nations competed. It was a windy year. In the opening race, Hong Kong came third, fourth, and fifth, which was the first time in history that one country had ever placed three boats in the team in the top five places—it was a new record, one that was emblazoned in headlines in the newspapers. It was fabulous.
>
> We didn't do so well in one or two other races but were still around third or fourth going into the Fastnet. The Fastnet of '79 was the yacht race of all time. That was when fifteen people were killed—the biggest loss of life in any ocean race by miles. We had a very tough race. With me at the helm, we rolled over, mast pointing at the ocean floor, stayed there a bit, and then came up: really heavy-duty stuff. This was described in the 'bible' of offshore racing, *Heavy Weather Sailing* by Peter Bruce: 'the boat turned broadside on in a trough to be rolled over by the breaking crest of the next wave. The entire watch on deck went

over the side to the limit of their lifelines, and all winch handles and torches on deck were lost overboard. Fortunately, the deck crew were able to climb back on board suffering only bruising and shock . . .'

While the majority of the competitors failed to finish the Fastnet, all of Hong Kong's three boats completed it, coming third overall. In 1981 Hong Kong entered the Admiral's Cup once more but 'we didn't do well, came tenth, I think, so it all came to an end'. For Esben Poulsson, though, there remain the albums of photographs, clippings, and other memorabilia. And he will always be able to relive that thrilling, unforgettable moment—the end of the third race in 1977—'when we led the race the entire way and were pipped in the last quarter of a mile, and I never in my wildest dreams imagined I would be in tears at coming second in an Admiral's Cup race.'

Just Another Chinese City?

Anyone inclined to think of the Handover as the end of an era would have found the last weekend of June 1997 rich in symbolic images. There was the rousing finale of *Rule Britannia* at the 'Last Night of the Proms', belted out amidst red, white, and blue streamers and Union flags by a largely Chinese choir. Or the lone piper playing *Auld Lang Syne* in pouring rain. Or the royal yacht sailing out of the harbour with the Patten family and Prince Charles on board. Or the flickering candles and shouts of 'Long live Democracy!' at a midnight political rally in front of the Legislative Council Building. Or People's Liberation Army troops crossing the border at Lok Ma Chau to the stirring serenade of a military band.

In the case of former civil servant James Hayes, the sense of finality struck on an altogether different occasion when, having retired to Sydney, he became an Australian citizen. At the mass naturalization ceremony, he was seen weeping by his daughter. 'Oh, Daddy,' she asked him, 'is it because you're overtaken by emotion at joining the kangaroos?'

'No,' he replied, 'it's because of the upsetting thought that we can never be citizens of an independent Hong Kong.'

The paradox for many long-term expatriates was that Hong Kong had been their home, and they took it home in their hearts when they departed. But some of them also believed they left much that was constructive behind. 'Like many of my friends in the Administrative Service and the Public Works Department,' writes James Hayes, 'I felt that we really had made a contribution to Hong Kong's internal development and external stature over the years of our stay. . . . It sounds egotistical, but wasn't really. . . . Whilst it is true that Hong Kong gave us opportunities, we rose to the occasion simply because Hong Kong had that effect on us!'

The 'Hong Kong effect', if one may call it that, still binds the thousand-strong membership of the Hong Kong Society, social arm of the Hong Kong Association, a business forum and lobby based in the UK. These are, broadly speaking, people who have spent the best part of their careers in Hong Kong and so retain for the place a range of feelings—from goodwill to fond attachment and perhaps even nostalgia. Above all, they relish the opportunity of seeing each other at lunches and dinners organized regionally and in central London—often a Chinese meal in Soho—at which they may relive their time in Hong Kong. One member, Anne Sorby, explains their close ties this way: 'When you live abroad your friends become your family.' Every so often these ties are exuberantly renewed. A Hong Kong Society millennial celebration—offering a Chinese dinner in a huge marquee on the lawns of the Honourable Artillery Company in the City of London, as well as stalls selling memorabilia, a beating retreat by a Gurkha band, and a lion dance—drew over a thousand participants. One of them, afterwards writing to the Society's executive director, David Turner, enthused: 'Surrounded by so many old friends, I felt transported back to Hong Kong where, as we know, all the best parties take place.'

One expatriate who did not leave at the Handover was Jason Wordie, a journalist and historian from Australia. In fact he took what some of his friends considered a 'completely mad' step and applied for a British National Overseas (BNO) passport, the document that replaced the British Dependent Territory Citizen (BDTC) passport formerly held by those born in colonial Hong Kong. He said he did it because

> I've made my home here. . . . Enough people were jumping off the ship; someone had to show that we're not all rats. If there's one thing I cannot abide it is the sheer number of Europeans who trumpet on loudly that 'Hong Kong is home' even though they maintain a residence elsewhere and can't speak a word of the language. . . .
>
> In 1996, when I'd lived here long enough to qualify, and when the opportunity came up, I took it. So there I was, in amongst the great long queues of people snaking round Immigration Department. My BNO passport was remarkably difficult to get. The immigration officers couldn't get over why someone with an Australian passport would want a Hong Kong one.
>
> So I had form after form, question after question, back and forth. At the end, they said, 'We have to ask you this: you're not doing it so you can claim a public assistance flat, are you?' When I said 'No, I'm not', they finally gave in.

In the same year, Stacy Mosher's Chinese publisher husband, Jin Zhong, was turned back at the border when trying to enter China and branded *persona non grata* in the land of his birth. His dissident status, her own situation, and their prospects as a childless couple of limited means 'all reinforced the necessity of beginning to plan for our long-term future. I was nearing forty and had spent my entire working life in Hong Kong, and I knew that if I waited too long to return to the US I would have difficulty establishing myself in reasonable employment.' But she was also homesick:

> I had begun to long for America. I can't pinpoint when this feeling began, but somewhere along the line I had hit the limit of my adaptability. It was as if I had spent my years in Hong Kong traversing a wide expanse on a giant trapeze. On the verge of reaching the other side, I was unable to release my grip on my American soul. And so I began an accelerated swing back to my homeland.

This swing back was eventually accomplished, but it took time because 'it was one thing to make such a decision, but quite another to carry it out. Jin Zhong wanted to continue publishing his magazine as long as possible, and could not conveniently do so from overseas. In any case, I had to see out the Handover of 1997.'

One evening after she had made the decision to leave,

> I rode on the upper deck of a bus passing through Yau Ma Tei and Mong Kok. Below me gleamed the lights that had so entranced me during my earliest days in the territory. I realized how much I would miss Hong Kong, the warm glow of the little restaurants, the raucous, jostling crowds, the incomparably expressive Cantonese language. At the same time I recognized that the part of Hong Kong I loved most, typified by Yau Ma Tei, was the part I could never entirely enter because of the barrier within myself. I would always be an outsider, and in the dim light of the bus's upper deck my eyes filled with tears at the recognition of my loss.

It comes as no surprise to learn that she chose to move to New York, 'the American city most similar to Hong Kong':

> I like to think that by ensuring a safe haven for Jin Zhong I make a small contribution to the independent spirit of Hong Kong that, unlike me, insists on holding its ground. When I hear an old Canto-pop tune in Chinatown or watch a Hong Kong movie on video I realize how much Hong Kong will always be a part of me. I don't deceive myself that my presence in Hong Kong had even the tiniest fraction of the effect that Hong Kong had on me. But I treasure the privilege I was given to add my measure to the collective consciousness, exemplified by those weeks in 1989 when I was literally one in a million, bound up in a common purpose impervious to surrender or defeat.

In New York she 'entered a new phase of the Hong Kong experience as part of an "astronaut" family', for Jin Zhong continues to publish his *Open Magazine*, unmolested by the authorities, and Stacy visits when she can. Like many long-term foreign residents of Hong Kong, she has noticed no obvious changes but feels that the chemistry of the place has altered somehow. 'So many people we knew—expatriate and Chinese—had left for political or professional reasons. It was a different mix of people contributing to the collective mentality, and the change was as subtle and unmistakable as the flags fluttering over the buildings downtown.'

China's red flag flying alongside its Special Administrative Region's own bauhinia-decorated one is indeed an unmistakable symbol of Hong Kong's post-colonial identity. An equally apparent change is the widespread reversion to the use of Chinese in public signs and printed advertisements.

So has Hong Kong cast off its hybrid East–West character and become more Chinese? Aman Mehta, Chief Executive Officer of HSBC, thinks so: 'I do feel that Hong Kong is a more Chinese city than when I first came [in 1976]. The expatriate community has declined in relevance . . . you'll find more turnover than previously. Today's expatriates will be working for multinational corporations, and so they tend to move around. The opportunity to sink roots and settle here is going to be percentage-wise lesser.'

Now that the civil service and police force have been substantially localized, there has certainly been a diminution of Britons in the expatriate community. Of course this is to be expected, but if there's one question that is invariably asked of a visitor from Hong Kong to the UK, it is 'How has Hong Kong changed since the Handover?' Underlying this query is the assumption that things cannot possibly be as good as they were under the British.

There are indeed many causes for concern: the erosion of the rule of law, the dawdling pace of democratic reform, the decline in the general standard of English, the environmental pollution and the authorities' conspicuous failure to tackle it, to list a few. Having said that, Hong Kong remains one of the most liveable of Asian capitals. Not least among its charms is a highly favourable corporate and personal tax regime (in fact, for tax reasons some British expatriates have gone so far as to adopt Hong Kong as their domicile, keeping a home address here even when they live elsewhere). Still, those who remember it 'in the good old days' will point to all the negative facets as symptoms of creeping 'Chineseness', a development which they think will make Hong Kong a less and less desirable city for non-Chinese to live in. What's more, this increased Chineseness is bolstered by the expanding presence of mainlanders.

Such a trend is contrary to the government's avowed intentions, for official policy comes firmly down on the side of enhancing Hong Kong's international standing. No longer able to compete on cost with the rest of the region, Hong Kong will maintain growth only by becoming an advanced knowledge-based economy and centre for capital and talent from around the world. This means bringing in more, rather than fewer, expatriates.

With Hong Kong's fate ever more tightly entwined with that of China, some of that imported talent is bound to come from the Mainland, especially Chinese who have been educated abroad. Attempts to attract such expatriates, however, come up against a severe skills gap in China itself. This lack is felt most keenly in Shanghai, China's leading city of business. Now bristling with skyscrapers, Shanghai dreams of assuming its historical pre-eminence as Asia's commercial hub and becoming a world-class city to rival Hong Kong and Singapore. This meteoric rebirth has indeed led some observers to predict its imminent usurpation of Hong Kong's crown; with Shanghai's ascendancy, they declare, Hong Kong will dwindle into just another Chinese provincial city.

This may happen—but not for a very long time, probably decades, according to pundits who have experience of both Shanghai and Hong Kong. (It's worth noting that Deng Xiaoping posited fifty years from 1997 for the Hong Kong–China merger to become seamless.) To corroborate their opinion, these pundits point to Shanghai's inadequate regulatory and business structures and the dearth of trained people to operate them, deficiencies that patently cannot be remedied in just a few years. It is true that multinationals have started to locate branch offices to Shanghai, but they generally prefer to employ local staff, and 'the reality is that they are very hard to find', according to Larry Wang, a recruitment specialist and author of a guide to career opportunities in China. 'The raw talent is there—intelligence, capability, innovation—but there is a gap among mainland Chinese just in the years of experience: their exposure, polish, insight, understanding, and professional maturity. They are still not at the management level yet.'

All the same, he adds, Western managers rushing in to fill the gap in Greater China (which includes Hong Kong and Taiwan) must offer rather more than in the past. To justify their expatriate packages—'a huge housing allowance, a premium on their salary for hardship, trips home, club memberships, and so on'—Western candidates 'have to prove their capabilities'. In Larry Wang's experience, it also helps if they possess a deeper cultural awareness, even a high level of bilingualism. Standards and requirements have been raised substantially, in other words.

Sensitivity to cultural differences cuts both ways, of course. If Emperor Qianlong had not been prevented by tradition and a sense of China's supremacy from overlooking Lord Macartney's refusal to kowtow, if some common ground of understanding had been found between the two nations, the history of Sino-British relations might have been entirely different. But out of this clash of cultures came the Opium Wars and the cession of Hong Kong. And in this little enclave of 'Europe in China' the cultural conflicts were steadily resolved—rather in the manner of flowing water smoothing out stone—until Hong Kong metamorphosed into the unique interface between East and West that it is.

This uniqueness must be understood and appreciated if Hong Kong is to retain its dynamism, suggests historian Carl Smith. Hong Kong may be at heart Chinese, he writes, but it has been stamped by a heritage whose 'dominant strand has been its possession by

Britain. . . . The British presence has produced a different political and judicial system from that of China. The whole is overlaid with a glaze of foreign features.' This past 'cannot be surgically severed from the present or the future', and as Hong Kong adjusts to life under Chinese sovereignty, 'a sense of history can help it avoid mistakes, build on its achievements, and profit from its various traditions'.

Of course all this will happen alongside the inexorable march of globalization, which is changing the world for everyone anyway. Part of this movement must be for Hong Kong, and indeed Shanghai, to become for good or ill more and more like cities in the West. Hong Kong's challenge is to remain true to its East–West nature but flexible enough to bend with the prevailing winds. It should ask no less of any foreigner who chooses to live and work here.

For those who like images, here are two that may stand as auguries for the continuing presence of expatriates in Hong Kong. Our first is a sight caught fleetingly on Handover night. The hour is late, the parties are over, and only a few worse-for-wear revellers still linger on the steamy streets. One of them is embracing a placard adorned with Deng Xiaoping's photograph, beneath which is printed this short caption in Chinese: 'Xiaoping, *fang xin*' (Rest assured, Xiaoping), suggesting that Deng's resolution for the territory's future will endure. The person with the placard, however, is not Chinese but a foreigner. And indeed, the expatriate who learns to live with his new rulers ensures his survival in post-colonial Hong Kong.

Since we started this book with a Scottish anniversary, let us end with one. The second image is of Alasdair Morrison (Jardines taipan, 1994–2000) delivering the Immortal Memory on Burns Night, 1990, and offering his manifesto of the Scots in Hong Kong, excerpted below:

> Let no man underestimate
> The race of Scots expatriate,
> Whose latent ardour flames apace
> When freed from Scotland's cold embrace.

'Twas Scots that formed from barren rock
This quintessential culture shock,
Where mainly East and West now blend
But Scots to special rank pretend. . . .

But now we're hoist, tho' held in high regard,
Upon our parsimonious petard;
For, in this one great error caught,
We leased the land we should have bought.
And now the Day of Judgement lowers
To test the Scots' adaptive powers,
For many say about the Scots
We cannot change our native spots.
But we shall not fail or be ignored
By drafters of the Basic Law . . .

And when by Tamar's waters play
Young cadres from the PLA,
We will not fear an empty sky
Or the lion dancer's dotted eye,
But from Shek O's shores to Tai Mo Shan
We'll summon Burns' immortal clan
And, if we must, in the SAR,
We'll toast our bard in Putonghua.

Notes and Sources

Our main source is the pile of transcripts accumulated from conversations and correspondence with those to whom this book is dedicated. Their names appear at the front of the book, and to all of them we express our deepest gratitude. Details of citations from memoirs, histories, and newspapers are given under the relevant chapter headings below. We are also indebted to several friends, also mentioned below, who have helped with suggestions and material.

Introduction: Who Are They?
This chapter quotes Charles Boxer, who was first quoted by Emily Hahn in her book *China To Me* (London: Virago Press, 1987). In 1935 Missouri-born Emily Hahn embarked on a world tour that lasted nine years, taking in Shanghai and Hong Kong, where she began an affair with a scholarly English officer working in military intelligence called Charles Boxer. Interned in Kowloon during the Japanese occupation, Charles Boxer later married Emily Hahn and, at the end of the war, became a history professor at London University.

1 'Braveheart' in China
Peter Edwards's culinary comment was taken from his speech on behalf of the guests at a Burns supper on 25 January 1991. John Lang kindly provided a copy of Hong Kong St Andrew's Society's Rules and a list of past chieftains. The first St Andrew's Ball was reported in the *China Mail* on 1 December 1877. Letters praising or criticizing the event appeared in the correspondence columns three days later.

2 Merchants
The extract from James Matheson's letter to William Jardine is quoted by Robert Blake in the authorized history, *Jardine Matheson: Traders of the Far East* (London: Weidenfeld & Nicolson, 1999).

Albert Smith's observations of merchants' monotonous life were published in his *To China and Back, being a Diary kept out and home* in 1859; the book was reissued by Hong Kong University Press in 1974. The editorial about 'four long coats' coming out of Yau Ma Tei is from the 14 December 1931 edition of the *South China Morning Post* and quoted by H. J. Lethbridge in *Hong Kong: Stability and Change: A Collection of Essays* (Hong Kong: Oxford University Press, 1978). James Clavell is the author of *Tai-pan* (London: Michael Joseph, 1966). For Sir John Keswick's reflections on his last days in Shanghai in 1951, see Maggie Keswick (ed.), *The Thistle and the Jade* (London: Octopus Books, 1982). Patrick Alexander graciously gave permission for May Holdsworth to quote from his China diary.

3 Ministers and Mandarins

Dan Waters kindly found the relevant issue of *The Overseas Pensioner* (Number 79, October 1999), in which the HMOCS commemoration at Westminster Abbey was reported, and Ian Lightbody drew May Holdsworth's attention to the article about cadets by H. J. Lethbridge in *Hong Kong: Stability and Change* (ibid.). The quote from Sir Ralph Furse about civil servants being the government in most colonies, and the one referring to the maxim *Pas trop gouverner*, may be found in that book. Anthony Kirk-Greene's *On Crown Service: A History of the Colonial and Overseas Services 1837–1997* (London: I. B. Tauris, 1999) is a useful guide to the background. Several generations of expatriates in Hong Kong have enjoyed Austin Coates, *Myself a Mandarin: Memoirs of a Special Magistrate* (Hong Kong: Heinemann Educational Books Asia Ltd, 1975). James Hayes talks about being a 'Father and Mother Official' in the preface to his autobiographical work, *Friends and Teachers: Hong Kong and Its People 1953–87* (Hong Kong: Hong Kong University Press, 1996). Thanks are also due to him for a copy of Cecil Clementi's memorandum about his rat-infested office (Hong Kong Public Records Office, CSO 1624/06). David Clementi's recollections of his grandfather were written for an earlier project by the authors. Phoebe May's portrait is included in an unpublished account of her childhood entitled *View from the Peak*. The poem celebrating Clementi's first sight of his future wife may be found in *A Journal in Song*, printed for private circulation by Basil Blackwell, Oxford, in 1928.

Reginald Johnston's head wagging is mentioned in *From Emperor to Citizen: The Autobiography of Aisin-Gioro Pu Yi*, translated by W. F. Jenner (Beijing: Foreign Languages Press, 1965). The quotations from James Hayes are taken from 'The Hong Kong History Project', published in the *Journal of the Royal Asiatic Society, Hong Kong Branch* (vol. 27, 1987), and from a letter to his parents dated 25 May 1959. Denis Bray's account of his days in the New Territories was part of a lecture he presented to the Royal Asiatic Society, Hong Kong Branch, in May 2000.

4 Some of the Governors

Chris Patten's comment on being the mayor of Hong Kong is a quote from his book, *East and West* (London: Macmillan, 1998), as is his remark about not having gained foreign experience through a conventional diplomatic career. Sir Frederick Lugard's tenure in Hong Kong is admirably covered by Margery Perham in the second volume of her biography, *Lugard: The Years of Authority 1898–1945* (London: Collins, 1960), the source of all his words quoted here. This chapter has also drawn gratefully from Sir Alexander Grantham's memoir, *Via Ports: From Hong Kong to Hong Kong* (Hong Kong: Hong Kong University Press, 1965).

Newspapers, particularly the *Hongkong Daily Press* of 4 and 8 March 1922, provided interesting perspectives on the seamen's strike.

5 Money Makes the World Go Round

Hong Kong's financial beginnings are traced in Maurice Collis, *Wayfoong: The Hongkong and Shanghai Banking Corporation* (London: Faber and Faber, 1965), from which Thomas Sutherland's quotes are taken. The chicanery of those involved in the Carrian case was reported extensively in the newspapers, including the *South China Morning Post*, which announced the guilty verdict on Ewan Launder on 26 March 2000.

6 Cops and Robbers

For material on grave inscriptions, see *Almost Forgotten: A Researcher's Guide to the Past Members of the Hong Kong Police Force*, which was compiled by Christine M. Thomas and shown to May Holdsworth by Mrs Margaret Leeds, archivist of the Royal Hong Kong Police Association in the UK. In this connection the help of Mrs Sylvia Mansell, the Association's Secretary, is also gratefully acknowledged.

The description of the early members of the constabulary as men who readily yielded to the temptation offered by public houses is from *Hong Kong: Stability and Change* by H. J. Lethbridge (ibid.), who was in turn quoting *The History of the Laws and Courts of Hong Kong* by J. W. Norton-Kyshe (Hong Kong: Vetch & Lee, 1971; first published in 1898).

We learnt about James Dodds from Mrs Margaret Leeds, who holds a copy of his short diary, *In the Days of Tiffin: Being an Account of Life in the Hong Kong Police Force in 1876*. The unpublished memoir of Henry May's daughter, Phoebe, yielded the account of the Central Police Station gaol.

The first section of this chapter has also relied upon an article published in *The Royal Hong Kong Police Association Newsletter* (No. 83, December 1999), 'The Contingent Input into the Hong Kong Police Force'. Its author asked to be identified as '1314'. Mark Simpson kindly provided a copy of the Newsletter.

George Wright-Nooth's stories were recounted at an interview with Libby Halliday for a documentary film, *The Hong Kong Story*, which she directed, and we thank her for allowing us to take excerpts from her transcript. The film, produced by Elaine Forsgate Marden, was broadcast worldwide around the time of the Hong Kong Handover in June 1997. A published account of the Japanese occupation, George Wright-Nooth with Mark Adkin, *Prisoner of The Turnip Heads: Horror, Hunger and Humour in Hong Kong, 1941–1945* (London: Leo Cooper, 1994), filled out the background.

No-one with an interest in the history of the police force can afford to miss Kevin Sinclair's *Asia's Finest* (Hong Kong: Unicorn Books Limited, 1983) and its sequel, *Asia's Finest Marches On: Policing Hong Kong from 1841 into the 21st Century*, by Kevin Sinclair and

Nelson Ng Kwok-cheung (Hong Kong: Kevin Sinclair Associates Ltd, 1997).

In the section on localization, the remark about expatriate policemen being thrown out on the scrap heap is from a *South China Morning Post* report on 16 June 1994.

7 Missionaries

Jackie Pullinger's description of her first sight of Hong Kong appears in her book *Chasing the Dragon*, written with Andrew Quickie (London: Hodder & Stoughton, 1980). Sister Helen Kenny kindly provided a copy of Penny Lernoux, *Hearts on Fire: The Story of the Maryknoll Sisters* (New York: Orbis Books, 1993). Mrs Shuck's comment on the Chinese predilection for things which concerned the world is from J. B. Jeter, *Memoir of Mrs Henrietta Shuck: The First American Female Missionary to China* (Boston: Gould, Kendall & Lincoln, 1846).

Carl T. Smith's collected writings may be found in *Chinese Christians: Élites, Middlemen and the Church in Hong Kong* (Hong Kong, Oxford University Press, 1985) and *A Sense of History: Studies in the Social and Urban History of Hong Kong* (Hong Kong: Hong Kong Educational Publishing Co., 1995). The latter reprints Ng Akew's story from *The Chung Chi Bulletin* (No 46, 1969).

8 The Quality of Life

Printed sources for this chapter include Karen Penlington's press cuttings and programmes of the Hong Kong Arts Festival and the Youth Arts Festival. The quote from Ted Marr is reproduced from an article, 'Lost Elite's Last Ball', written for *Hong Kong iMail* by Winsome Lane and published on 14 March 1999.

9 Fish Climbing Up a Tree

In *Verandah: Some Episodes in the Crown Colonies 1867–1889* (London: Century Publishing, 1984), the author James Pope-Hennessy quotes Isabella Bird's reflections on foreigners' misuse of the Chinese to illustrate the state of race relations in 1870s Hong Kong. For Lord Redesdale's view, see A. B. Freeman-Mitford, *The Attaché in Peking*

(London: Macmillan and Co., 1900). The quotation from Sir Hercules Robinson appears in G. B. Endacott, *A History of Hong Kong, Second Edition* (Hong Kong: Oxford University Press, 1973).

China Mail, 12 April 1877, is the source of the letter in which it was predicted that the Chinese would eventually buy foreigners up 'lock, stock and barrel'. For the letter containing the idiom 'fish climbing up a tree', thanks are due to Carl T. Smith, who first reproduced it in 'A Sense of History' in the *Journal of the Royal Asiatic Society, Hong Kong Branch*, (Vol. 26, 1986). It is also from this article that much of the information about the City Hall and cricket ground meeting is drawn.

Marjorie Chui, *Justice Without Fear or Favour: Reflections of a Chinese Magistrate in Colonial Hong Kong* (Hong Kong: Ming Pao Publications Ltd, 1999) is instructive on racial discrimination in legal and judicial circles. The bullying magistrate described by Jan Morris may be found in the pages of her *Hong Kong: Epilogue to an Empire* (London: Viking, 1988; Second edition, London: Penguin, 1993).

Jean Gittins' autobiography, *Eastern Windows—Western Skies* (Hong Kong: South China Morning Post Ltd, 1969) is the source of her story about being spurned by European children when out with her governess. Han Suyin's remarks about being Eurasian are taken from *Love is a Many-Splendoured Thing* (Harmondsworth: Penguin Books, 1952). Emily Hahn's entertaining record of colonial snobbery in the 1940s, which includes the story of Captain Osgood and Miss Bartholomew, is from *Hong Kong Holiday* (New York: Doubleday & Company, Inc., 1946).

'Protected women' as a term is defined in the *Hongkong Government Gazette* of 1880 and cited in Stephen Frederick Fisher, *Eurasians in Hong Kong: A Sociological Study of a Marginal Group*, an M.Phil thesis submitted to the University of Hong Kong in 1975. John Smale's comments on beautiful Eurasian children and their degradation are from the same source.

The account of the battle for the Peak is drawn from memoranda held on microfilm (CO129/347) at the Hong Kong Public Records Office. The *Hongkong Daily Press* published Man-kam Lo's letter on 23 November 1917 and that by 'S.L.' the day after.

It was again the *Hongkong Daily Press* (7 June 1902) which yielded the letter about the two kinds of Eurasians. James Hayes graciously allowed extracts to be taken from his 'East and West in Hong Kong: Vignettes from History and Personal Experience', in *Between East and West: Aspects of Social and Political Development in Hong Kong*, edited by Elizabeth Sinn (Hong Kong: Centre of Asian Studies, University of Hong Kong, 1990), including his comment about the Chinese and European communities' mutual disdain. For references to Vandeleur Grayburn and his views on staff marrying non-British women, readers should look up *The Hongkong Bank Between the Wars and the Bank Interned 1919–1945: Return to Grandeur*, the third volume of Frank H. H. King, *The History of the Hongkong and Shanghai Banking Corporation* (4 vols, Cambridge: Cambridge University Press, 1988–91).

Peter A. Hall's *In the Web* (Heswall: Peter Hall, 1992) is an indispensable guide to the 'tangled up' kinship links of the oldest Eurasian families in Hong Kong. He kindly wrote to May Holdsworth about his own experience of tracing those links. Thanks are due to Veronica Needa for the Reverend Guy Shea's poem, in both Chinese and English translation, and for much else besides. In her programme notes to *Face*, she provides extracts of conversations with Mr Shea, to whom she had turned for information on Eurasian families, as well as her own description of what her play is about ('Tracking our personal journeys, mapping out our place . . .'). She also graciously said that this book might draw from the preview article she wrote for the *South China Morning Post* weekend entertainment section, 23 October 1998.

10 Trailing Spouses and Single Women

For Somerset Maugham's account of how an Englishwoman transformed a Chinese temple into 'a nice place in England', see *On a Chinese Screen*, reissued with an Introduction by H. J. Lethbridge (Hong Kong: Oxford University Press, 1984). Maugham described expatriates in Asia, their clubs and their little flirtations, in *Collected Short Stories, Volume 4* (Harmondsworth: Penguin Books, 1963). Karen Pittar kindly gave permission for the quotation about making tea for her maid to be reproduced from her article in the magazine of the Hong Kong American Women's Association, *Aware*.

11 A Small World

A letter in the Hong Kong Public Records Office (CO 129/311) from the Registrar-General, A.W. Brewin, and Inspector of Schools, Edward A. Irving, to Major-General Sir William Gascoigne, then Officer Administering the Government of Hong Kong, throws light on how Ho Tung's donation of a school in Kowloon was viewed within the civil service. Ho Tung's letter giving reluctant consent is cited by Vincent H. G. Jarrett, 'Old Hong Kong', a series of articles from the *South China Morning Post* published between 17 June 1933 and 13 April 1935. Charles W. Dull's remark is taken from Hong Kong International School's current prospectus. David C. Pollock and Ruth Van Reken, *The Third Culture Kid Experience: Growing Up Among Worlds* (Houghton, New York: Interaction Inc.) explores the experiences of children raised outside their parents' home country and offers suggestions on ways of dealing with the challenges and benefits of expatriation.

12 Healthy Pleasures

Captain Champion's collection is described in George Bentham, *Flora Hongkongensis: A description of the Flowering Plants and Ferns of the Island of Hong Kong* (London: Lovell Reeve, 1861). It was G. A. C. Herklots who mentioned the naming of *Rhododendron Championae* after Captain Champion's wife, in his *The Hong Kong Countryside Throughout the Seasons* (Hong Kong: South China Morning Post Ltd, 1951). Robert Fortune is quoted from E. H. M. Cox, *Plant-hunting in China* (Hong Kong: Oxford University Press, 1986). Details of the Botanical Gardens' music programme were gleaned from the *China Mail*, 25 July 1877. The definitive work on butterflies is M. J. Bascombe, G. Johnston, F. S. Bascombe, *The Butterflies of Hong Kong* (London: Academic Press, 1999).

Lord Charles Beresford's account of his visit to China appears in *The Memoirs of Admiral Lord Charles Beresford* (London: Methuen

& Co., 1914). A report of the Taikoo Club sports day was published in the *Hongkong Telegraph*, 2 January 1897.

J. Dickson-Leach kindly supplied a copy of Sir John Masson's letter about the inconveniences of Shek O. Esben Poulsson quoted from the 'bible' of offshore sailing, *Heavy Weather Sailing* by Peter Bruce (London: Adlard Coles Nautical, 1991).

Just Another Chinese City?

When we were in danger of not seeing the wood for the trees, David Dodwell kindly pointed out a path through the forest of our perplexity. Carl T. Smith's Introduction to *A Sense of History: Studies in the Urban and Social History of Hong Kong* (ibid.) is a timely reminder that the past cannot be severed from the present or future. Larry Wang was interviewed by Benedict Rogers in *Hong Kong iMail* on 12 April 2001. His book is *The New Gold Mountain: The Success of Chinese Americans in Greater China . . . And What You Need to Know to Get There!* (Hong Kong: Andiremar Publications, 1998). Alasdair Morrison's Immortal Memory speech, from which the verses reproduced in this chapter are gratefully taken, was delivered at the St Andrew's Society Burns supper on 19 January 1990.

Illustrations

Some illustrations are from private albums; others are either in the public domain or provided by the institutions named. In a few cases it has not been possible, despite every effort, to trace owners of material possibly still in copyright. If omissions come to light after publication, the publisher would be glad to make appropriate acknowledgement in any future editions. The credits which follow show, in order, the page number on which an illustration appears, explanatory caption, and source of the illustration (in brackets), except where the illustrations are the authors' own.

Introduction: Who Are They?
p.xi: Visible and 'invisible' expatriates in the central business district.
p.xii: Expatriates in nineteenth-century Hong Kong (print from *The Graphic*, Wattis Fine Art, Hong Kong).

1 'Braveheart' in China
p.1: St Andrew's Ball, the Regent Hotel, Kowloon, 1999. pp.4 and 6: Scenes from an earlier St Andrew's Ball, City Hall, Hong Kong (from an engraving, courtesy of Nicci and Mike Button). p.9: Robert Burns.

2 Merchants
p.11: East Point (courtesy of the Martyn Gregory Gallery, London). p.13: 'China in Scotland'—a dragon wall encloses a Chinese-style garden at Portrack, Maggie Keswick's house in Dumfries (courtesy of Charles Jencks). p.14: John Lang (courtesy of Harry Wilken). p.17: Cricket match, Wayfoong (Hongkong Bank) vs. Taikoo (Swire), 1936 (courtesy of HSBC). p.18: Canton trade fair, late 1970s (courtesy of Magnus Bartlett). p.24: Chinese poster urging modernization, early 1980s (courtesy of Magnus Bartlett). p.28: Cartoon, the *South China Morning Post*, 29 December 2000 (courtesy of Chris Young).

3 Ministers and Mandarins

p.33: The Queen and the Duke of Edinburgh meet HMOCS members at the Westminster Abbey service, 25 May 1999 (courtesy of Tariq Chaudry and *The Overseas Pensioner*, UK). p.39: Penelope Clementi. p.41: James Hayes at a Shau Kei Wan Kai Fong refuge (courtesy of James Hayes). p.44: Sham Shui Po prison camp during the Japanese occupation (drawn by Michael Wright). p.48: Squatter shacks, Ma Tsai Hang, 1965 (courtesy of Ko Tim Keung). p.49: The Queen, the Governor, and Ian Lightbody, Beacon Hill viewpoint, Kowloon, 1975 (courtesy of Ko Tim Keung).

4 Some of the Governors

p.56: Sir Frederick Lugard, sitting, second from right; his Colonial Secretary, Francis Henry May, standing in the row behind him, second from left. p.58: Sir David Wilson takes the salute, Queen's Pier, 9 April 1987 (courtesy of Information Services Department, the Government of the Hong Kong Special Administrative Region; hereafter Information Services). p.67: Cultural Revolution poster (*Hong Xiao Bing*, Shanghai). p.69: Dr David Wilson (left), Sir Murray Maclehose (centre), and Sir Yuet-keung Kan (right) at the Great Wall, 1979 (courtesy of Information Services). p.71: Canton–Kowloon through train arrives at the border, 1979 (courtesy of Information Services). p.74: Sir Alexander Grantham.

5 Money Makes the World Go Round

p.81: The history of Hong Kong's growth as a financial centre as reflected in the Hongkong Bank's headquarters building, beginning with this colonnaded, domed, and balconied Victorian edifice. p.85: Spanish dollars minted in South and Central America were used in the China trade, such as this silver coin (courtesy of HSBC). p.88: This Bank building was redeveloped during the early part of the 'Roaring '80s' (courtesy of HSBC). p.97: International officers, junior mess guest night, late 1930s (courtesy of HSBC). p.99: A global bank, with an architecturally distinctive building for its Hong Kong headquarters.

6 Cops and Robbers

p.104: The Colonial Police included Europeans, Indians, and Chinese. p.110: When the grain harvest failed following the Great Leap Forward, posters like this one were produced to encourage greater effort on the farms. p.113: Quelling rioters at a housing estate, 1967. p.116: Peter Moor in retirement at his house in Sussex (courtesy of Peter Moor). p.121: Ritchie Bent (front) during his time with the PTU (courtesy of Ritchie Bent).

7 Missionaries

p.128: The Bradbury Hospice opening, 1992; Sister Helen Kenny (third left) looks on as Mrs Lavender Patten and Prince Charles chat to a patient (courtesy of the Keswick Foundation). p.134: Children receiving BCG vaccination, 1953 (courtesy of Ruttonjee Sanatorium). p.135: Sister Mary Gabriel (courtesy of the Missionary Sisters of St Columban). p.138: A Vietnamese refugee camp in Hong Kong. p.139: Father Peter Newbery, prison chaplain (courtesy of Peter Newbery). p.143: Missionaries in China used to dress in Chinese clothes. p.147: Reverend Carl Smith and his filing cabinets.

8 The Quality of Life

p.154: Allan Zeman (courtesy of Nick Shearman, *South China Morning Post*). p.160: Michelle Garnaut (courtesy of Michelle Garnaut). p.167: Hong Kong Youth Arts Festival logo and participants (courtesy of Hong Kong Youth Arts Festival). p.170: Allen Youngblood (courtesy of Terry Duckham/Asiapix). p.171: Oil on canvas, 'Shameless: Wings', by Du Xinjian (courtesy of Arts Scene China, Hong Kong).

9 Fish Climbing up a Tree

p.176: Tai Ping Shan, late 1860s. p.179: Cartoon, *The Correspondent/ 50th Anniversary 1949–1999* (courtesy of Chris Young). p.184: Mountain Lodge on the Peak. p.191: The wedding of Victoria Ho Tung and Man-kam Lo, 1918. p.195: Nancy Kwan. p.198: Veronica Needa (courtesy of Veronica Needa).

10 Trailing Spouses and Single Women
p.201: Henrietta Shuck's grave, Hong Kong Cemetery. p.205: Anne Sorby in her garden, Kent, England, 1999. p.207: Sitting room in Bunker House (courtesy of Sally Lo). p.211: Boat party (courtesy of Ian Howard). p.224: Sedan-chair race 2000 (courtesy of Matilda Sedan Chair Race Charities Fund).

11 A Small World
p.232: Liz Dewar with Tamzin (courtesy of Lauralynn Goetz). p.234: Tamzin (right) and Zoe (left) Dewar (courtesy of Vanda Cole). p.236: Expatriate child with Chinese amah, 1930s. p.240: A painting of Sir Robert Ho Tung in old age (courtesy of Jardine Matheson). p.243: Hong Kong International School, (courtesy of HKIS). p.245: Future global citizens (courtesy of HKIS). p.248: Third-culture kids at a party.

12 Healthy Pleasures
p.249: *Rhododendron Championae* (from *The Hong Kong Countryside* by G. A. C. Herklots, illustrated by the author and A. M. Hughes). p.252: Caspian tern, a regular visitor to the Mai Po Marshes (from *Birds of Hong Kong* by Clive Viney and Karen Phillipps). p.256: Cricket in Central, 1960s (courtesy of Ko Tim Keung). p.260: At the Hong Kong Rugby Sevens. p.264: Trailwalker 1992; (from left) Jonathan Hugo, Esben Poulsson, Nick Harbinson, David Holdsworth, Martin Spurrier. p.268: Esben and Jo Poulsson at the Tsing Yi boatyard (courtesy of Esben Poulsson). p.270: *Vanguard* in the lead, Admiral's Cup 1977 (courtesy of the *Times*).

Just Another Chinese City?
p.273: Lone piper at the Handover. p.277: End of Empire cartoon (courtesy of Gavin Coates). p.281: A change of flag.

Index

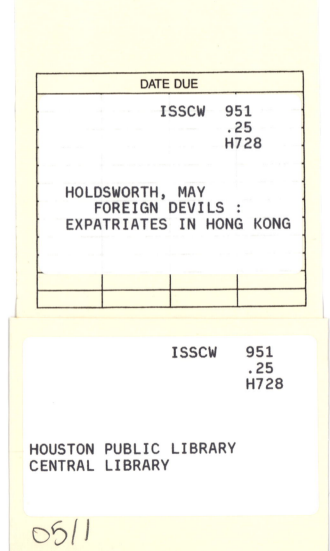